15 ST. MARY STREET
TORONTO ONTARIO, CANADA
M4Y 2R5

JOURNAL FOR THE STUDY OF THE NEW TESTAMENT
SUPPLEMENT SERIES

6

Consulting Editors

Ernst Bammel, James Dunn, Birger Gerhardsson, Anthony Hanson
David Hill, Barnabas Lindars, Howard Marshall
Robert Tannehill, Anthony Thiselton, Max Wilcox

Executive Editor

Bruce D. Chilton

Publishing Editor

David J.A. Clines

Department of Biblical Studies
The University of Sheffield
Sheffield S10 2TN
England

Let our brethren then, who desire to shed their blood for Jesus Christ, be of good courage, and anticipate their future joy. For behold a seminary of martyrdom is ready for them; and they will have wherewithal to satisfy their longings.

(Francis Xavier)

PERSECUTION
AND
MARTYRDOM
IN THE
THEOLOGY
OF
PAUL

John S. Pobee

Journal for the Study of the New Testament
Supplement Series 6

TO

MY THEOLOGICAL TEACHERS WHO HAVE
INFLUENCED MY THINKING AND LIFE

C.F.D.M.
N.Q.K.
J.P.M.S.
E.B.
W.O.C.
S.G.W.

Published by JSOT Press
Department of Biblical Studies
The University of Sheffield
Sheffield S10 2TN, England

Printed in Great Britain
by Redwood Burn Ltd., Trowbridge, Wiltshire.

British Library Cataloguing in Publication Data

Pobee, John S.
    Persecution and martyrdom in the theology of
Paul.—(Journal for the study of the New testament
supplement series, ISSN 0143-5108; 6)
    1. Bible. N.T. Epistles of Paul
    2. Persecution—Biblical Teaching
    I. Title   II. Series
    272'.1   BS2655.P5/

ISBN 0-905774-52-3
ISBN 0-905774-52-1 Pbk

CONTENTS

PREFACE

This volume takes its origin from research begun in the University of Cambridge in the early sixties. Three things worked together to direct me to the subject of persecutions and martyrdom. Though a happy and privileged sojourner in Cambridge, my heart was bleeding for my motherland, Ghana, which had come into the grip of a corrupt and ruthless tyrant and government. While I laboured to follow my calling as a New Testament scholar, I also agonized over the fate of loved ones back home, my parents and the Church of God. The government had even expelled the Anglican bishop of Accra for criticizing attempts to divinize the head of state—which gave one to think more deeply about the Church and persecution.

Just about that time I had the privilege of hearing the lectures of Professor Owen Chadwick, Master of Selwyn College, Cambridge, on the Church in Nazi Germany and of Dr Ernst Bammel on the Revelation of John and the other Johannine writings. Needless to say these courses focused my attention on the subject of persecutions, firing my imagination and also answering some of my questions concerning the circumstances of my motherland. As if to confirm me in a study of persecutions, I had the further privilege of studying, with my beloved teacher and mentor, Professor Charles F.D. Moule, then Lady Margaret Professor of Divinity, the influence of historical circumstances on New Testament eschatology. Once more, the question of persecutions came up. At that point I resolved to prepare this study of the theme of persecution and martyrdom.

I wish to dedicate this volume to those six scholars who have deeply influenced my theological thinking and development. Professor C.F.D. Moule impressed me with his cautious, meticulous scholarship; he represented for me an island of liberal evangelicalism in an age in which it was almost fashionable to be radical. But above all, he forced me to work through the biblical texts systematically. Professor Noel Q. King, who had been my Professor in the University of Ghana, was my first teacher, and the one who persuaded me to read Divinity. The Revd J.P.M. Sweet was my director of studies at Selwyn. But he was also my friend. Dr Ernst Bammel was my

'Arbeitsvater' who introduced me to the world of German scholarship. He too became a friend. Professor W. Owen Chadwick was the Master of my College in Cambridge, Selwyn. He took a keen interest in my development and he became a friend. My last teacher was the late Revd Dr S.G. Williamson. In my second year at the University College of Ghana, I had him for my supervisor. He made me work; he opened up the subject to me; he forced me to think through issues. These six men have been some of the greatest influences on my life, particularly my theological and religious development. I wish, by dedicating this volume to them, to express my deepest gratitude for all that they have done for me.

I wish to thank Dr E. Bammel for encouraging me to publish this study, Professor Moule and the Revd J.P.M. Sweet for reading and criticizing different drafts of the study. Furthermore, it is fitting to express gratitude to the Institute for Ecumenical and Cultural Research, St John's University, Collegeville, Minnesota, the University of Ghana and the Theological Education Fund (London) for their varying contributions to the preparation of this work for publication.

I am pleased to express my gratitude to the Battume-Baker Fund of the Divinity School, University of Cambridge for the 'grant of £200 to subvent the publication costs' of this monograph in the JSNT Supplement Series.

Finally I wish to thank Mr Michael Folivi, Administrative Assistant to the Dean of Arts and Miss Evelyn Tetteh, Secretary to the Dean of Arts in the University of Ghana, for their patient and careful typing of the manuscript.

ABBREVIATIONS

BA	*Biblical Archaeologist*
BJRL	*Bulletin of the John Rylands Library*
BR	*Biblical Research*
BZ	*Biblische Zeitschrift*
CAH	*Cambridge Ancient History*
CBQ	*Catholic Biblical Quarterly*
CGB	Cambridge Greek Bible
CSEL	*Corpus Scriptorum Ecclesiasticorum Latinorum*
DLZ	*Deutsche Literaturzeiting*
EB	*Encyclopaedia Biblica*
ETL	*Ephemerides Theologicae Lovanienses*
ExpT	*Expository Times*
EQ	*Evangelical Quarterly*
HDB	Hastings, *Dictionary of the Bible*
HJ	*Hibbert Journal*
HTR	*Harvard Theological Review*
HUCA	*Hebrew Union College Annual*
ICC	International Critical Commentary
IEJ	*Israel Exploration Journal*
JAOS	*Journal of the American Oriental Society*
JBL	*Journal of Biblical Literature*
JE	*Jewish Encyclopaedia*
JEH	*Journal of Ecclesiastical History*
JJS	*Journal of Jewish Studies*
JRS	*Journal of Roman Studies*
JQR	*Jewish Quarterly Review*
JSS	*Journal of Semitic Studies*
JTS	*Journal of Theological Studies*
LAB	*Liber Antiquitatum Biblicarum*
MGWJ	*Monatsschrift für Geschichte und Wissenschaft des Judentums*
NJKAG	*Neue Jahrbücher für des klassischen Altertums Geschichte*
NTS	*New Testament Studies*
REG	*Revue des études grecques*
RHPR	*Revue d'Histoire et de Philosophie Religieuses*
RQ	*Revue de Qumran*
RSR	*Recherches de Science religieuse*

SAB	*Sitzungsberichte der preussischen Akademie der Wissenschaften*
BSNTS	*Studiorum Novi Testamenti Societas Bulletin*
SJT	*Scottish Journal of Theology*
TDNT	*Theological Dictionary of the New Testament*
TLZ	*Theologische Literaturzeitung*
TQ	*Theologische Quartalschrift*
TR	*Theologische Rundschau*
ThStKr	*Theologische Studien und Kritiken*
TTZ	*Trierer Theologische Zeitschrift*
ZAW	*Zeitschrift für die alttestamentliche Wissenschaft*
ZKG	*Zeitschrift für Kirchengeschichte*
ZNW	*Zeitschrift für die neutestamentliche Wissenschaft*
ZRGG	*Zeitschrift für Religions- und Geistesgeschichte*
ZSysTh	*Zeitschrift für Systematische Theologie*
ZTK	*Zeitschrift für Theologie und Kirche*

Chapter 1

FORMS OF PERSECUTION MENTIONED OR
ALLUDED TO IN THE PAULINE LITERATURE

The letters of Paul contain references to institutions and events
which were associated with persecution. Some of these are references
to actual persecutions; others are a figurative use of them to set forth
various ideas. Therefore, a survey of those forms of persecutions
should be a useful background study to the theme of persecution and
martyrdom in the Pauline letters.

The Arena
According to 1 Cor. 4.9 the apostles are 'like men condemned to
death in the arena' (ὡς ἐπιθανατίους, ὅτι θέατρον ἐγενήθημεν). Paul
compares the circumstances of the apostles of Christ with those of
men condemned to death through combat with gladiators or wild
beasts in the theatre. The theatre was the meeting place of the δῆμος
which had legislative and judicial functions (Josephus, *Bell.* 1.654; cf.
Josephus, *Ant.* 18.160f.; Acts 19.29).[1] There judicial sentences were
carried out.

The amphitheatre was an oval or circular building. In its interior
was the 'arena' which derived its name from the fact that it was
strewn with sand. That section, the scene of the contests, was
surrounded by the cages of the beasts and the rooms of the
combatants. These rooms were really gaols because the combatants
were largely recruited from among condemned criminals, prisoners
of war and slaves, though there were sometimes volunteers (Josephus,
Ap. 1.43; 2.53-54; Tacitus, *Ann.* 15.44).[2]

Condemnation to the arena did not always spell death. Though
sometimes the criminals were tied to stakes and thereby made
defenceless against starved wild beasts, on other occasions they were
allowed the use of weapons which, more often than not, only

prolonged the torment.[3] However, those who survived the beasts were handed over to either private or imperial establishments. If at the end of three years they had not fallen dead in the arena, they were given a wooden cross to signify relief from the arena. Some were given a hat after five years to signify manumission.[4]

Condemnation to the arena was reserved for the worst offences, i.e. robbery, sacrilege, murder, arson and mutiny (Callistratus, *Dig.*48.28; Paulus, *Sent.* 6.7.3.1; Quintilian, *de Cognit.* 6.9, 21). However, on certain occasions, for example when there was a shortage of combatants for the arena, the imperial caprice consigned others besides the worst offenders to the arena. Indeed, although as a rule a Roman citizen could neither be made to fight as a 'bestiarius' or 'venator' in the arena, nor be flung *ad leonem*,[5] some emperors compelled citizens to perform in the arena. For example, the emperor Caligula (AD 37-41) compelled Esius Proculus, a Roman citizen, and others to perform in the arena (Suetonius, *Caligula* 18). Similarly, Piso-Caesonimus, proconsul of Macedonia, sent a number of innocent men to Publius Clodius for his aedile games.

In New Testament times condemnation to the arena was predominantly a Roman form of penalty. It is estimated that there were some two hundred and seventy Roman amphitheatres all over the empire, the notable ones being the Colosseum at Rome, and those at Scaurus and Pompeii. But Herod Agrippa is reported to have made one thousand and four hundred criminals in his realm fight in his amphitheatre at Berytus (Josephus, *Ant.* 19.7.5). The punishment was resented as a form of Romanizing or hellenizing.

1 Cor. 4.9 is obviously a figurative use of the amphitheatre imagery to capture the life and death struggle in which apostles of Christ were engaged in the pursuit of their commission to preach to the whole world. Similarly, the reference to Paul fighting beasts at Ephesus (1 Cor. 15.32), whatever its interpretation, also reflects the life and death struggle and danger that accompany the apostolic ministry. It underlines the ignominy and humiliation involved in being disciples of Christ. But they by the same token became a spectacle to the world: through them Christ is 'placarded'.

Crucifixion

A central proclamation of the earliest community of believers was the crucifixion of Christ (1 Cor. 1.23; b*Sanh.* 43a). Many other Christians subsequently died on the cross for their convictions about Jesus

Christ (Tacitus, *Ann.* 15.44; cf. Josephus, *Ant.* 18.63-64; Eusebius, *H.E.* 1.11.7-8). Crucifixion in the manner Jesus experienced it was never really a Jewish mode of execution. In the canonical Old Testament literature, Ezra 6.11 is unique in its reference to the impalement of a living body when it refers to the decree of Cyrus that 'whosoever shall alter this word, let a beam be pulled out from his house, and let him be lifted up (*zqyp* = ὠρθωμένος)[6] and fastened thereon'. That, of course, was decreed by a Persian. We know that Alexander Jannaeus (104-78 BC) crucified about eight hundred captives in Jerusalem (Josephus, *Bell.* 1.97, 113). Otherwise the nearest to this predominantly Roman form of execution in Jewry was the impalement which occurred after the person had been executed by stoning[7] (Philo, *De Spec. Leg.* 28). The point of such impalement was to propitiate God and warn men against the evil that brought on this punishment (Deut. 21.22; 2 Macc. 15.35; Josephus, *Bell.* 4.317). It was meant to be an additional disgrace and not the punishment itself (Jos. 10.26; 1 Sam. 31.10). It was the hanging and not the death which brought the ignomiy on the sufferer and also the defilement of the land. And it is this aspect which makes an easy transition to the use of the word crucifixion for Jewish hangings.[8]

However, crucifixion in the proper sense of the word is predominantly a Roman form of cruel execution and punishment (e.g. Philo, *Flacc.* 72; *Midr. Teh.* 11.7) for hardened criminals, e.g. the one who commits sacrilege by robbing a temple; the soldier who deserts; the one who is guilty of high treason and insurrection.[9] In principle crucifixion was reserved for slaves and according to the *Lex Porcia* and *Lex Sempronia* a Roman citizen could not be crucified.[10] However, there were occasional violations of this law. For example in about AD 66 Florus 'ventured . . . to do what none had ever done before, namely, to scourge before his tribunal and nail to the cross men of equestrian rank, men who, if Jews by birth, were at least invested with that Roman dignity' (Josephus, *Bell.* 2.308).

The actual mode of execution need not detain us here, as it is adequately dealt with elsewhere.[11] But for our purposes it is enough to emphasize that the execution was as a rule carried out by soldiers; for the imperial governors were military administrators and the judicial power flowed out of *coercitio*,[12] a military authority. As Suetonius puts it, *saepe, in conspectu prandentis vel comissantis . . . miles decollandi artifex, quibuscumque et custodia capita amputabat*

(Suetonius, *Cal.* 32). This point, if taken seriously, raises questions about Paul's claim that it was the Jews who killed Jesus (1 Thess. 2.15). The fact that Jesus was crucified means that the Roman authorities accepted responsibility for his death and did execute him for some alleged criminal act. The early church's claim that it was the Jews who crucified Christ may, therefore, not be the whole truth; it may be in part tendentious and a piece of anti-Jewish propaganda. The cross was for the Jew and Gentile alike the most terrible fate that could overtake a man. For the Roman view Cicero and Tacitus may be taken as typical: according to the former, crucifixion is 'crudelissimum taeterritumque supplicium' (*In Verr.* 5.64). Tacitus refers to it as 'supplicium servile' (*Ann.* 4.3, 11). Crucifixion is a despicable death.

It was considered equally terrible by the Jews. The most eloquent evidence lies in the various translations of Deuteronomy 21.23: *ky qllt 'lhym tlwy*. This Hebrew text is rather ambiguous because *'lhym* may be either a subjective or an objective genitive. Thus there are two main translations. First, the LXX translated it thus: ὅτι κεκαταραμένος ὑπὸ θεοῦ πᾶς κρεμάμενος ἐπὶ ξύλου, i.e. 'he who hangs is accursed in the sight of God'. This translation, which is followed by Paul (cf. Gal. 3.13), states in no uncertain terms that crucifixion is the worst disaster; it is to be rejected by God. However, the second translation, which does not deny that it is a disaster, is a little more positive in its understanding of crucifixion. That translation is represented by Jewish writers such as Aquila, Theodotion, Symmachus, and the Targum of Jonathan—as well as by the Syriac Peshitta. These interpret Deut. 21.23 as 'he who hangs is a contempt, a reproach/insult to God'. Lightfoot explained that this second interpretation bears the marks of the experience of persecution by the Jews as the people of God: they found it difficult to believe that the crucified heroes of faith were under the curse of God.[13] Therefore, for them the experience of the most shameful punishment by men of faith was a challenge to the Almighty God whom they served.

There appear to be three reasons for the very negative attitude to the cross: first, the most intense pain that went with it; second, the shame due to its servile associations; and third, in the case of the Jews, the curse that may attach to it. It is therefore, hardly any wonder that the Christians' claim that the idea of the crucified Jesus as Lord was difficult for Jew and Gentile alike to accept.

The Sword

At Rom. 8.35 Paul asserts that not even the sword can separate devotees of God from God's love through Christ. The citation of Ps. 44.22, 'For thy sake we are killed all the day long . . . ', makes it more than likely that he is thinking of persecution by the sword.

In the Jewish world the sword was used in times of war to despatch the vanquished after a blow or spear had been used; in peacetime it was used to execute malefactors. According to Jewish law the inhabitants of an apostate city, adulterers and murderers were to be killed by the sword (Deut. 13.13-19; Num. 25.7; 1 Kgs 18.40; 2 Kgs 23.20; b*Sanh.* 50a, 52b). It appears to have been essentially a royal form of execution (2 Kgs 6.31; Jer. 26.23; Acts 12.2; Josephus, *Bell.* 1.367; Est. 13.6).

In theory the Christians could be condemned to the sword for supposedly being apostates. But, of course, in New Testament times the Jewish authorities had no authority to condemn to death; the death penalty was the prerogative of Caesar or his representative.

The Romans practised *decollatio*, i.e. beheading by the sword, in place of beheading by the axe which was a common practice under the empire (Suetonius, *Nero* 49; Tacitus, *Ann.* 2.32).[14] The execution was in the hands of the military. That authority was in the time of Domitian known as the *jus gladii* and goes back to the early principate (cf. Josephus, *Bell.* 2.117).[15] Execution by the sword was so characteristically Roman that R. Judah stigmatized it as a Roman practice (Mishnah, *Sanh.* 7.3):[16] 'The ordinance of them that are to be beheaded [is this]: they used to cut off his head with a sword as the [Roman] government does'.

Stoning

Stoning as a mode of capital punishment is predominantly Jewish (1 Kgs 20.13; 2 Chron. 10.18; 24.21).[17] It was not always a legal matter; popular anger and mob-violence often were expressed in this form of execution (Philo, *Flacc.* 66).

As a Jewish capital punishment, no details are preserved with regard to the manner of stoning in the period before the Mishnah. The only stipulation was that it should take place outside the city (Lev. 24.14; Num. 15.36; Josephus, *Ap.* 2.217). According to Mishnah *Sanh.* 6.1, 'When sentence (of stoning) has been passed they take him forth to stone him. The place of stoning was outside (far away from) the court, as it is written, "Bring forth him that hath cursed outside the camp".' There is, however, one example of stoning within the temple-precincts, namely that of Zechariah the son of Jehoiada the priest (2 Chron. 24.20-21; cf. Mt. 23.35; *Proph. Vit.* 44 line 8; 71 lines 1-2). But that looks like a conspiracy rather than a legal procedure. The witnesses were obliged to cast the first stone (Deut. 17.7; cf. Acts 7.50). But in rabbinic times one witness cast the first stone on the chest of the convicted man. If this failed to kill him, others joined in to complete it. And the execution was often followed by hanging (Josephus, *Ant.* 4.24).

Stoning was administered to the following assortment of offenders: (a) a blasphemer, i.e. anyone who made an attack on the fundamental belief of Judaism—Lev. 24.15-16; Deut. 17.2-5; b*Sanh.* 49b; (b) a necromancer and wizard—Ex. 22.18; Lev. 20.27; (c) a desecrator of the sabbath—Ex. 31.14-15; Num. 15.32-36; (d) a *msyt*, i.e. one who incites individuals to idolatry—Deut. 13.6-10; 1 Macc. 2.24-26; Philo, *De Spec. Leg.* 1.54-57; b*Sanh.* 50b; (e) the *maddiaḥ*, i.e. the one who seduces a whole town to idolatry—b*Sanh.* 49b, 53a. For our purposes, it is of interest to emphasize that messengers of God who seemed to challenge the ecclesiastical *status quo* could easily be caught under one of these offences (cf. Josephus, *Ant.* 20.197f.: the stoning of James the Just).

However, the references to the stoning of Paul at Lystra (Acts 14.8-20) and of Stephen in Jerusalem (Acts 7) are so vague that it is difficult to be sure whether they were legal executions or mob-violence.

Burning

Burning as a legal mode of punishment is not usual in the Greek and Roman world, though *The Twelve Tablets* recommend burning for the arsonist. Whether this is a matter of retaliation as distinct from a legal form of execution is not clear. Again, the burnings of Christians at the orders of Nero may have been at the whim of a dictator rather than a legal procedure (cf. Tacitus *Ann.* 15.44; Dio Cassius, 65.6.3; Mart. Polyc. 5.2; 11.2; 15.1, 2; 16.1, 2; Eusebius, *H.E.* 5.1.41-43).

Before the Romans[18] the Seleucids appear to have punished rebellious Jews by burning them (Dan. 3.28; Song of the Holy Children; 2 Macc. 6.11; 7; 13.4-8; 4 Macc. 6.27; Ass. Mos. 6.9; 8.4; Josephus, *Ant.* 10.213; Josephus, *Bell.* 1.100; 2.152; 7.48; Philo, *Flacc.* 67). The problem here is that it is difficult to distinguish fact from fiction. For example, later tradition reports that the patriarch

Abraham was thrown into the fire for refusing to worship Nimrod's gods.[19] But such elaborations probably indicate the later interest in martyrdom. However, in Jewry execution by burning was customary. It was either a penalty in itself, as in the case of a harlot or of the adulterous daughter of a priest (Gen. 38.24; b*Sanh.* 49b-50a) or a measure to enhance the death penalty (Lev. 20.14; Josh. 7.25; Mishnah *Sanh.* 9).

In view of the nature of the offences for which burning was prescribed in Judaism, it is most unlikely that burning as a form of persecution would be Jewish in origin. This, however, does not deny that it could have arisen from a mob-violence or have had the form of even a religious suicide as happened when Faustus Cornelius, Furius and Fabius marched into Jerusalem to take it for Pompey (cf. Josephus, *Bell.* 1.150-151, 655; 6.271-272; 7.385-387; 4 Esd. 10.22).

Let us turn from capital punishment to other forms of persecution such as imprisonments, excommunication and corporal punishment.

Imprisonment
This form of penalty is in abundant evidence in both the Jewish and Roman worlds. Among the Jews, initially it was not a punishment for crime but a restraint of freedom (Jer. 20.2; 29.26; 1 Kgs 22.24, 26; 2 Chron. 16.10; 18.25f.). But after the exile of 586 BC it was recognized as a legal form of punishment to be awarded by a judge (Ezr. 7.26; 3 Macc. 4.25; 5.6), although even during the first commonwealth it was already becoming a punishment (1 Kgs 22.27; Jer. 37.15f.). But in this latter case it was more like an arbitrary punishment inflicted by kings and magistrates on those who incurred their displeasure.

The rabbis did recommend imprisonment for murder: 'If a man committed murder but there were no witnesses, they must put him in prison and feed him with the bread of adversity and the water of affliction' (Mishnah, *Sanh.* 9.5). If a man is found guilty for the same offence, he is to be imprisoned: 'If a man was scourged (and committed again the same transgression) and was scourged a second time, (if he transgressed a third time), the court must put him in a prison-cell and feed him with barley until his belly burst' (Mishnah, *Sanh.* 9.5). On other occasions it was a temporary imprisonment while one awaited trial (b*Sanh.* 78b; cf. Mishnah *Sanh.* 9.1). According to Mishnah b*Hag.* 9.4, when a victim is on the danger list, his assailant is kept in prison until the result is known. R. Nehemiah (c. 140-165) also taught incarceration, but allowed that the assailant may be released if the victim survives or, having been thought likely to die, seems to recover and then deteriorates and dies. In the latter case, the assailant is to be executed. The last two categories, i.e. persistent offences and temporary imprisonment while awaiting trial, would be most applicable to the Christians.

On the other hand, *abductio in carcerem* or *in vincula* was not recognized as a penalty in Roman law. But it played a dual role in the *coercitio*: (a) It was a way by which the magistrates defended their dignity and secured obedience from both private citizens and lower magistrates and senators.[20] Thus according to *Dig.* 48. 19.8, 9, *carcer enim ad continendos homines non ad puniendos haberi debet*; (b) It was sometimes a 'precautionary measure to secure the appearance on trial of one whom they accused'.[21] This gives the preventive detention a quasi-punitive character in Cicero's day. For example, Paul's 'imprisonment' referred to in his letter to the Philippians was a custody until the trial.

However, in Roman law there also was provision for safeguarding the rights of a Roman citizen. A praetorian interdict *ad exhibendum* could order that an imprisoned private man be produced. On the other hand, where a magistrate had detained a citizen, only the *auxilium* of another magistrate of equal or higher authority could save him from his plight. During the last century of the Republic the *provocatio ad populum* protected the citizen against death, flogging and imprisonment. This privilege was reaffirmed by the *Lex Julia de vi publica*, which forbade anyone invested with *imperium* or *potestas* to condemn or put in bonds a Roman citizen who appealed to the people, or to prevent a defendant from presenting himself in Rome within a certain period of time.[22] Of course, there were departures from this norm, as Cicero's *In Verrem* shows.

Expulsion (Excommunication)
In Jewish society, excommunication, i.e. exclusion from the religious community, was the highest ecclesiastical censure. Jewish excommunication during the time of Christ grew out of the *ḥrm* (the ban), which meant devotion to destruction. In pre-exilic times idolatry was punishable by death (Is. 34.2, 5; Mic. 4.13; Jer. 50.21). But this law was modified out of humanitarian considerations to excommunication (Ezr. 10.8). Indeed, in New Testament times excommunication was the regular punishment for serious moral and religious offences. For example, the Samaritans were excommunicated from the temple for

desecrating it with the bones of dead men (Josephus, *Ant.* 18.30). Thus in New Testament times excommunication was an institution which aimed at the preservation of the solidarity of the Jewish people and of the authority of the synagogue.

The application of it in the Qumran community is of interest. The Qumran community excommunicated those who lied about their property (1QS 6.24), those who arrogantly transgressed the Law (1QS 8.17, 22), and those who recanted under persecution (1QS 7.1; cf. Josephus, *Bell.* 2.143f.). Furthermore, in the Qumran community excommunication was either for ever, as in the case of those who 'commit (an offence) with a high hand' (1QS 9.1), or a temporary expulsion, as in the case of those who commit 'accidental sins' (1QS 9.2).

Between AD 90 and AD 100 the Jews inserted a twelfth petition into the *Shemoneh Esreh* so as to exclude the Christians from the synagogue. It read: 'For apostates (*mšmdym*) let there be no hope, . . . And let the *Notsrim* (i.e. Christians) and the *Minim* (i.e. the heretics) perish as in a day'.[23] This petition became in effect the test of whether the worshipper in the synagogue was Christian or not.[24] A man who could not repeat that twelfth petition was thereby recognized as an apostate from Judaism and therefore excommunicated.

Excommunication was, therefore, by and large a legal measure to which resort was made by a judicial court for prescribed offences, although individuals were allowed to pronounce it on particular occasions.[25] Although it was legal, the procedure was not very formal or rigorous, for circumstantial or hearsay evidence was admissible.[26] There also was a lighter informal punishment called *nzyph*.

Expulsions were of two types: (a) the *ndy* or *smt'* which lasted up to thirty days; and (b) the severer *hrm* which lasted much longer.[27]

The Talmud mentions twenty-four cases for which excommunication could be administered (cf. b*Ber.* 19a). But later authorities enumerate among them the following: (a) insulting a learned man, (b) calling an Israelite a slave, (c) refusing to appear before a court at the appointed time, (d) dealing lightly with rabbinic or Mosaic precepts, (e) refusing to abide by the precepts of the court, (f) causing others to profane the name of God, (g) preventing a community from performing some religious act, (h) being made the subject of a scandal (in the case of a rabbi). Various charges, of those mentioned above, could be the ground for Christians' being prosecuted and expelled from the synagogue.

Roman society also offers examples of expulsions. A Roman citizen could choose *exilium* so as to avoid final condemnation (Sallust, *Catiline* 51.21, 40).[28] Sometimes too it was a penalty in itself, as was the case in the exile of Flaccus Avillius (Philo, *Flacc.* 147f.), Seneca (*Ad Polybiam* and *Ad Helviam*), the banishment of Herod Archelaus to Vienne in Gaul in AD 6 (Josephus, *Bell.* 2.39f.) and the exile of Cumanus (Josephus, *Bell.* 2.245). However, all these are juridically different cases. Nearer home, we have the expulsion of the various *collegia*, e.g. of Isis in 58 BC.[29] In the period under study we have the expulsion of the Jews from Rome in AD 49 (Acts 18.2).[30] Later still, Domitian banished Flavia Domitilla to the island of Pandataria for 'atheism' (Dio Cassius, *Epitome* 67.14).[31]

Corporal Punishment
The Apostle Paul was subjected to corporal punishment by both the Jews (2 Cor. 11.24) and the Roman authorities (Acts 16).

Scourging seems to be the only corporal punishment mentioned in the Pentateuch.[32] According to Deut. 25.2-3, the number of strokes should not exceed forty and the punishment was to be administered in the presence of the judges. Later, however, the number was specified as forty less one—hence the description of this corporal punishment as the 'forty save one' (2 Cor. 11.24; Josephus, *Ant.* 4.231, 233).[33] That figure was settled on for two reasons: (a) by this time the three-thonged scourge had replaced the rod[34] and thirteen strokes with that gave thirty-nine; (b) to avoid any error in counting.

In the Old Testament the only offence for which corporal punishment was explicitly adminstered is an unjust charge against a newly married bride (Deut. 22.13f.). However, those who challenged the religious *status quo*, e.g. the prophets, were sometimes treated to corporal punishment (Acts 5.40; Is. 53.6). In rabbinic times stripes were recommended for the breaking of 'negative commands' and for crimes for which the Torah decreed excision from the people (cf. Mishnah, *Makkoth* 2.4, 10, 12; Mishnah, *Hullin* 12.4).

The actual mode of this penalty need not detain us here, as it is clearly spelt out elsewhere.[35] The point of interest for our purposes, however, is that once the culprit had been flogged, his civil rights were restored to him.[36]

There is considerable evidence of corporal punishment adminstered by the Roman authorities (Acts 16.22, 23, 27; 22.24-25). In the Roman legal procedure flogging belonged to police action[37] and was, therefore, administered by the lictors (i.e. the attendants on the magistrates) with the *fasces*.

There appears to have been gradations of beatings: *fustes, flagella* and *verbera*.[38] But these were never punishments by themselves but were always associated with other reproof.[39] Thus, for example, the *fustigatio*, which is the lightest form of corporal punishment, was accompanied by the magisterial warning, when the governor considered a formal *cognitio* unnecessary. It was thus an act of *coercitio*, as for example in a case of fire due to negligence (Paulus, *Dig.* 1.153.1). Paul's experiences at Philippi (Acts 16.22-24) and Jerusalem (Acts 22.24) were examples of the cautionary flogging under the *coercitio*.

The *Lex Porcia* and the Valerian Law exempted Roman citizens from being flogged because that was *scelus*. But, as Cicero's indictment against Verres shows, this norm was sometimes violated.[40] And, of course, Paul protested at his flogging by the Roman authorities at Philippi (Acts 16.37) and had his right as a Roman citizen upheld (cf. Acts 22.25).

This survey of a number of punishments has suggested a legal dimension to these courses of action. However, persecutions need not always have had a juridical basis. Sometimes it was the outcome of caprice on the part of those in authority; at other times it could have been mob-violence with perhaps a quasi-legal flavour. For example, the mob in Jerusalem attacked Paul, invoking a law of 'instant death without appeal' against anyone who profaned the temple (Acts 21.28, 29, 32; cf. Philo, *Leg.* 307).[41] It was legal only in so far as they were invoking Jewish customary law; but considered from the standpoint of the Roman overlords of Palestine, it was illegal because it was the Roman practice to reserve the *jus gladii* for the procurator and a death sentence had to be approved by the Roman authorities.[42]

However, it is reasonable to suppose that Rome was sometimes indulgent as long as the victim was not a Roman citizen or a non-citizen of some rank. The reaction of the authorities to the martyrdom of James the Just shows that Rome was apt to intervene in the case of a non-citizen of some importance (Eusebius, *H.E.* 2.23.1-19).

Lynching was in general for apostasy and blasphemy. According to Philo, *De Spec. Leg.* 1.54-57, 'If any of the Nation fall away from honouring the One, they ought to be punished with the most extreme penalties . . . So then it is fittingly enjoined upon all who have a zeal for virtue that they should immediately and out of hand execute the penalties, taking the culprits to no court, to no council, indeed to no ruler of any kind.'[43] Similarly according to Mishnah, *Sanh.* 9.6, 'If a man stole a sacred vessel or cursed by *kosem* or made an Aramaean woman his paramour, the zealots may fall upon him. If a priest served [at the Altar] in a state of uncleanness his brethren the priests did not bring him to a court, but the young men among the priests took him outside the Temple Court and split open his brain with clubs.' So lynching was a recognized institution in Jewish society, its application having a quasi-legal nature and being dependent on the mood of the mob. The implication is that a persecution may not always be the result of due process of the law to punish an offence but also a mob action.

Certain deductions may be made as from this survey of the forms of sufferings the Christians underwent. First, since the *jus gladii* was held by the Roman authorities, cases of capital punishment, e.g. the crucifixion of Jesus, indicate that the Romans accepted responsibility for those punishments. Second, it follows from the first point that the picture given by the New Testament books, particularly the Gospels and the Acts of the Apostles, that the Jews were the *fons persecutionis* is a tendentious statement which needs to be taken *cum grano salis*.

Chapter 2

TOWARDS A THEOLOGY OF MARTYRDOM IN JUDAISM

1. *Introduction*

The letters of Paul together with other New Testament writings presuppose *inter alia* a Church under attack, e.g. 1 Thessalonians, Philippians, Revelation and 1 Peter. The apostle himself met with so much persecution that he could describe himself as ἐν κόποις περισσοτέρως, ἐν φυλακαῖς περισσοτέρως, ἐν πληγαῖς ὑπερβαλλόντως, ἐν θανάτοις πολλάκις (2 Cor. 11.23). Since theology emerges from the experience of a people, it would be a surprise if the experience of attack, indeed persecution, did not leave its mark and did not influence the documents of the Church. As C.F.D. Moule has observed, the documents embody 'defence or counter-attack'.[1] It could even be argued that experiences of persecution provided the language and imagery suitable for describing Christian experience.

The Church was not the first institution to experience opposition and attack. Judaism, the matrix in which Christianity was born, had her full share of sufferings. Ps. 129.1-2 tell the story of Jewish suffering:

'Sorely have they afflicted me from my youth',
    Let Israel now say—
'Sorely have they afflicted me from my youth,
    yet they have not prevailed against me'.

Israel's history was one long tale of oppression and suppression and violence both from within and without. In this connexion the Graeco-Roman period of Israel's history is the classic example, because that age of Judaism, which emerged from the Babylonian captivity as a church-state, had a traumatic experience of persecutions to a degree unparallelled in its history. Our task in this chapter is to examine that experience of the Jews as a background to our study of the Pauline corpus.

Scholars have long pointed out the connexion between persecutions and the literary genre of apocalyptic.[2] The golden age of apocalyptic literature, from about 200 BC to about AD 135, falls during the period stretching from the conflict between the Jews and the Seleucids over the issue of how much Hellenistic culture could be accommodated by Judaism, into the first two centuries of the Christian Church's existence. It would be a miracle if apocalyptic literature and, through that, the ideas emerging from persecution and martyrdom did not make some impact on the Church. Indeed, Schlatter has suggested that this apocalyptic Judaism, with its presupposition of the trauma of the experience of martyrdom, did significantly influence the early Church,[3] even if it was only one stream in the development of Christianity.

The crucial importance of the Maccabaean martyrs is more than a hypothesis; it is well borne out by the spread of literature relating to them. This brings us to a brief survey of the literature.

The primary source is the book of Daniel which was originally composed in Aramaic and Hebrew in Palestine in about 165 BC. There are numerous references to Daniel as the prototype and ideal martyr–1 Macc. 2.60; 4 Macc. 13.9; 16.3, 21; 18.13; Heb. 11.34; Jos. *Ant.* 10.260-263; *Gen. R.* 34 and b.*Ab. Zar.* 8b. There are also numerous talmudic and midrashic references to the three companions of Daniel, namely Hananiah, Mishael and Azariah—*Sanh.* 93a; *Ab. Zar.* 3a; *Ta'an.* 18b; *Pes.* 118a, 94a; 1 Macc. 2.5; 4 Macc. 13.9; 16.3, 21; 18.12; *Cant. R.* 7.8; Pal. Targumim Gen. 38.25.[4] More striking are the amplifications of the text of Daniel which heighten the martyrological aspect. Thus in the LXX there is added at the end of Daniel *Bel and the Dragon*, which probably goes back to an Aramaic or Hebrew original.[5] Further, the Greek versions followed by the Syriac, Latin and Arabic versions interpolate the *Song of the Three Children* at Dan. 3.3.

These numerous references to Daniel, Hananiah, Mishael, and Azariah and the amplifications of the text of Daniel in the LXX, Syriac, Latin and Arabic versions attest a lively interest in the Maccabaean martyrs, some of the references being contemporaneous with Paul and the NT. The Maccabaean martyrs are cited in these Jewish sources as examples to posterity of total and uncompromising dedication to God, the Torah and ancestral tradition, even though it meant sufferings and/or death for themselves.

Of the documents from Palestine showing interest in the Maccabaen martyrs we cite especially 1 Maccabees, which later came to be appropriated by the Christian Church. That document dates between 105 BC and 64 BC[6] and claims to trace the history of the persecution of the Jews from Antiochus IV (c. 175-163 BC) to Antiochus VII (Sidetes).

2 Maccabees, also dating from the first century BC, is, unlike 1 Maccabees, a religious rather than a purely historical book. It looks at the historical facts of the Maccabaean times from a religious perspective and interprets them theologically.[7]

3 Maccabees, purporting to be a historical narrative, tells the story of how Ptolemy IV's attempt to enter the Jerusalem sanctuary at the time of the battle of Raphia (c. 217 BC) was frustrated and how he, consequently, wrought vengeance on the Alexandrian Jews. But the work has more of fiction than history about it, and had a primarily religious purpose, being intended to be read in the synagogues of Egypt at some festival celebrating their deliverance (3 Macc. 6.30-41; 7.19).[8] The book itself dates from early in the first century AD.[9]

4 Maccabees dates from the first half of the first century AD[10] and was composed probably at Antioch in Syria.[11] It seeks to argue that the four cardinal virtues of prudence, justice, courage and temperance may be attained through strict adherence to the Jewish law, such as that exemplified by the lives of the Maccabaean martyrs. There are similarities between 2 Maccabees and 4 Maccabees, but for our purposes it is enough to assume that the two works have drawn independently on an older source or tradition.[12]

Another book dealing with the Maccabaean martyrs is the book of *Enoch*. It is a composite work, but the section covering chs. 1–104 probably dates from Maccabaean times.[13] Needless to say, for our purposes the most important section will be chs. 91–104 which deal with persecutions.

Let us now draw together the threads of the literature relating to the Maccabaean martyrs. First, there appears to have been interest in the Maccabaean martyrs in both Palestinian and Hellenistic Judaism. The former is adequately represented by 1 Maccabees, while the latter is represented by 2 and 4 Maccabees. Secondly, the interest in the Maccabaean martyrs appears to have been keener in the diaspora, especially in Syria—as is evidenced by the embellishments, literary and theological, in 2 and 4 Maccabees, on the simpler Palestinian tradition. The embellishments seem to us to presuppose a situation in which the martyrs were revered.

This surmise, based on the existence of documents interested in the Maccabaean types, is usually borne out by the historical facts. There is evidence of a cult of the martyrs at Antioch right up to the fourth century AD when Christians took it over from the Jews.[14] Such a cult is evidence of continuing interest in martyrs, particularly the Maccabaean martyrs. Finally, there were some feasts which commemorated the martyrs as the giants and heroes of faith. Two such feasts were Hanukkah and Purim. Hanukkah, for example, which originally celebrated the recapture of the Jerusalem temple from the Seleucid ruler Antiochus Epiphanes and its rededication, now came to celebrate *inter alia* the giants of faith who shed their blood in defence of their ancestral religion.[18] Similarly, the seven Maccabaean brothers were commemmorated in the synagogue on the ninth of Ab (cf. b.*Ta'an.* 30a; Mishnah, *Soph.* 18.5, 9).[16]

The survey of the Maccabaean literature has suggested that there was a heightened interest in the cult of the martyrs particularly in the diaspora, notably Syria. This detail is not without interest for our Pauline studies. For not only was Antioch in Syria a great centre of and for Christian mission[17] (Acts 11.19f.; 13.1f.), but also Paul had a significant connexion with Antioch of Syria (Acts 11.25f.; Gal. 1.21-22). Thus it is not impossible that Paul, who himself had his full share of persecution and suffering for the sake of the gospel and preached Christ crucified for others, may have been influenced by the martyrological ideas of the world in which he travelled and taught and suffered.

We have spent a good deal of time on the Maccabaean martyrs and the sources for the related theology. That may give the impression that the basis for our claims concerning martyrdom is only the Maccabaean martyrs. That is far from our intention, for there are several other sources on other martyrs, at which we should now briefly glance.

Quite a few examples of the literature from the inter-testamental period and the first century AD show interest in martyr theology.

Ecclesiasticus is one such case. The Greek text which has survived to us dates from about 132 BC, although it is probably a translation from a Hebrew original dating probably from 190-180 BC.[18] For our purposes ch. 2 is of great importance. So much is it a martyrological text that Codex Vaticanus 346 gives that chapter the heading περὶ ὑπομονῆς; ὑπομονή is one of the marks of the martyrs. And, of course, the martyrs are included in the list of 'famous men' whose praises are sung in Ecclus 44ff., notably at 44.14, 45.23 (Phinehas the son of Eliazar), 48.12-13, and 50 (Simon Maccabaeus).

The *Wisdom of Solomon* dates from sometime in the first century AD.[19] For our purposes ch. 2, particularly vv. 10-21, dealing with the oppression of the righteous by the ungodly, are of interest. Those verses reveal more of a literary than a circumstantial character of the book: it does not bear the marks of originating from a very deep patriotic or religious feeling; it is dramatically inartistic, cool and in measured language. These facts make the book all the more interesting as evidence for current martyrological ideas.

The *Psalms of Solomon* are the outpouring of the soul of a troubled worshipper of Yahweh. It dates from sometime in the first century BC.[20] There are also the Qumran documents, particularly 1QS, 1QH and CD. These date from the second century BC to the first century AD,[21] and contain several references to persecution, e.g. 1QS 8.4; 1QH 2.12ff.; 1QpHab 7.

There are a number of relevant documents also from the first and second centuries AD—the *Assumption of Moses*, the *Martyrdom of Isaiah*, and the writings of Philo and Josephus.

The *Assumption of Moses* dates from the first three decades of the first century AD.[22] It purports to be a prediction by Moses of the history of the Jews from their entry into Canaan to the author's own day. That span of history is divided into three periods: (a) down to 170 BC (chs. 1–5); (b) Antiochus Epiphanes (chs. 8–9); (c) Antiochus Epiphanes to Herod the Great (ch. 6); (d) God's decrees concerning the End (ch. 7.10ff.). In content the history is one long tale of suffering by the Jews, for in each epoch the righteous suffer at the hands of either their compatriots or foreigners (3.1; 8.1, 5; 9.6; 6.3). The author's purpose in telling the story of the sufferings of their forebears was to encourage his contemporaries to embrace death rather than be disloyal to their God. Hence the author presents the epoch of Antiochus Epiphanes as the typical precursor of the final age.

The *Martyrdom of Isaiah* is most interesting because in actual history Isaiah did not die a martyr. But the book reflects a Jewish midrash on 2 Kgs 21.16. The date of the midrash is uncertain. But the *terminus ad quem* of the tradition, whether oral or written, may be put in the middle of the first century AD, because the epistle to the Hebrews (at 11.37) appears to have been acquainted with the legend. The *terminus a quo* is more difficult to ascertain. But it may be put sometime in the first century BC because it is implied in Ecclus 48.25.[23] Be that as it may, the appearance of the midrash is evidence of an interest in martyrdom and martyr theology.

The works of Philo of Alexandria which concern us are of different literary types. His *In Flaccum* and *Legatio ad Caium* form the two volumes of a history of the Jewish people under Caligula. They are straightforward history-writing. On the other hand, *De Providentia* and *Quod omnis probus liber sit* are treatises on particular themes, and martyrdom comes in only in so far as it illuminates or illustrates those themes. Philo was born between 20 and 10 BC and was a contemporary of Paul. The writings cited date from the first century AD and are almost certainly before AD 70.

As for the works of Josephus, our primary concern will be with his *Bellum Judaicum*, dating from AD 75-79, *Antiquitates*, written in AD 93-94 and *Contra Apionem* which dates after AD 94. The first two are basically histories, while the last one is a polemic against Apion. His references to martyrdom are incidental and meant to be illustrations of his theme of the 'instinct with every Jew from the day of his birth, to regard [the Scriptures] as the decrees of God, to abide by them and, if need be, cheerfully die for them' (Josephus, *Ap.* 1.42; *Bell.* 2.196, 197, 198; 3.360).

This survey of select Jewish literature from the period between 200 BC and AD 200 shows that there is some interest in martyrs and martyrdom in different areas, from both Palestine and the diaspora. They have been of different literary types—some history, some history written from a religious perspective; others are tractates and sermons. But throughout these works one is aware that Israel had an acute sense of persecution and suffering which inevitably left a mark on the documents of the Jews. Those marks will be isolated later on in this chapter.

Before we proceed to an analysis of the Jewish background there are some terms on which there is need for comment. We refer to persecution, martyr and confessor. By persecution we understand disabilities imposed or encountered because of one's convictions, particularly religious convictions. Such disabilities were not always violent or bloody; sometimes they involved intolerance like the prohibition by Antiochus Epiphanes of temple worship (1 Macc. 1.45), of the observance of the Sabbath and other feasts (1 Macc. 1.42, 45; 2 Macc. 6.6, 11); the prohibition of circumcision as a rite of Jewish national identity (1 Macc 1.60; 2 Macc. 6.10); and the establishment of the 'desolating abomination' in the temple. It is another question whether the one who inflicted these disabilities saw them as acts of persecution or merely as the due process of the law as it caught up with violators of that law. It is submitted that the use of the word 'persecution' presupposes the viewpoint of the one who experiences disabilities and/or that of his sympathizer.

From about the second century AD a distinction has been drawn between the martyr and the confessor. According to this distinction the word 'martyr' has been reserved for the one who paid with his life for his religious faith. Examples are Stephen (Acts 7), James Boanerges (Acts 12.1ff.), Antipas of the church of Pergamon in Asia Minor (Rev. 2.13), Ignatius of Antioch, and Polycarp of Smyrna. The other term, 'confessor', has been reserved for those who came under disabilities in consequence of their religion but did not pay the ultimate price of death.

However, that distinction was not drawn from the first.[24] The μάρτυς was one who witnessed to God. A man could witness to God by abiding in the commandments of God, whether with or without discomfort. It seems to us, therefore, that in the NT we should be prepared to see a fluidity about the word martyr, not distinguishing too sharply between the martyr and the confessor. For our purposes the word martyr will be used with two elements of meaning within it: witness to or confession of God and an element of suffering whether it ends in death or not.

2. *Historical Framework: The Maccabaean Martyrs*

Since the Maccabaean martyrs are demonstrably important in Jewish history and theology, we begin with the historical framework within which the Maccabaean martyrs are to be studied. Our sources are the book of Daniel, 1–4 Maccabees, and their elaborations like the *Song of the Three Children* and *Bel and the Dragon*. And, of course, use will be made of external records, coins, etc.

In the fourth century BC Philip of Macedon conceived the idea of one empire with one culture, Hellenism.[25] By Hellenism was meant the Greek way of doing things: using the Greek language as a *lingua franca*, adopting Greek habits like the Greek games in honour of Greek gods, and so on. Hellenization was intended as an instrument for welding together the vast empire which had absorbed all sorts and conditions of men. It was a grand concept pressed into the service of a political organization. Philip of Macedon did not live to realize his vision, but his successor, Alexander the Great, embraced the idea and in his extensive conquests attempted to make it a reality.

The efforts of the Hellenizers were by and large attended with much success, except with one group, the Jews. Judaism had emerged from the Babylonian exile of 586 BC as a church-state with an exclusivist attitude. Since the Jewish people escaped being submerged in the superior culture of Babylon only by closing their ranks and holding fast to Yahweh, their God who brooked no rivals, Judaism after the exile was very exclusivist, rejecting any outside influence. It was inevitable that Hellenism and Judaism should soon be in a head-on collision.

The collision came to its height in the second century BC, during the reign of the Seleucid king, Antiochus IV, otherwise known as Antiochus Epiphanes. It appears that Hellenism made some gains from Judaism, even in Jerusalem itself. For the Jewish nationalist author of 1 Maccabees reports that 'In those days went out of Israel wicked men, who persuaded many saying, Let us go and make a covenant with the heathen that are round about us: for since we departed from them we have had much sorrow' (1 Maccabees 1.11). The author of 1 Maccabees, supporting the exclusivist position vis-à-vis the Hellenists describes the collaborators with the Hellenists as 'wicked men' simply because they had been accommodating in their attitude towards the Hellenizers. The pro-Hellenists embraced Hellenism as a means of advancing their nation without necessarily denying Judaism, at least in its essential elements. Thus the divisive issue within the Jewish church-state was the question, 'What has Greece in common with Judaea?'; or, 'What has King Antiochus IV in common with high-priest Onias?'; 'What has Hellenism in common with the Torah?'

The pro-Hellenist Jews adopted Greek ways of life and thought. For example, they built a gymnasium in Jerusalem, the holy city itself (1 Macc. 1.14; 4.12-13). The reaction of the anti-Hellenist Jews to the gymnasium was one of hostility and horror, because a gymnasium was not only a place of exercise but also had idolatrous associations. For the games organized there were also in honour of the gods. Besides, the nudity which was commonplace in the gymnasium was a matter of utter disgrace and horror to most Jews, a heathen practice. It was unforgivable for Jews to indulge in the games of the gymnasia.

The pro-Hellenist Jews again 'made themselves uncircumcised' (1 Macc. 1.15). Circumcision was a mark of the Jew as a member of the people of God with whom Yahweh had entered into a covenant relationship through the patriarch Abraham (Gen. 17.10). Therefore, defacing the marks of their circumcision amounted to eschewing Jewish nationality and going back on the covenant relationship with Yahweh, the God of Israel.

The examples taken up in the preceding two paragraphs show beyond doubt that Hellenism made some gains from Judaism and within Judaism itself. Later still, we shall see how some of the leadership had Hellenist sympathies and openly gave their support. On the other hand, in about 168 BC there began a long and bitter war between the loyal Jews led by the house of Mattathias and the Hellenizers. That war was not only a war between the Jewish church-state and the foreign power represented by Antiochus Epiphanes, but it was also a civil war between conservatives and reformists within Judaism.[26] It was, indeed, a holy war (cf. War Scroll of Qumran).

But why did the disagreement turn into a full-scale war? The answer lies in the man Antiochus Epiphanes. In his genuine zeal to promote Hellenism, he brought extra pressure to bear on the Jews with a view to making Judaism yield itself up to Hellenism. But it backfired. His over-zealousness for Hellenism was what triggered off the open war.[27] And what measures bear witness to the over-zealousness of Antiochus Epiphanes?

First, Antiochus interfered with the holy institution of the high priesthood. That office had been confined to a particular family, and the incumbent was appointed for life. Now Antiochus deposed the legitimate high priest Onias and replaced him with Jason, Onias' relative. Jason bought that position (2 Macc. 4). Devout Jews could not take kindly to a Gentile ruler interfering with the sacred institution of the high priesthood. But that was not the end. Since the office of the high priesthood had been offered to the highest bidder, money had become an issue and an important factor in the appointment, rather than lineage or depth of religious conviction. So when Menelaus offered a still higher sum, Jason, who was at least of the high priestly family, was deposed and the office was turned over to Menelaus (2 Macc. 4.24ff.). This was too much for the devout Jews: it was bad enough for a heathen ruler to interfere with Jewish religious institutions, even if Jason was of the right family; but it was worse still when a total outsider, one outside the high priestly family, was appointed. So, the Jews set in motion a rebellion once they saw Antiochus occupied elsewhere; and Antiochus' first attack on the city of Jerusalem was in reprisal for that rebellion. This story reveals the two sides to the story of persecution: from Antiochus' view-point he was taking action to check rebellion and restore his authority, while from the standpoint of the devout Jews it was a persecution on account of their religion. Antiochus' purpose in selling the high priesthood was to install suppporters of radical reform in Jerusalem itself, with a view to transforming the Holy City of Jerusalem into a Hellenistic polis under the name of 'Antiocheia' (2 Macc. 4.9).

Secondly, Antiochus IV made an attack on the temple-treasury (1 Macc. 1.21-23). This was not peculiar to his relationships with the Jews. For Antiochus ransacked non-Jewish sanctuaries as well. Thus he laid claim to a 'dowry' from the temple of Atagartis at Bambyrce. He robbed Egyptian temples while on his campaign in 168 BC.[28] Finally, he died while attacking the temple of Namia near the Parthian border. Thus his attack on the temple-treasury of Jerusalem was of a piece with similar attacks on other temples. His aim in these attacks was not so much to destroy their religions as to replenish the state coffers which had become almost empty as a result of the numerous wars and payments made to Rome. It had been, in part at least, for the same reason that he had interfered with the high priesthood. But, of course, in the eyes of the Jews the action of Antiochus IV toward the temple of Jerusalem was a religious persecution, an attack on their religion and upon a central institution of their national life.

Thirdly, Antiochus IV issued an edict of intolerance which touched central issues of religion. He forbade temple-worship (1 Macc. 1.45). Temple-worship centred on sacrifices and was the heart of Jewish national and religious life. The temple was the symbol of God's presence with his chosen race, a presence which was the assurance of God's continued blessings on the church-state of Israel. Thus to forbid temple-worship amounted to an attempt to destroy the national and religious life of the Jewish people. He also prohibited the observance of the Sabbath and other feasts (1 Macc. 1.42, 45; 2 Macc. 6.6, 11). The sabbath, of course, was a day of rest appointed by God (Exod. 20.8; 31.13; Deut. 5.12). Thus the prohibition of the observance of the sabbath amounted to forcing the Jews to disobey their God and to deny their national identity. But no *force majeure* could absolve a

Jew from observing the law which was of divine authority and origin. Further, Antiochus IV prohibited circumcision (1 Macc. 1.60; 2 Macc. 6.10) a national and religious mark for the Jew, as we have noted above.

All the measures discussed in the preceding paragraph were attempts to destroy the national consciousness of the Jews by destroying everything that supported that consciousness. The dynamism of the Jewish church-state was derived from its religion and all that had to be destroyed if the Jews were to be submissive to Antiochus Epiphanes. But to the Jews the struggle was a holy war,[29] first to regain religious liberty and secondly 'the concentration of Palestinian Judaism'.[30] Much as the divinity of the emperor was the current idea of kingship in the orient, it was downright idolatry to the Jews to whom there was only one God, namely Yahweh, the God of Israel (1 Macc. 1.10; 2.62).

Finally, Antiochus IV established in the temple what the biblical writer described as the 'abomination of desolation' (*šiqqûṣ mᵉšōmēm* = τὸ βδέλυγμα τῆς ἐρημώσεως; Dan 11.31; 1 Macc. 1.54; cf. Mk 13.14). The resentment of the Jews at this abomination was so great that thereafter it became the paradigm of idolatry (Mk 13.14; cf. 2 Thess. 2: the mystery of lawlessness).[31] The abomination is to be seen as part of the tradition of the divinity of the emperor. According to numismatic evidence Antiochus IV was at the beginning of his reign described as 'King Antiochus'. That was normal and harmless. But in 169 BC he took the title Θεὸς Ἐπιφανής (i.e. god manifest), to which he added Νικηφόρος (i.e. victorious) in 166 BC. Thus from 169 BC Antiochus saw himself as the incarnation of divinity, the Olympian Zeus to be precise. Indeed, on a coin dating from 166 BC Antiochus wore the beard and laurel wreath of Zeus.[32] The point of the divinization of the emperor, excesses apart, was to legitimize his political power.[33]

This is the broad historical canvas on which the martyr theology of the Maccabaean period is to be painted, the historical context within which the normative theology of martyrdom in Judaism appeared. What has emerged is that the crisis of the second century BC was as much a struggle between the Jewish church-state on the one hand, and the Hellenist and hellenizing Seleucids on the other, as it was a civil and holy war between the conservative Jews represented by Mattathias and his sons Judas Maccabaeus, Jonathan and Simon, on the one hand and the reformists represented by personalities such as

Jason and Menelaus on the other. Further, there would have been dispute as to what word to apply to what was going on: from the point of view of the Jews it was persecution on account of their faith; but from the point of view of Antiochus IV it was justifiable punishment for the recalcitrance and subversion of the Jews, their challenge to his authority as king. The question now is, What theology emerges from this experience of the Jews?

3. *Who is the Martyr?*

In the course of surveying the historical framework of the Maccabaean struggle, we learnt that to describe someone as a martyr involves a subjective and sympathetic evaluation. What we seek to do now is to give content to that subjective and sympathetic evaluation.

The first element is that of suffering, whether it be in the form of disabilities or death. The second element—and perhaps the more important element—is that the suffering should be consciously regarded as a witness to God. By the suffering, the victim gives witness (μαρτύριον) to God; he gives witness that he is a devotee of God alone. This aspect we term the zealot-theme. That calls for extended comment.

In our brief outline of the historical background, we discussed Antiochus' legislation against some Jewish customs rooted in the Torah, e.g. the observance of the Sabbath and the practice of circumcision. To the Maccabaean martyrs it was more than a question of overlooking some laws; it was an assault on their existence as the covenanted people of God. The reaction to this assault on the theocracy was to show zeal for the Lord through devotion to his commandments. The word often used for this reaction is some form of *qānā'* (= ζηλόω), e.g. 1 Macc. 2.24, or *qināh* (ζῆλον), e.g. 1 Macc. 2.54; cf. Ps. 44.23; Jer. 20.9; 15.15. Thus according to 1 Macc. 2.24 Mattathias 'was inflamed with zeal (ἐζήλωσεν)' in his opposition to the agents of Antiochus IV who had come to Modein to enforce Antiochus' decrees. The Hebrew root *qn'* describes the enthusiasm of exclusive devotion amounting to fanatical intolerance of anything that runs counter to one's beliefs,[34] e.g. 1 Kgs 19.10; 2 Kgs 10.16. The martyr then is one who comes into suffering as a result of his zealous devotion to God. Thus the valedictory speech of Mattathias exhorted the Maccabaeans: 'Now therefore, my sons, be ye zealous for the law, and give your lives for the covenant of your fathers' (1 Macc. 2.50). They are to show zeal for the Lord by giving their lives in defence of the covenant.

It was by design that we earlier referred to the theocracy. Against that background the object of the zeal is variously expressed: zeal for God, which is synonymous with 'fear of the Lord' and love of God (cf. 1 Macc. 2.54; 1 Kgs 19.10; cf. Josephus, *Ant.* 8.330, 334, 347; 2 Chron. 24.20; Jer. 18.12, 13; 20.7, 8, 9; 26.15; Ps. 44.17, 22; 69.26; 73.15; Ecclus 2.2, 15); zeal for the covenant (1 Macc. 2.50), which is synonymous with zeal for the laws or God's commandments (1QS 1.17; 5.1, 8; 9.24), zeal for all God's words (1QS 1.4; 3.11), zeal for the precepts of righteousness (1QS 4.4), zeal for what has been revealed (1QS 1.8-9; 5.9; 8.1, 15; 9.13, 19; 1QpHab 12 on 2.17). All these are aspects of the idea of theocracy for which the martyrs were zealous. Thus the battle- and rallying-cry of Mattathias was 'whoever is zealous of the law and maintaineth the covenant, let him follow me' (1 Macc. 2.27).

It is instructive to turn to the specific examples of zeal for the Lord which are cited by the Maccabaean literature—Abraham, Joseph, Phinehas, Joshua, Caleb, David, Elijah, Ananias, Azarias, Misael and Daniel (1 Macc. 2.51-60). Of this list Ananias, Azarias, Misael and Daniel hardly need comment as paradigms of utter devotion to the God of Israel in the face of hostile attack from the enemies of the God of Israel. But perhaps some comment should be made on Abraham, Phinehas and Elijah.

The reference to Abraham as an example of zeal for the Lord is often explained in terms of Abraham's faith in God, both in leaving his secure home for an unknown destination and in believing the promise to multiply his seed as the sand of the seashore when all external indications made the promise ridiculous (Gen. 12). No doubt that element is there. Besides, he became an example of perfect obedience to God, showing great love of God when he was willing to sacrifice Isaac, his only son (Gen. 22). But in the Maccabaean writings this explanation is inadequate not only because of the context of persecution from which they were written but also because of the existence of a fully developed theology about Abraham's martyrdom. According to legend, Nimrod threw Abraham into a fiery furnace. Notwithstanding that, Abraham remained faithful and 'hallowed the Name of the Holy One' (*Gen. R.* 38 near the end; *Tanḥuma* [ed. Buber], Lek Leka 2; *Num. R.* 1.12; b.*Git.* 57b). Needless to say the motif of the the fiery furnace is common to this story and to that of Daniel and his friends. So in late Judaism Abraham was *inter alia* an example of a martyr.

Similarly, Phinehas was regarded in late Judaism as a martyr. Thus according to the Haggadah on Num. 25.6-8, Phinehas exposed himself to obloquy and peril when he killed the two defiant sinners (cf. Sifre Num. 25.13 which even cites Is. 53.12 to clinch the argument). Further, Phinehas's zeal for God led to the identification of Phinheas and Elijah (Targum 25.2; *Pirke de R. Eliezer*, 47).[35]

Elijah's fame, of course, stems from his conflict with Ahab and Jezebel, whose marriage meant the appearance in Israel of the Phoenician despotic concept of royalty as well as the national deity of Jezebel. She was zealous to spread the worship of the Phoenician god in Israel, and had influenced Ahab to demolish the altars of Yahweh and to kill ardent loyal Yahweh-worshippers who resisted the apostasy (1 Kgs 18.22; Josephus, *Ant.* 8.316-354). Elijah and a few others refused to 'forsake thy covenant' (1 Kgs 19.10). To forsake the covenant of God was to forsake God.[36] Elijah then was the prototype of zeal for the Lord. The height of his fanatical devotion to God was his massacre of the prophets of Baal at Mt Carmel, which, he must have realized, would incur the wrath and vengeance of Jezebel.

From the examples surveyed above, it becomes clear that suffering out of zeal for God or his 'covenant with the fathers' is a mark of the martyrs.

It is equally instructive to study the language used of the opponents of these martyrs. Unlike the martyrs who are zealous for the Lord and suffer for it, the persecutor is πονηρός, παράνομος, ἄνομος–1 Macc. 1.43, 52; 2.14; 7.5; 9.23; Ass. Is. 2.4, 5, 8; 4.2-3; Ecclus 4.12, 23; 12.1; 15.8; 17.11. The epithets πονηρός, παράνομος and ἄνομος are used in contrast to δίκαιος (Ecclus 2.35; 3.3; 13.7, 8), ὅσιος (Ecclus 2.36; 8.28, 40; 13.10) and πτωχός (Ecclus 15.2; Ps. 109.12). Thus the contrast makes clear that the παράνομος and ἄνομος are the enemies of the law of God of which the righteous martyrs are the champions. By virtue of being opponents of the law of God they are πονηροί. That epithet, though a perfectly normal adjective, may be intended to indicate an affinity with Satan whose other name is ὁ πονηρός. Thus the three epithets draw a sharp contrast with the faithful zealots of the Lord. Unlike the arrogant, blasphemous and lawless persecutors who have set themselves against the will of God, the martyrs have declared themselves by word and deed for the will of God.

Equally instructive is the description of persecutors as 'beasts'—
Heb. *ḥyh* = Aramaic *ḥyw'* = Greek θήρ or θηρίον. It is used to
describe the opponents of Israel as non-doers of the will of God—Ps.
74.19; Jer. 12.9; 2 Macc. 4.25; 4 Macc. 9.28; Dan. 4.12; 7.5; Philo,
Quod Omn. 89; *Flacc.* 66. Apart from a general description of them as
beasts, certain creatures become symbols for them: (a) bull—Ps.
22.12, 21; (b) dog (*klb* which is used in three senses: i. as a term of
contempt–1 Sam. 17.43; 2 Kgs 8.13; *Lachish Ostraca* 2.4; 5.4; ii. the
enemy—Ps. 22.16, 20; 56.10; Enoch 89.41-50; iii. the wicked—Is.
56.10-11; Rev. 22.15.[37] (c) dragon (δράκων = Heb. *tnyn*). This last
figure originates in Sumerian creation myths. It appears in the Old
Testament as the Leviathan, the monster of the sea, which is
symbolic of chaos. In this sense the dragon came to be used of any
entity which opposed the will of God. Thus it is used of Egypt at Ps.
74.14, of Nebuchadrezzar (Jer. 51.34) and of the persecutors of the
churches of Asia (Rev. 12.7, 13, 16, 17). Other references are Est.
10.7; 11.6; Ps. 74.13; Ps. Sol. 2.29; Ezek. 29.3; 32.2. (d) lion—Ps.
22.13, 21; Est. 14.13; 1QpHab 1.1ff.

All these animals signify ferocity, savagery and cruelty, thus
implying their enmity to what God demands, in contrast to the
devotion of the martyrs to the will of God.

Related to the zealot-theme is the upholding of the prophets as
prototype martyrs. This theme appears again and again in the New
Testament where the Jews are accused of murdering the prophets
(Mt. 23.31, 34-35, 37; Lk. 13.34; Rom. 11.3; 1 Thess. 2.15). To the
genesis of the idea we now turn.

Prophets arose in times of national crises, whether in the form of
national apostasy or in the form of imminent war. In such crises
anyone who did not reflect the current and predominant outlook was
naturally considered a saboteur and consequently came under disabilities and hardship. It should, therefore, occasion no surprise that
many a prophet met with bitter opposition and personal violence,
some even meeting death. Historically speaking, several prophets
suffered maltreatment or, to use later terminology, they were 'confessors', e.g. Elijah, Jeremiah, Micaiah (1 Kgs 22.20), Amos (Neh.
9.26, 30, 32; Lam. 2.20; 4.16). Few prophets were actually done to
death for their faith like Zechariah (2 Chron. 24.20f.; cf. Josephus,
Ant. 9.168-171; Mt. 23.35; Lk. 11.51; Heb. 11.37) and Uriah (Jer.
26.20-23; cf. Neh. 9.26). Many are unknown by name (1 Kgs 19.10;
cf. Josephus, *Ant.* 8.330, 334; 2 Kgs 21.16; cf. Josephus, *Ant.* 20.38).

However, in later Jewish tradition this motif underwent a development. At this stage martyrdom became a *sine qua non* of the
prophetic vocation and, therefore, every prophet was regarded as
having undergone a martyr's death. And so, now Micaiah not only
suffers but dies a martyr (Ass. Is. 2.16); Jeremiah dies by stoning in
Egypt (Vitae Prophetarum 71.3f.; 119.12f.; Acts of Philip 83).[38]
Similarly, Isaiah was sawn asunder by Manasseh.[39] Even Abel, who
was killed by his brother Cain for reasons other than religious, came
to be referred to as a martyr-prophet (4 Macc. 18.14; cf. Mt. 12.35).[40]
So was Jonah according to a tradition dating from AD 350,[41] as well
as Amos and Ezekiel who were allegedly executed.[42] Indeed, according
to a midrash standing in the name of R. Jose b. Nehonai, the
following were the persecuted prophets: Abel, Noah, Abraham, Isaac,
Jacob, Joseph, Moses, Saul, David and Israel.[43]

Clearly at this point the prophet-martyr motif has moved from the
realm of sober history to that of theology. The appearance of this
theological motif is interesting because it bears witness to an
increased interest in martyr theology by the time of the golden age of
apocalyptic literature. The explanation of the equation of the prophet
and the martyr may be through the zealot-theme: if the prophet was
raised up in an age of apostasy to be the true witness to Yahweh in
the midst of a stiff-necked people, standing *contra mundum*, then he
must have been a martyr. Thus the prophet-martyr motif is another
expression of the zealot-theme—exclusive devotion to God, even if it
means suffering and/or death.

There is a third stage in the development of the prophet-martyr
theme. Here every martyr is a prophet. The starting point of this idea
is the belief that every *moriturus* had a vision. Hence Stephen's vision
of the son of man standing at the right hand of God (Acts 7.55-56).
This may also be a background to the problematic Lucan passage of
an angel appearing to strengthen Jesus during the agony in the
Garden of Gethsemane (Lk. 22.43). It is as though at the point of
death the *moriturus* is reminded of the heavenly council into which
he was introduced and which guided him to that end. However, the
theology goes beyond the vision of a *moriturus* to invest the vision
with the same force as the words of prophecy. Thus a dying martyr's
testimony is 'esteemed like precious oracles or even the words of
classical prophecy'.[44] With this emerges the significance attached to
sermons or speeches attributed to martyrs, often being a testimony of
unflinching and uncompromising devotion to Yahweh, e.g. 1 Macc.

2.49ff.; Acts 7 (Stephen's speech). Hence also the emergence in history of the literary genre called the *Marturion* and the *Passio*.

In our effort to define the martyr's role, we have discerned two elements: zeal for the Lord and suffering and/or death in consequence of that zeal for the Lord. There is a third element: a looking beyond the present and earthly and human circumstances to the kingdom of God. The zeal for the Lord which refuses to count the cost is rooted in a deep conviction about the sovereign omnipotence of the God who is the object of the zeal. In that sense the zeal for the Lord is eschatologically rooted. Later we shall outline the types of eschatological teachings that emerge from the various martyr-situations. But for the present our concern is the theme as it affects the zealot-theme. Some of the transcendent appellations of God[45] in this connection are: the God of gods (ὁ θεὸς τῶν θεῶν)—Dan. 3.93 (LXX), Lord God of spirits (ὁ κύριος ὁ θεὸς τῶν πνευμάτων)–2 Macc. 3.28, 29; the ruler of all authorities (ὁ πάσης ἐξουσίας δυνάστης)–2 Macc. 3.24; Lord (κύριος)–3 Macc. 2.2; 5.7; Almighty (παντοκράτωρ)–2 Macc. 3.30; 3 Macc. 2.2; 5.7; the ruler of all creation (ὁ δεσπότης πάσης κτίσεως)–3 Macc. 5.7; the creator of the world (ὁ κτίσης τοῦ κόσμου)–3 Macc. 3:14; Most High (ὁ μέγιστος θεός = Aram. *'lh' 'ly*)—Dan. 4.2, 17, 24, 29, 32, 34; 5.18, 21; 7.18, 22, 25, 29; 3 Macc. 1.9, 16; 4.16; 5.25; ὁ ὕψιστος–3 Macc. 3.31; the king of the heavens (ὁ βασιλεὺς τῶν οὐρανῶν)–3 Macc. 2.2; living God (Aram. *'lh' ḥy'*)—Dan 6.10.

Apart from the straightforward use of appellations that speak of the transcendent omnipotence of God, the point is also made in circuitous ways. Thus the book of Daniel, for example, makes sweeps into history in order to establish that the God of the martyr is the sovereign Lord of history; we may note the symbolic significance of the colossal image (Dan. 2), or the successions of creatures (Dan. 7), representing the various kingdoms of the world. At other times the sovereignty of God is established dramatically by the intervention of God, most often through his angels, to protect the zealots. Thus for example, Shadrach, Meshach and Abednego were delivered from the fiery furnace (Dan. 3) or Daniel from the den of lions (Daniel 6; 3 Macc. 4.21; 5.12-13, 27-28; 6.18-21). At other times, the persecutor comes to recognize and acknowledge the power of God. Thus in Daniel Nebuchadrezzar after the incident of the fiery furnace shouts 'there is no other God who is able to deliver in this way' (Dan. 3.29). Other passages are Dan. 6.26-28; 1 Macc. 6.11-14; 3 Macc. 6.28;

Philo, *Flacc.* 170-175. Sometimes also the point is made that the persecutor's power is limited to the body, unlike the power of God which extends even to the soul—Jer. 1.19; 15:ll; 20.11, 13; 4 Macc. 13.14; Ass. Is. 5.10; Philo, *Quod Omn.* 6; Mt. 10.28.

In view of what has been said above with respect to zeal, perseverance and the eschatological rooting of the martyr's stance, it is hardly surprising that athletic and military metaphors are sometimes used of the martyr. The martyr is as an athlete because of his zealous perseverance in straining towards the eschatological goal—4 Macc. 6.10; 9.23; 11.20; 12.15; 15.29; 16.16; 17.16; Acts of Thomas 39.[46] The martyr is a soldier who fights on God's side—4 Macc. 11.8; 16.14.

The burden of our argument so far is that the biblical martyr is characterized by three things: first, suffering, whether it issues in death or not; secondly, by his suffering being seen as a witness to his zeal for or devotion to God or the theocracy of Judaism; thirdly, by his devotion being rooted in a conviction about the omnipotence and transcendence of God. The question that may be raised by all this is the difference between the martyr and the suicide.

The line of division between the suicide and the martyr is a very thin one. Let us take the example of Elijah whom 1 Maccabees and late Judaism portrayed as a martyr. When Elijah slaughtered the Baal prophets, he must have known that Jezebel with her ideas of oriental despotism would be sure to retaliate. Thus to slaughter the prophets of Baal was in effect to court death, which Elijah barely managed to avoid by his flight. Again the refusal of Mattathias to offer the sacrifice ordered by Antiochus IV was to court reprisal and punishment from Antiochus. Again, some of the 'zealots' refused to take to flight on the sabbath when the Hellenists attacked and in consequence were slaughtered. Their reason was that they could not violate the law of the sabbath by taking to flight or fighting on the sabbath.[47] Others in the name of religion went further to take their own lives rather than wait for the enemy to seize them. For example, at the capture of Masada and Jerusalem, some threw themselves into the fire.[48] The suicide of the mother of the seven martyrs was, according to 4 Macc. 17, applauded by a heavenly voice.

Apparently the issue of suicide and/or martyrdom was debated in Judaism. We find two antithetical attitudes in late Judaism. One school of thought approved religious suicide. The classic example is the Assumption of Moses from about the first century AD. The author's purpose in telling the tale of Moses in Egypt (3.11), of the Jews under the Seleucids, especially Antiochus Epiphanes (8.1, 5; 9.6), of the surviving families of the Maccabaeans and of the forty-five of the Sadducean aristocracy at the hands of Herod (6.3) was to encourage his contemporaries to embrace death rather than be disloyal to God and the law. The religious suicide is a hero, indeed a martyr. There is hardly any difference between the religious suicide and the martyr!

Further evidence for some sympathy with religious suicide comes from the rabbinic debates which tried to restrict martyrdom. Thus during the Hadrianic persecutions the rule appears to have been 'live through (the Law) but do not die through (it)'.[49] That there should be such advice presupposes that there were some who favoured religious suicide, which was considered a martyrdom.

The issue was thrown into relief almost at the beginning of the Maccabaean struggle when Mattathias and his followers had to decide whether to fight back on the sabbath when the Seleucids attacked them. The text speaks clearly, so we quote it *in extenso*: 'Let us [i.e. Mattathias and his followers] die all in our innocency; heaven and earth shall testify for us, that ye put us to death wrongfully. So they [the Seleucids] rose up against them in battle on the sabbath, and they slew them, with their wives and children, and their cattle, to the number of a thousand people' (1 Macc. 2.37-38). These were obviously religious suicides, even if they are also considered martyrs. But this was a traumatic experience for the nationalists and the devout Jews who realized that these were unnecessary deaths. So they revised their position and decided to fight back even on the sabbath. Here there emerges a second school of thought.

The second school of thought is represented by the Maccabaean literature, which is critical of religious suicide and would rather encourage fighting in self-defence. And so now they say: 'If we all do as our brethren have done, and fight not for our lives and laws against the heathen, they will now quickly root us out of the earth . . . Whosoever shall come to make battle with us on the sabbath day, we will fight against him; neither will we die all . . . ' (1 Macc. 2.40-41). In other words, zeal for the Lord need not lead to death. One should not be too eager for death to show one's zeal for the Lord.

Similarly, the third generation Tanna, R. Elazar b. Perata, taught: 'Danger to life annuls the Sabbath, for man is to live by doing God's commandments and not to die by them'.[50] We have also cited above the statement from the Hadrianic persecutions advising the Jews to 'live through (the law) but not die through (it)'. Another tradition is particularly instructive because it allowed idols to be worshipped to save life, although martyrdom was preferable to public profession of idolatry.[51] This brings us to a consideration of two terms, *hallul ha-shem* and *hillul ha-shem*.

The issue to which the two schools of thought in Judaism with regard to religious suicide and martyrdom addressed themselves was evangelism. When Jewry was in the midst of Gentiles, every Jew was obliged to 'sanctify the Name of the Lord' (*hallul ha-shem*). From that obligation no *force majeure* could absolve them. Thus the greatest test to this obligation came during times of persecution. For example, according to *Cant. R.* 7.8.1, the refusal of Hananiah, Mishael and Azariah to worship the image set up by Nebuchadrezzar was to give 'their lives for the sanctification of the Name'.[52] Similarly, according to *Gen. R.* 38, Abraham by remaining faithful and steadfast to God when he was thrown into a fiery furnace, 'hallowed the Name of the Holy One'.[53] Indeed, in another tradition Abraham himself said, 'I will give my life for the hallowing of the Name'.[54]

The opposite of 'sanctification of the Holy Name' is 'profanation of the Holy Name', or *hillul ha-shem*. Thus according to Ass. Is. 5.4-8 Belchira or Satan tries to get Isaiah to commit *hillul ha-shem* by compromising with Manasseh. This was considered the unforgivable sin, amounting to idolatry. Thus the third generation Tanna in Rome called Rabbi Eleazar b. Azariah said in reply to R. Matthia b. Heresh: 'If he has been guilty of profanation of the Name, then penitence has no power to suspend punishment, nor the Day of Atonement to procure atonement, nor suffering to finish it . . . Only death finishes it' (b.*Kid.* 40a). Similarly, the third generation Amora by the name of Rabbi Abbahu said: 'Better had a man secretly transgress than publicly profane God's name, for . . . (Ezek. 20.39)' (b.*Yoma* 86a). Compromise with a persecutor amounted to idolatry.[55]

The concept of *hallul ha-shem* is really another way of stating the zealot-theme. This is probably amply demonstrated by *Midrash Ps.* 68.13 which compares Israel to a dove because she does not struggle when 'they are slaughtered for the sanctification of the Name'.[56] The martyr was the zealot who by his suffering advertised his God. He was a missionary. Consequently the time of suffering, particularly the trial and the point of death, became the occasion for a discourse on God and exhortations to faithfulness to God. Such speeches are really *apologia pro Deo*. Thus according to Dan. 3.16-18, Shadrach, Meshach and Abednego, before being thrown into the fiery furnace for refusing to worship the golden image set up in the plains of Dura, gave a short speech affirming their devotion to God, his power and ability to deliver them from the hands of the persecutor. Similarly at 2 Macc. 7.37 one of the brothers being martyred said: 'I, as my brethren, offer my body and life for the laws of our fathers, beseeching God ... that thou by torments and plagues mayest confess, that he alone is God'. Again Eleazar made a speech in which he affirmed the almightiness of God (2 Macc. 6.24-28). 4 Maccabees has even more of such *apologiae pro Deo*—4 Macc. 5.14-37; 6.31–7.25; 9.1ff.

We have so far sought to demonstrate that the martyr by his sufferings bears testimony to God. This is more than just demonstrating that the martyr himself is a devotee of God. He is also engaged in a missionary endeavour. By his witness through suffering he seeks to witness to God and to convert others to his God. Consequently, several of our documents tell stories of the conversion of the persecutor as a result of the suffering. Thus according to Dan. 3.26-29, Nebuchadnezzar as a result of the deliverance of the three men from the fiery furnace came to acknowledge them as 'servants of the Most High God'; he also blessed the God of Shadrach and he passed a decree to destroy all who spoke evil of this God of Shadrach, Meshach and Abednego. Similarly King Darius also came to recognize the God of Daniel (Dan. 6.25ff.). Other examples are Bel and the Dragon 41, 1 Macc. 6.11-14; 2 Macc. 3.28f.; 3 Macc. 6.28; Philo, *Flacc.* 116, 121, 125, 170-74. The martyrdom by crucifixion of Rabbi Jose b. Joezer,[57] identified by some with the Qumran Teacher of Righteousness,[58] so affected his persecutor, Jakim, identified by some scholars with Alcimus, the pro-Hellenist high priest of the time of the Seleucid King Demetrius I (c. 162 BC) that the latter repented and religiously committed suicide. Clearly martyrdom is a witness with a view to conversion. This is where we return to the distinction between martyr and suicide.

There is no easy distinction between the martyr and the religious suicide, as became obvious from the discussion of the concept of *hallul ha-shem*. Such distinction as there is depends in part on how sympathetically the suffering is viewed. The distinction may also in part be based on how far the personal element obtrudes in the

decision to die or not. If the personal and private element pre-
dominates, it becomes suicide. It is martyrdom when the glorification
of God is the sole and paramount consideration.

4. *The Theodicy of Martyrdom*

A martyr is a zealous devotee of God, who is willing and able to
undergo suffering because of his deep-rooted conviction that Almighty
God is the ultimate authority and ruler of the world who alone
matters. The suffering of devotees of God at the hands of Gentiles
raises problems for faith. Since atheism was almost unknown in
Judaism, the problem was not the existence of God; rather it was a
question of what God, who is almighty sovereign, good and just, was
doing when his chosen race and more, those who were zealous for
him and his laws, were trampled over, or indeed done to death, by the
heathen. It is even more difficult to understand the situation when it
is borne in mind that the persecutor, who is apparently the victor by
the standards of the world, is an unbeliever and a heathen. It is to
that aspect of martyr-theology that we now address ourselves.

Several diverse solutions are proferred to this problem.

(a) *Chastisements* (παιδεία = *musar*)
Though martyrs are zealous for the Lord, that is not the same thing
as an affirmation of their sinlessness. Consequently, sometimes the
sufferings of the martyrs were understood as a way of expiating their
sins. Of course in late Judaism suffering, whether in the sense of
martyrdom or not, could atone for sins. For example, according to
b.*Ber.* 5a, 'chastisements wipe out all a man's wickedness' (cf. *Sifre
Deut.* 32 [ed. Friedmann, f.73b near the top]). Even a criminal's
death expiates his offence (Mishnah, *Sanh.* 6.2; 9.5). However, the
sufferings of the martyrs came to be looked upon as being especially
of atoning efficacy for their own sins. Thus the fifth of the seven
brothers in 2 Maccabees told the king, 'We suffer these things for
ourselves, having sinned against our God' (2 Macc. 7.18, 32, 33; cf.
Wisd. 3.5).

However, more often than not, their sufferings are considered
chastisements for the sins of the Jewish nation, the covenanted
people of God. For example, in Daniel's prayer in connexion with the
mystery of seventy years, the following confession is made: 'To us, O
Lord, belongs confusion of face, to our kings, to our princes, and to

our fathers, because we have sinned against thee' (Dan. 9.8). In other words, the untold suffering of Daniel and his companions was God's punishment for the sins of the Jewish church-state, high and low alike. The sentiment is expressed again at Dan. 9.16: 'O Lord, according to all thy righteous acts, let thy anger (ὀργή) and thy wrath turn away from thy city Jerusalem, thy holy hill; because for our sins, and for the iniquities of our fathers, Jerusalem and thy people have become a byword among all who are round about us'. Οργή or wrath is the divine wrath expressed in the affliction of Israel by the Seleucidae. That aspect is given greater emphasis in the LXX. Thus, for example The Song of the Three Holy Children adds that their plight was the 'true judgment' of God (v. 5), 'for we have sinned and committed iniquity . . . In all things have we trespassed' (v. 6). The message is that the persecutions and martyrdom of Maccabaean times are the punishment of God for the nation's sins and waywardness.

Perhaps one more example, this time from 2 Maccabees, should clinch the point for us. At 2 Macc. 7.38 the last of the seven brothers who died for the faith said: 'In me and my brothers the wrath of the Almighty, which is justly brought upon our nation, may cease'. The striking thing is the admission that their circumstances represent the wrath of God which was justified and well deserved. The persecutions and martyrdom were God's punishment for the sins of the nation of Israel. This introduces the idea of *chastisements of love*.

Although their affliction was considered God's just punishment for their sins, yet the sufferings were seen as evidence of the love of God. 2 Maccabees again puts it quaintly and in a manner which hardly needs comment: 'Now I beseech those that read this book, that they be not discouraged for these calamities, but that they may judge those punishments not to be for destruction, but for a chastening of our nation. For it is a token of his great goodness, when wicked doers are not suffered any long time, but forthwith punished. For not as with other nations, whom the Lord patiently forbeareth to punish, till they be come to the fulness of their sins, so dealeth he with us, lest that, being come to the height of sin, afterwards he should take vengeance on us. And therefore he never withdraweth his mercy from us; and though he punish with adversity, yet doth he never forsake his people' (2 Macc. 6.12-16). A number of points emerge from this text. First, Israel's calamities were God's punishment for their sins. Secondly, they are evidence of God's goodness in the sense that God does not tolerate evil or sin. Thirdly, their calamities are not just vindictive punishment, but corrective in intent, 'for the chastening of our nation'. To that extent they are evidence of God's love for the Jews. Fourthly, their early punishment is in fact a blessing or a mark of God's special favour to them because instead of letting them continue in their wickedness like all the other nations who will realize only at the last day that they are doomed for destruction, God has made a timely intervention to arrest their progression to final destruction and to put them on the right path to fellowship with himself. Thus, their calamities are 'chastisements of love'.

Rabbinic literature as well has much to say on 'chastisements of love'. Thus, for example, the second generation Tanna by the name of Rabbi Eliezer b. Jacob, commenting on Prov. 3.12, says: 'Whom God loves (*y'hb*) he chastens (*ykyḥ*) even as the father chastens the son of whom he is fond What causes the son to be loved by his father? Sufferings.'[59] Their sufferings are termed 'chastisements of love' primarily because they are considered to be corrective in intent and purpose. But it is also a privilege they had over the rest of the world, one which made them more fit to share in the glory of God. If we may make a parody of a popular saying, 'Those whom God loves, he punishes early'.

Thus one line of theodicy is to explain the persecutions and martyrdom as a divine punishment (παιδεία or ὀργή or δίκη) for the sin of the martyrs themselves and/or their nation.[60] This was otherwise known as 'chastisements of love'. It was a pain inflicted for moral ends and with remedial intent.

(b) *Sacrifice*
Next door to the idea of chastisements is the idea of sacrifice. Martyrdom or faithful witness to God through and despite suffering was considered a means of atoning for sins. Several images are used for describing this. One metaphor is that of refining. Thus, for example, Ecclus 2.4-5: 'Whatsoever is brought upon thee take cheerfully, and be patient when thou art changed to a low estate. For gold is tried in the fire, and acceptable men in the furnace of adversity.' The metaphor of refining occurs several times in biblical writers, e.g. Is. 48.10; Prov. 17.3; 27.21; Zech. 13.9; Mal. 3.3; Wisd. 3.6; James 1.12; 1 Pet. 1.7; 4.12. Classical writers had a similar idea. For example, Ovid, *Trist.* 1.4.25: 'Scilicet ut fulvum spectatur in ignibus aurum. Tempore sic duro est inspicienda fides.' Similarly

Seneca talked of 'refining' at *De Prov.* 5: 'Ignis aurum probat, miseria fortes viros'. So it was a metaphor found generally in Jewish and Gentile societies. Δοκιμάζειν has the notion of proving a thing to see whether it is worthy to be received or not.[61] It often implies that the proving has been victoriously surmounted. e.g. Ecclus 44.20; 1 Thess. 2.4; Mt. 26.39; Mk 14.36; 1 Tim. 3.10. Though the metaphor of refining highlights the aspect of proving whether the martyr is worthy or not, yet there is the implied idea of purifying that comes through the refining. This is where it links up with the sacrificial interpretation of martyrdom.

Another metaphor is that of cleansing—καθαρίζειν = Heb. *ṭhr* For example, Dan. 11.35: 'some of those who are wise shall fall [i.e. martyrs], to refine and to cleanse (καθαρίσαι) them, and to make them white . . . ' Their martyrdom is a cleansing. Other passages are Dan. 9.42; 12.10; 4 Macc. 1.11; 6.29; l7.21; Ps. Sol. 10.1; 1QH 7.30. As is evident from Ex. 29.37, καθαρίζειν sometimes is a translation of *kpr*, the word so often used for atoning.

Expressing the sacrificial idea is the root *'šm*. Martyrdom is *'āšām*—Is. 53.5, 10, i.e. a guilt offering. In this connexion it is interesting to consider the use of Is. 53.10 by R. Huna: 'In whom God delights him he crushes with chastisements, Is. 53.10; I might think that it was so even if he did not accept them for love; therefore it says in Is. 53.10: *'m tsym 'šm npšw*, just as guilt-offering is brought with intention, so chastisements must be accepted with assent. If he accepted them, what is his reward? Is. 53.10: He will see seed, prolong his days; and even more, his learning will be preserved in him.'[62] Martyrdom is a type of guilt offering, a sacrifice that atones for sin. Another interesting example of the idea of martyrdom as a guilt-offering is 1QpHab 9 (on 1.12-13): 'God will execute the judgment of the nations by the hand of his Elect. And through their chastisement (*btwkḥtm*) all the wicked of his people shall expiate (*y'tṣmw*) their guilt who keep the Commandments in their distress (*bzr*).' The suffering of the zealous nation has atoning efficacy. Another interesting example is 1QS 8.3f.: 'They shall preserve the faith in the land with steadfastness and meekness and shall atone for sin (*wlrzwt 'wn*) by the practice of justice and by the sorrows of affliction (*wzrt mzrp*)'.

One last example is most interesting from the point of the New Testament. 4 Maccabees describes the suffering of the Maccabaean martyrs as ἱλαστήριον and ἀντίψυχον (4 Macc. 17.22), as making atonement for sin. Furthermore, it was a vicarious suffering which had atoning efficacy. Martyrdom acquires a treasury of merits, so to speak, which is available for the covering of the sins of others. It is a vicarious atoning offering.

To summarize the sacrificial interpretation of suffering and martyrdom, we begin with the idea that sins may be expiated by sufferings— 'Chastisements wipe out all a man's wickedness' (b.*Berakot* 5a [end]; cf. *Sifre Deut*. 32 [ed. Friedmann f.73b near top]). Even a criminal expiates his sins by death to which he is sentenced (Mishnah, *Sanh.* 6.2). However, especially the sufferings and death of the righteous have propitiatory or piacular[63] value not only for themselves but also for others—Song of the Three Children 15, 16; 2 Macc. 6.13-16; 7.18, 32f., 37, 38; 4 Macc. 6.27-29; 9.20; 10.8; 17.20-22.[64]

(c) *Eschatology*

The dilemma of 'zealots' of the Lord suffering with no apparent vindication was often resolved in eschatology. This is to be expected for two reasons. First, as we suggested above, the zeal of the martyr was rooted in his convictions about God as the sovereign Lord of history. That conviction sooner or later had to be justified, if it was not to be an empty hope. Secondly, eschatology is best seen in the context of the view of history: as held by the Jews, history is a straight line steadily moving towards a climax or τέλος, the Day of the Lord. On that day, it was believed, the sovereignty of God as the Lord of history would be fully exercised and seen to be a reality. One aspect of it is, of course, the judgment at which is demonstrated the accountability of the creature man to God the Creator. Another aspect is the twin-idea of reward and punishment. Every point on that straight line stands in some relation to that eschaton of the Day of the Lord.

The eschatological theodicy takes diverse forms and involves several ideas which we shall now proceed to outline.

i. *Messianic Woes*. One approach, especially in apocalyptic Judaism, is to interpret the sufferings as 'eschatological woes' (*ḥblw šl mšyḥ* = Aram. *ḥblyh dmšyḥ* = Greek ὠδινες). The Messianic Woes are the eschatological birthpangs out of which the Messianic age is to be born. The Messianic Woes are marked by apostasy and persecution.[65] In the period just before the Day of the Lord evil is expected to come to a height because in God's inscrutable purpose the full sum of sins must be completed before the eschaton. Persecutions and martyrdom are part of the evil that goes to complete that full sum of sins necessary for the arrival of the Day of the Lord. From the literature of the Maccabaean period this theology is articulated by Dan. 8.23: 'at the latter end of their rule, when the transgressors have reached their full measure, a king of bold countenance, one who understands riddles, shall arise'. This passage was the explanation of the vision of the succession of the ram representing the kings of Media, the he-goat representing the king of Greece and the horn representing one of the Seleucid kings. The author of Daniel expected the Kingdom of God to succeed the wicked kingdom of the Seleucidae. But that would be only when the Seleucidae had incarnated the height of wickedness. And that was precisely the experience of the Jews under Antiochus I. Thus the persecutions of Antiochus IV were a Messianic Woe making up the full measure of sins required to herald in the Messianic age.

Similarly, in Dan. 9 the reply of God to Daniel's ardent prayer was: 'Seventy weeks of years are decreed concerning your people and your holy city, to finish thy transgression, to put an end to sin, and to atone for iniquity, to bring in everlasting righteousness . . . ' (Dan. 9.24). The eschaton can come only when the full measure of sins has been filled up. And the experience of persecution and suffering and martyrdom was part of the process of filling up the full measure of sins.[66] In the Qumran writings persecutions are said to take place in the 'dominion of Belial' (*mmšlt bly'l*) which is the period preceding the age of the Messiah–1QS 1.23,28; 2.19; 3.23; CD 1.5 (*wbqṣ ḥrwn*).

Thus one of the ways of explaining why those zealous for the Lord may suffer without any apparent vindication is to explain their suffering as an eschatological woe which is ushering in the Messianic age or the Day of the Lord.

ii. *Rewards or Punishments.* A second approach to theodicy through eschatology is the promise of Rewards and Punishments, often beyond the grave or death. Hebrew religion was for a very long time silent on life beyond death. Beyond death was shadowy existence in Sheol, an area below the earth that was cut off from God.[67] The classic statement is Ps. 115.17:

> The dead do not praise the LORD,
>> nor do any that go down into silence.

As such death was by no means welcome: it was 'the valley of the shadow of death' (Ps. 23.4), a state of sorrows (Ps. 18.4).

However, although there are one or two hints at an after-life as in Isaiah and Ezekiel, it was in the course of the traumatic persecution under Antiochus IV that the book of Daniel enunciated clearly a doctrine of individual survival after death. It may not be without significance that that note was struck in a time of affliction and tribulation. For the numerous martyrdoms in the struggle between the Seleucidae and the loyal Jews raised a question mark against the goodness and justice of God. Thus teaching with regard to the after-life was essentially focused on the divine justice and vengeance. Thus, for example, the slaughter of Andronicus is considered as his punishment for his murder of Onias and the comment is, 'Thus the Lord rewarded him his punishment, as he had deserved' (2 Macc. 4.38).

Punishment was reserved for the persecutor or whoever compromised with him. His plight takes the form of shame (*hrpwt*, Dan. 12.2) and contempt (*dr'wn*, Dan. 12.2). Contempt described the horror of the damned, such as was inspired by decomposing dead bodies. To be consigned to eternal contempt is to be denied fellowship with God which to the Jew was essential to man's well-being.[68] This looks like reserving the old concept of Sheol for the persecutors. It is, therefore, not surprising that in Enoch a quarter of Sheol is reserved for persecutors (Enoch 91.11, 19; 94.1, 6, 7; 95.6; 96.1,6, 8).

Sometimes the eschatological fate of the persecutors was realized in this world through some catastrophe that overtook them in this life. Thus 1 Macc. 6.12-13 interprets the set-back of Antiochus IV at Elymais as the punishment for his persecution of the faithful Jews. Similarly the paralysis and death of Alcimus were interpreted by the author of 1 Maccabees as God's punishment on him for his effrontery in attempting to pull down the temple of the Jews (1 Macc. 9.55-56). 2 Maccabees has an even more spectacular case of punishment, when Heliodorus 'by the hand of God was cast down and lay speechless without all hope of life' (2 Macc. 3.29), because of his attacks on the Jews. What happened to Heliodorus spoke of the power and vengeance of God. Indeed throughout the literature there is the tendency to explain the misfortunes of persecutors as the punishment of God for their attack on the devotees of the God of Israel–1 Macc. 2.62, 67-68; 6.22; 7.38, 42; 2 Macc. 3.24-28, 36; 4.38; 9.25, 28; 3 Macc. 6.28; Philo, *Flacc.* 116, 121, 174-175; *Leg.* 206; *Quod Omn.* 89; Mart. Is. 2.14; 2

Chron. 24.22; cf. Josephus, *Ant.* 11.171 (where the murder of Joash is treated as the punishment for his murder of Zechariah); Est. 7.10; 16.18; cf. Josephus, Ant. 11.267-268.

Two ideas appear to lie behind the expectation of punishment for persecutors. First, in the sovereignty of God, evil cannot go unpunished. Thus, for example, when Heliodorus was struck down as he tried to enter the temple, he himself, reportedly through that experience, came to acknowledge the power of God (2 Macc. 3.24-28, 36). In other words, the punishment of the persecutor is an eloquent testimony that the history of the world lies under the scrutinizing sovereignty of God. Secondly, the blood of the martyrs always cried for vengeance because such acts of wanton pain and bloodshed were in fact perpetrated against God himself (2 Macc. 8.3-4). The classic example is the blood of Abel, considered in late Judaism as the first martyr, which cried for vengeance so much that even the earth refused his blood (*Gen. R.* 22.22; Sibyl. Or. iii.311). It is almost a theology of *lex talionis*. For in 2 Maccabees the fifth brother had this to say: 'abide a while, and behold his great power, how he will torment thee and thy brother' for what he had done to them (7.16-17). The same idea emerges from 2 Macc. 8.3, 4; 4 Macc. 9.24. In this connexion j.*Ta'an.* 68d is interesting: 'When Bar Koziba slew R. Elazar of Modi'im, the second generation Tanna, for allegedly plotting to betray the city to Hadrian, a heavenly voice said, "Thou hast slain R. Elazar, the arm of all Israel and their right eye, therefore shall thine arm be dried up, and thy right eye utterly darkened". At once Bethar was captured and Bar Koziba slain'.[69] Clearly Bar Koziba reaped what he had sown.

The eschatological fate of the martyr presents a very diverse array of ideas. They are to be rewarded. But the nature of the reward is of great variety. They may be exalted to share in the Messianic age, appearing as assessors at the judgment. An example of this theology is Dan. 7.22 (21 LXX): the 'little horn', symbolizing Antiochus Epiphanes, made war against 'the saints', i.e. the Maccabaean martyrs, 'until the Ancient of Days came and judgment was given for the saints of the Most High'. The language here is most striking. The 'Ancient of Days' and the 'one like a son of man', i.e a man-like figure, stand in striking contrast to the description of the other *dramatis personae* as beasts. This by itself may already be suggesting the superiority of the son of man and the Ancient of Days to the rulers of the other kingdoms which will ultimately be subject to man, as Ps. 8 would put it. The 'Ancient of Days' further contrasts with the man-like figure in the sense that sovereignty and perhaps eternity properly belong to the former. We there read that τὸ κρίμα ἔδωκεν ἁγίοις ὑψίστου. That clause is capable of two interpretations: (a) judgment was given in their favour; (b) he gave judgment to them, i.e. they were judges. Ewald, followed by Bevan,[70] has conjectured that *ytb wšltn'* dropped out by homoeoteleuton before *ytb*. That is, the original would have read 'the judgment sat and dominion was given to the saints'. This conjecture of Ewald argues for the second interpretation and appears to have the support of the RSV, which has as the next clause 'and the time came when the saints received the kingdom'. Though both interpretations are perfectly reasonable, we on balance favour the second interpretation because the view is enunciated independently at Dan. 12.13 where the martyrs 'shall stand in (their) allocated place at the end of days'. Thus the vindication of the Maccabaean martyrs would consist in part in their appearing with God, as assessors at the judgment.

Elsewhere in Jewish literature the idea is repeated, for example at Wisd. 3.8. The righteous who had experienced so much torment would 'be greatly rewarded: for God proved them and found them worthy for himself' (3.5). That reward is further elaborated in these words: 'in the time of their visitation (ἐπισκοπή = *bywm pqwdh*) . . . they shall judge the nations and have dominion over the people . . . ' Judging the world is an element of having dominion. God is the judge of the world as the sovereign Lord of history. But he delegates some of that power and authority to those who prove zealous for the Lord, despite their persecutions.[71]

Another idea in the area of rewards is the expectation of immortality—ἀθανασία and ἀφθαρσία. The doctrine of immortality is found mostly in the hellenized writers. Thus 4 Maccabees, which is thoroughly hellenized, promises immortality—4 Macc. 16.13; 14.5; 15.3; 17.12; 18.3. So too Wisd. 3.1-6; Ps. Sol. 3.11; 13.11; 14.2-3; Josephus, *Bell.* 2.152-153, 515; 7.344, 346. Αθανασία, which does not occur in the Greek versions except in Aquila's version of Ps. 49.15, seems to waver between two ideas: first, continual and continued personal existence (Wisd. 3.3, 4, 8, 17; 15.13; Ecclus 19.17) in fellowship with the Lord in heaven (Wisd. 3.23; 6.18-19; 4 Macc. 9.22, 23).[72] As such it is synonymous with αἰώνιος ζωή (4 Macc. 15.3; 17.12; 18.3). Secondly, however, *athanasía* sometimes seems to mean an immortality of remembrance, a survival in the memory of posterity; so e.g. Wisd. 8.13, 'I shall obtain immortality, and leave behind me an everlasting memorial to them that come after me'. In the parallelism of the passage immortality is the everlasting memorial. Immortality appears to be an untarnished reputation and descendants to maintain that reputation[73] (Ecclus 2.10-11; 40.15; 41.6). This brings us to the major theme of martyrs being a memorial.

By virtue of the fact that the martyr showed zeal for the Lord of Israel, he became an example to his contemporaries as well as posterity. The martyr became a venerable figure and example. He was invoked by posterity directly as an example. Thus Mattathias cited the example of Abraham, Phinehas, Elijah, Ananias, Azarias, Misael and Daniel in these words: 'Be ye zealous for the law, and give your lives for the covenant of your fathers. Call to remembrance what acts our fathers did in their time; so shall ye receive great honour and an everlasting name' (1 Macc. 2.50-51; cf. 2.64). Thus there is an immortality of remembrance as a result of their zeal for the Lord. Indeed, it became a literary genre to draw up a catalogue of the spiritual heroism of the martyrs as examples of zeal for the Lord to the Jewish people.[74] The martyrs were celebrated as examples not only of zeal for God but also of manliness (ἀνδρεία–4 Macc. 1.11; 8.15; 10.14; 14.4; 6.20-21), courage (εὐτυχία–2 Macc. 6.30; 4 Macc. 6.11; 10.4), nobleness of spirit (εὐγενῶς–4 Macc. 6.22; 9.13; 12.14; 13.10), boldness or frankness (παρρησία–4 Macc. 10.5), patience (ὑπομονή–4 Macc. 1.11; 5.23), (καρτερία–4 Macc. 6.13; 11.12), cheerfulness and joy (4 Macc. 5.23; 8.17; 10.2). As such he is a pioneer or guide (κυβερνήτης–4 Macc. 7.1) and a hero.

The idea of immortality is expressed in indirect ways as well. Thus the martyrs were honoured and commemorated by the erection of tombs over their graves. For example, Simon immortalized the memory of his father and brothers by erecting a sepulchre at Modein for a 'perpetual memory' (1 Macc. 13.27-30; 4 Macc. 17.8-10; b.*Yoma* 87a). Daniel was also commemorated by the erection of a tomb at Ecbatana (Josephus, *Ant.* 10.264).[75]

The martyrs were also immortalized through feasts. The two significant ones were the feasts of Hanukkah and Purim. Hanukkah originally celebrated the rededication of the Temple on the 25th of Kislev, 165 BC (1 Macc. 4.54). But that date was deliberately chosen because it was exactly three years after Antiochus Epiphanes profaned the temple by setting up in it the statue of the Olympian Zeus, the *šiqquṣ meʾšōmēm* (1 Macc. 1.20). Thus the feast of Hanukkah came to celebrate the triumph of right over evil might and through that, the Maccabaean martyrs. Indeed, E. Bammel[76] has suggested that 4 Maccabees itself was probably a homily to be read at a feast of Hanukkah to celebrate the martyrs. The seven brothers were also commemorated in the synagogue on the ninth of Ab.[77] Similarly, the feast of Purim commemorated the triumph of faith over might in the Persian diaspora when Ahasuerus (Xerxes) afflicted the Jews in about 483 BC (Est. 3).[78] Later still, the prayers for fast days contain a litany which celebrates the biblical prophets and the deliverance from persecution, danger or martyrdom. The martyrs were remembered in the liturgy.[79]

Whatever immortality meant, it was said to involve εἰρήνη (peace) which had two elements: rest (ἀνάπαυσις—Wisd. 4.7) and blessedness under God's protection (Wisd. 3.1-6; Enoch 102.10; Philo, *Jos.* 43; *Mos.* 39).

In the more Jewish writings the expectation of the martyr's vindication takes the form of a resurrection. Thus the second of the seven brothers mocking at the king said: 'Thou [the king] like a fury takest us out of this present life, but the King of the world [God] shall raise us up, who have died for his laws, unto everlasting life' (2 Macc. 7.9).[80] That was a resurrection beyond the grave—as becomes clear from the exhortation of the mother to the seventh brother: 'Take thy death, that I may receive thee again in mercy with thy brethren' (2 Macc. 7.29). The curious thing is that the resurrection is thought of in a literalistic, material sense. It is a personal resurrection to life and personal consciousness. Resurrection was also a new creation. Thus the mother again exhorted her children in these words: 'I cannot tell how ye came into my womb; for I neither gave you birth nor life, neither was it I that formed the members of every one of you. But doubtless the Creator of the world, who formed the generation of men and found out the beginning of all things, will also of his own mercy give you breath and life again, as ye now regard not your own selves for his laws' sake' (2 Macc. 7.22-23). There is hardly any speculation about the nature of the resurrection life. But it is regarded as something like a replica of this life and also entirely the work of God in recognition of or in response to the martyr's dedication to God.

On the subject of the expectation of a resurrection it is difficult to make statements that will do justice to the very diverse statements that appear in late Judaism and in the Intertestamental period. In the book of Daniel, for example, there is no promise of a general resurrection. Only many of the dead (*wrbym myšny 'dmt 'pr*) are to be raised. Again it is not all mortals who died who would be raised 'to everlasting life', but only those who are described as *mśkylym* (Dan. 12.3, 10; 11.33). Some scholars like Heaton and Vermes[81] have interpreted these words of the scribes and sages. However, in view of ἐννοούμενοι τοῦ ἔθνους συνήσουσιν εἰς πολλούς of Dan. 11.33, it is better with Porteous[82] to interpret *mśkylym* of 'the wise leaders of the people', namely those who came forward in the Maccabaean crisis and showed courage and loyalty at the cost of their lives (cf. 1 Macc. 2.42; 7.13; 2 Macc. 6.18ff.). Thus one group to be raised are those whose extraordinary goodness is attested by their martyrdom. On the other hand, those whose extraordinary wickedness is attested by their persecution of true religion are also raised for punishment (Dan. 12.2). It seems, therefore, that in Daniel, at any rate, the resurrection theme is brought up in order to make retribution possible. Resurrection is thus a sign of the decisive victory of the cause of Yahweh and his own over evil.[83]

At the other extreme is the Book of Enoch. While in the OT Sheol simply awaits all and sundry, in Enoch, Sheol is the abode of dead souls until the judgment (ch. 22). It has four sectors, one for the righteous, another for the wicked, presumably the most wicked, a third quarter for the wicked who escaped punishment on earth, and the last quarter for the wicked who met their deserts and therefore have no further judgment (22.13). The moral law of Yahweh is supreme even in Sheol, because all the different types of wicked ones have a foretaste of their final destinies. There does not appear to be a general resurrection in Enoch.

(d) *The Cosmic Battle*

We have so far seen three theodocies of martyrdom, namely chastisements, sacrifice and eschatology. We now turn to a fourth. In this theodicy persecutions and martyrdom are seen as earthly manifestations of a cosmic battle in heaven itself. Thus, for example, in the book of Daniel the plight of the Maccabaeans was explained as the earthly manifestation of the war between the angel of Persia (10.13) and the angel of Greece (10.20) on the one hand, and the angel of the Jews on the other. Precisely because it is the war between the forces of God and the forces of Satan, angels of God are sent to intervene on the side of the martyrs. Thus the angel of God intervened to protect

Shadrach, Meshach, and Abednego from the fiery furnace (Dan. 3.28f.; Song of the Three Children, 26). Similarly, the angel of the Lord intervened to save Daniel from the jaws of the lion (Dan. 6.22f.; cf. Josephus, *Ant.* 10.262).

Again 'the little horn' 'grew great even to the host of heaven (Δύναμις τοῦ οὐρανοῦ); and some of the hosts of the stars it cast down to the ground, and trampled upon them' (Dan. 8.10). δύναμις τοῦ οὐρανοῦ often, as here, means the stars (e.g. Deut. 4.9; Jer. 33.22). But in this context they are closely associated with the martyrs. Indeed, they are the martyrs who form part of God's army against the infidel. There is an assimilation between the stars and the men on the earth.[84] Thus the plight of the Maccabaean martyrs was an earthly manifestation of a fight going on at the cosmic level.

The same idea is enunciated by the claim sometimes made that the persecutor acted as he did because Satan had inhabited him. Thus the martyrdom of Isaiah is because Manasseh was allegedly inhabited by Belchira or Satan (cf. Martyrdom of Isaiah).[85] Consequently, the predicates of Satan are applied to persecutors so as to show their affinity with Satan; thus, for example, πονηρός—Est. 7.16; 14.9; διάβολος—Est. 8.1; ἐχθρός—Est. 7.6; 9.10, 22; 14.6; ἀντικείμενος—Est. 9.2. Depicting the persecutor as a dragon serves the same purpose—Est. 11.6; cf. 10.7; Ps. Sol. 2.29; Ps. 74.13.

From this brief survey of the Intertestamental period there has emerged a body of ideas which constituted a widely known martyr-theology which grew out of the long history of the Jews as a much persecuted people of God. It is thus antecedently not impossible that some aspects of Jewish martyr-theology should have contributed towards the Christian understanding of their message. Whether or not there actually was such influence can only be decided by looking at the NT literature—which for our purposes will be restricted to the Pauline corpus.

Chapter 3

THE SCANDAL OF THE CROSS OF GLORY

The central message of Paul's missionary enterprise was the cross of Christ. As he himself put it in his letter to the church of Corinth, 'I decided to know nothing among you except Jesus Christ and him crucified' (1 Cor. 2.2). The focus on the crucifixion of Jesus is confirmed by 1 Thess. 5.9-10. Salvation is a future experience and at the same time irrevocably linked with Jesus' death on the cross, even though the resurrection may be implied. And yet precisely that message of the cross was the problem: 'We preach Χριστὸν ἐσταυρωμένον, to the Jews σκάνδαλον, to the Gentiles μωρίαν' (1 Cor. 1.23). To Gentiles it was folly[1] precisely because in their conception of God they could not take seriously any God who was ignominiously condemned and executed. Further, Christianity preached a scandal of particularity, fastening on the cross of Christ as the turning point in the history of the world and of salvation. To the Greek who held a cyclic view of history, such teaching was sheer folly, while in Roman society crucifixion was a cruel mode of execution and punishment reserved for slaves and hardened criminals like the man who committed sacrilege by robbing a temple, the soldier who deserted, the man who committed high treason and caused insurrection.[2] It was 'the most cruel and terrible penalty' (Cicero, *In Verr.* 2.64). The crucifixion of Jesus ruled him out of court for any serious consideration as a man of God and the turning point of history.

The cross was equally offensive to the Jews. Though a predominantly Roman mode of execution and, therefore, a reminder of foreign domination and oppression of the Jews, 'crucifixion had been used in Palestine since the second century BC—even by Jewish courts. Because it was a particularly gruesome form of execution it was used especially in political cases—like those branded by the Romans with the term λῃστεία.'[3] Whoever had the authority to consign to execution by the cross and for whatever crime it was administered, crucifixion was for the Jews as well 'the most wretched of deaths' (Josephus, *Bell.* 8.203). It brought ignominy on the sufferers and also defilement of the land (Deut. 21.22f.).

There was a further consideration where the Jews were concerned: the cross dramatized the curse of God: 'a hanged man is accursed by God' (Deut. 21.23). Consequently, for the Jews too the cross of Christ was a σκάνδαλον,[4] i.e. an insult to the Messianic hopes of the Jews who before the third century AD had no idea of a suffering Messiah.[5] It appears that Paul was conscious of this difficulty, as becomes evident from his citation of Deut. 21.23 at Gal. 3.13 (cf. 5.11). From the biblical and historical standpoints, therefore, the message of the cross could not be taken seriously by Jew or Greek.

Against this background, it is most striking that Paul like the rest of the Christians saw the cross in a brighter light without ever arguing, it seems, for his positive interpretation of the cross. How was it possible for Paul to envisage the cross more positively than others saw it? This chapter seeks to argue that it was the martyrological interpretation of it that made sense of the crucifixion of Jesus, at least in Jewish circles.

The first evidence is the phrase δοῦναι ἑαυτόν. Its cognate is παραδιδόναι ἑαυτόν (Eph. 5.2). Other occurrences of the two phrases are at Gal. 1.4; 2.20; Eph. 5.2, 25; 1 Tim. 2.6; Tit. 2.14. These phrases appear in two senses in the Pauline letters. They are used in their normal secular sense of 'to devote oneself to duty or service'.[6] For example, at 2 Cor. 8.5, Paul commends the churches of Macedonia for giving themselves over to the Lord (and to Paul) by caring for the poor saints. However, in most occurrences of the phrase it has the force of ἐσταυρώθη (1 Cor. 1.23; 2.2) or ἐσταυρωμένος or some form of ἀποθνῄσκειν (1 Thess. 5.10; Rom. 5.6f.; 14.15; 1 Cor. 15.3; 2 Cor. 5.15). For example, at Gal. 1.4 τοῦ δόντος ἑαυτόν can only mean 'him who surrendered himself in death'. This special application of the phrase could have been obvious to the Christian conscience and have belonged to the apostolic tradition.

The phrase δοῦναι ἑαυτόν corresponds exactly to the Hebrew phrase *ntn 'ṣmn* (b.*Shab.* 130a). The same idea is sometimes rendered *ntn npšw 'l* or *mṣr npšw 'l* which corresponds to παραδιδόναι (τιθέναι) τὴν ψυχὴν ὑπέρ. The basic idea is putting oneself at great risk for the sake of God, a risk which often culminated in death. Thus Mattathias in his valedictory speech to his children said 'be zealous for the law, and give your lives (δότε τὰς ψυχὰς ὑμῶν) for the covenant of your fathers' (1 Macc. 2.50).[7] It was an exhortation to martyrdom in defence and pursuit of the will of God. Giving oneself in death in obedience to God was evidence of one's zeal for the Lord. The phrase underlines the voluntariness with which that death is undertaken. In the words of Büchsel, ψυχὴν διδόναι (which is paraphrased as διδόναι ἑαυτόν, e.g. at 1 Macc. 6.44) is an expression 'current among the Jews for the death of martyrs, among the Greeks for the death of soldiers'. That aspect is really a part of the obedience to the will of God. It is a voluntary action which is also in obedience to God and out of zeal for the Lord. All these are characteristic aspects of the martyr. Jesus, therefore, by this phrase is depicted as a martyr with an emphasis on his self-surrender in obedience to the will of God.

Schlier[8] has suggested that δοῦναι ἑαυτόν recalls the Servant of the Lord who suffered immensely because of his obedience to the divine commission to him to witness to the truth. However, there is no need to pin down the phrase to Isaiah's servant. For not only is it absent from the Servant passages, but the idea is so general that it cannot be connected to a particular passage.[9] The idea of vicarious suffering and propitiation was not unfamiliar to pre-Christian Judaism, as 2 Macc. 7.18, 32, 38 and 4 Macc. 6.28-29 amply demonstrate.

The phrase δοῦναι ἑαυτόν and its cognate παραδιδόναι ἑαυτόν are therefore synonymous with the dying or crucifixion of Christ. Further, they underline the voluntary nature of the death of Christ and, through that, Christ's zeal for God.

A second passage draws out the zealot-theme in relation to the life and death of Christ. We refer to Rom. 15.3. In his exhortation to the stronger brethren to have consideration for the weaker brethren, to bear with their difficulties, Paul used the example of Jesus Christ to clinch his argument: 'For Christ did not please himself (οὐχ ἑαυτῷ ἤρεσεν); but, as it is written, οἱ ὀνειδισμοὶ τῶν ὀνειδιζόντων σε ἐπέπεσαν ἐπ' ἐμέ'. The phrase οὐχ ἑαυτῷ ἤρεσεν by itself focusses on the total devotion of Jesus to the will of God and underlines Jesus' zeal for the Lord. Christ willingly submitted himself to the sufferings caused by his compatriots' inexcusable hostility to God.

Paul goes further to illustrate that devotion to the Lord with a citation from Ps. 69.9, which describes the sufferings of the typically righteous man at the hands of the ungodly. With such a story to tell, it is hardly surprising that the Psalm became a martyrological proof-text.[10] And in the NT as a whole, it is, after Ps. 22, the most quoted, especially in the Passion apologetic:[11]

Ps. 69.4	=	Jn 15.25
69.8	=	Jn 1.11; 7.5
69.9a	=	Jn 2.17
69.22	=	Rom. 10.9-10
69.22b	=	Mk 15.36; Mt. 27.48
69.22	=	Jn 19.28-30
69.25	=	Acts 1.20.

This list betrays a general as well as detailed application of the psalm to the Passion of Christ.

In the passage under review from Paul's letter to the Romans, the ὀνειδισμοί are the humiliations of Christ which came to their culmination in his crucifixion. Thus his sufferings are here treated as evidence of his zeal for the Lord. Paul cites a martyrological proof-text to argue that Christ's submission to suffering and ultimately to the death on the cross in obedience to the will of God was evidence that he 'did not please himself' and was, therefore, devoted to God. Further, the use of Ps. 69 is meant to show that that shameful death was part of a divine plan which was unfolding. This removes some of the scandal of the cross.

The third passage is the kenotic passage of Phil. 2.5-11. This is primarily an appeal to the example of Jesus Christ and is only incidentally christological. Thus that hymn with its great doctrinal statements subserves ethical exhortations to humility. Indeed, it is of a unity with Phil. 2.1-4: μὴ τὰ ἑαυτῶν ἕκαστοι σκοποῦντες (2.4) = ἑαυτὸν ἐκένωσεν (2.7); ταπεινοφροσύνη (2.3) = ἐταπείνωσεν (2.8); ἐριθείαν, μηδὲ κατὰ κενοδοξίαν (2.3) = per contra ὑπήκοος (2.8). Clearly 2.1-4 and 2.5-11 are of a piece. Further, the fact that the section begins with οὖν (2.1) means that there is a close connexion with what goes before (1.27ff.). Thus 2.5-11 are integral to the paraenesis. In that paraenesis it is stated *inter alia* that 'it has been granted to you that for the sake of Christ you should not only believe in him but also suffer for his sake . . . ' (1.29). So the notes of suffering and martyrdom are already struck.

Some scholars[12] have discerned Is. 52–53 behind the second strophe of the hymn:

2.9	ὁ Θεὸς αὐτὸν ὑπερύψωσεν	52.13	ὑψωθήσεται
2.8	ἐταπείνωσεν ἑαυτὸν	53.7	καὶ αὐτὸς διὰ τὸ κεκακῶσθαι οὐκ ἀνοίγει τὸ στόμα
2.8	ὑπήκοος μέχρι θανάτου	53.3	ἤχθη εἰς θάνατον (LXX)
2.6	ἑαυτὸν ἐκένωσε	53.12	ἀνθ' ὧν παρεδόθη εἰς θάνατον ἡ ψυχὴ αὐτοῦ
2.10	'That at the name of Jesus every knee shall bow, should bow . . . and every tongue should confess . . .'	45.23	'That unto me every knee shall bow, every tongue shall swear.'

Davies concludes: 'In view of the above we shall assume that Paul identified Jesus, the Messiah, with the Suffering Servant of Deutero-Isaiah'. The assumption is far from convincing for a number of reasons. First, verbal similarities and coincidences are at a minimum, as becomes clear from a comparison of the texts in the Greek. If Paul had in mind Isaiah's Servant one would have expected more and closer verbal coincidences, especially since Is. 52–53 was a proof-text in the early Church. Second, where there appear to be similarities and coincidences, they are not in regard to the main and obvious characteristics of the Servant, namely the prophet of true religion of which he is a confessor and ultimately a martyr, whose martyrdom has vicarious expiation attaching to it. Third, in the general theology of Paul, there is extraordinarily little application of Is. 52–53 to the ministry of Jesus. Only Rom. 4.25, 10.16 and 15.21 seem to refer to Is. 53. Of these, Rom. 10.16 and Rom. 15.21 are about evangelism. Fourth, there is something odd about such a use of Is. 52–53 here. For as Davies himself suggests convincingly, Paul switches in this short passage from the LXX to the Hebrew text. This is not his custom.[13] The assumption of Davies that in Phil. 2 Jesus is identified with the Suffering Servant of Isaiah is forced and not borne out by the facts.

Jeremias also has argued that 'the decisive proof of the connexion of Phil. 2.6-11 with Is. 53 lies in the fact that ἑαυτὸν ἐκένωσεν, attested nowhere else in the Greek and grammatically harsh, is an exact rendering of *h'rh . . . npšw* (Is. 53.12)'.[14] Consequently, the self-emptying concerns the surrender of life rather than self-limitation in the incarnation.

Jeremias's interpretation is not satisfactory either, for a number of reasons. First, an active verb with a reflexive pronoun is a perfectly normal way of expressing reflexive action. Thus in the Lucan version of the exhortation of Jesus to men to deny themselves in order to come after him, we find ἑαυτὸν δὲ ἀπολέσας: i.e. if he loses himself (Lk. 9.25). Jeremias's conclusion that ἑαυτὸν ἐκένωσεν is 'grammatically harsh' is unconvincing. Second, the fact that κενοῦν chances not to be found elsewhere may be due to nothing more abstruse than that self-emptying is not an every-day occupation. Third, still less is it clear that ἐκένωσεν is a natural translation of *h'rh*. It seems to us that Is. 32.15 and perhaps Ps. 37.35 are the only biblical passages clearly conducive to the translation 'empty' rather than 'strip bare'.[15] Nothing in the phrase ἑαυτὸν ἐκένωσεν compels us to go back to Is. 53.

For our purposes three phrases are essential to our understanding of the hymn: μορφὴν δούλου λαβών, γενόμενος ὑπήκοος μέχρι θανάτου and ἑαυτὸν ἐκένωσεν. First, μορφὴν δούλου λαβών and γενόμενος ὑπήκοος μέχρι θανάτου are coincident with ἑαυτὸν ἐκένωσεν and are, therefore, the content of it. Second, μορφὴν δούλου clearly stands in conscious contrast to μορφὴ θεοῦ, especially so when ἀλλά is used, thereby indicating the antithesis between the two phrases. What then does δοῦλος mean?

It has sometimes been argued that δοῦλος is an allusion to Is. 53 and therefore recalls Isaiah's Servant of the Lord. Jeremias[16] has shown that παῖς and δοῦλος are synonymous, even though the LXX normally renders *'bd* with παῖς, while Aquila's translation renders it δοῦλος. Thus the use of δοῦλος would not argue against any allusion to Is. 53. However, δοῦλος was a common term in the Roman Empire for one who had no legal rights to himself. He was a *res*, a thing. This normal sense is the more appropriate and obvious meaning in our context because it fits better the contrast drawn by Paul between the role of Jesus as a δοῦλος and the glory of God. Again, while *'bd* of Is. 53 is a title of honour, denoting the special relationship between God and the Servant,[17] δοῦλος in our context is not a title and rather 'denotes the dishonour and limitations of the human body'.[18] That this is the right interpretation is borne out by the phrase ἐν ὁμοιώματι ἀνθρώπων γενόμενος, the plural ἀνθρώπων[19] emphasizing his solidarity with the rest of humanity.

One aspect of Jesus' genuine humanity was in being ὑπήκοος μέχρι θανάτου. The man Jesus was characterized by obedience to the will of God. He was zealous for the Lord. That humility of Jesus was epitomized in the death on the cross of shame. The cross is, therefore, the expression of total obedience to the will of God. Like the deaths of the prophets, his death was the last stage of the 'Zeugnis und Bekenntnis auf der Seite Gottes'.[20] As Davies puts it, 'martyrdom for the sake of the Torah was considered to be the acme of obedience or, in other words, obedience to the Torah was being thought of in terms of death'.[21]

In our exposition of ἑαυτὸν ἐκένωσεν two elements have stood out: Jesus' devotion to the will of God and his death on the cross of shame as an expression of that devotion to God's will. The two elements qualify Jesus to be looked upon as a martyr. Indeed, the text clearly sets Jesus forth as a martyr because his humiliating death on the cross portrays him as one zealous for the Lord. It is, therefore, this understanding of his death which transforms the shame of the cross into a thing of glory.

Our study of the phrase δοῦναι ἑαυτόν (Rom. 15.3 and Phil. 2.5-11) has revealed that the death of Jesus is not only stated as a historical fact but interpreted as a voluntary death undertaken out of zeal for the Lord.

The interpretation outlined above is implicit in the terminology. But it is explicitly stated in other passages and phrases. The first is the ὑπέρ-formula which usually follows δοῦναι ἑαυτόν and its synonyms. The ὑπέρ formula may be classified as follows:

(a) With the personal pronouns: ὑπὲρ ἐμοῦ (Gal. 2.20); ὑπὲρ ἡμῶν (Rom. 5.2, 8; Eph. 5.2); ὑπὲρ ὑμῶν (1 Cor. 1.13; 11.24; 2 Cor. 5.21); ὑπὲρ αὐτῆς (Eph. 5.20); ὑπὲρ οὗ (Rom. 14.15).

(b) With an adjective: ὑπὲρ πάντων (2 Cor. 5.14; 1 Tim. 2.6); ὑπὲρ ἀσεβῶν (Rom. 5.6).

(c) With a substantive: ὑπὲρ τῶν ἁμαρτιῶν ἡμῶν (1 Cor. 15.3; Gal. 1.4).

Before we examine the meaning of the phrase, let us briefly examine the cognate preposition περί. Sometimes also περί appears instead of ὑπέρ. Thus we have such phrases as περὶ ἡμῶν ἀποθανόντος (1 Thess. 5.10) and περὶ ἁμαρτίας (Rom. 8.3): that is, in respect of our sins. A close examination of the uses of ὑπέρ and περί in these contexts reveals that the two prepositions are used synonymously.[22] For example, the manuscript evidence with regard to Gal. 1.4 is most instructive: while p,[51] B and H read τοῦ δόντος ἑαυτὸν ὑπὲρ τῶν ἁμαρτιῶν ἡμῶν, p,[46] A, D, F, and G read περί for ὑπέρ. In hellenistic Greek, too, περί and ὑπέρ are interchangeable.[23] The only difference between the prepositions is that Paul tends to prefer ὑπέρ when the object is persons and περί when the object is sins.

The issue now is the meaning of the ὑπέρ-formula. Although ὑπέρ primarily has a local sense, in the NT it means 'on behalf of' or 'for the benefit of'. Thus the death of Christ was on behalf of us or our sins. In this connexion 1 Cor. 8.11 is interesting. In that passage Paul exhorts the stronger brethren not to allow their strong convictions to be a stumbling-block to the weaker brother δι' ὃν Χριστὸς ἀπέθανεν. The use of διά confirms that the death of Christ was on account of others. Thus ὑπέρ, περί and διά are synonymous in these contexts. They show the thrust of the work of salvation.[24] In view of the fact that the object of ὑπέρ is sometimes 'sins', the ὑπέρ-formula interprets the death of Jesus of Nazareth as a vicarious sacrifice. For the phrase interprets the death as being in respect of our sins (Rom. 8.3), or on account of the sins of men, namely, in order to atone for them (Rom. 3.23ff.; Gal. 3.12ff.). The idea of satisfaction is implied not in the signification of the preposition, but in the context.

The concept of sacrifice to remove sins was familiar to Judaism, in which the sacrificial system was a central religious institution. De Vaux has written 'Because sacrifice is a homage to God and establishes or re-establishes good relations between God and those who are faithful to him, so too, sacrifice appeases the anger of God against the sinner and averts punishment. For this reason every sacrifice has expiatory force.'[25] That sin could be atoned for by a sacrifice, therefore, would not be in dispute. What could be in dispute is whether a death on the cross could qualify as a sacrifice. But the Christians could cite the examples from the Maccabaean martyrs to substantiate their martyrological interpretation of the cross of Christ. And this is where we come back to the phrase δοῦναι ἑαυτόν.

The combination of δοῦναι ἑαυτόν with περὶ ἁμαρτίας removes the sacrifice from that of bulls and goats to a very personal level—to the level of the sacrificial death of the martyrs. For whereas in the OT and Judaism the slaughter of the victim did not constitute the chief act and was, consequently, not performed by the priest himself,[26] in the Pauline letters there is an emphasis on the dying. Thus Paul is thinking of sacrifices other than the temple sacrifices that made for atonement. And the only other sacrifice which could atone for sin—

and that outside the temple—was the martyr's death. For human sacrifices had never been permitted by OT law and the only sacrifice in Jewish thought that involved man as the victim was the death of the martyr.

The task now is to draw together the threads with regard to τὸ δοῦναι ἑαυτὸν ὑπὲρ ἡμῶν and its variants. First, that phrase highlights the voluntary nature of the death of Jesus on the cross, which emphasis is another expression for the theme of total devotion to the will of God, a characteristic feature of the martyrs. Secondly, that voluntary death is interpreted as a sacrifice. Thirdly, that sacrifice is personal in the sense that in contrast to the sacrifice of the life of bulls and goats in the Old Testament, it was the life of a human being which was expended. Fourthly, it was a vicarious sacrifice. These four elements highlighted by the phrase τὸ δοῦναι ἑαυτὸν ὑπὲρ ἡμῶν indicate a martyrological understanding of the death of Jesus. That interpretation was an effort to redeem the scandal of the cross.

Before leaving this topic, three passages in Paul or the deutero-Pauline literature call for special comment: Gal. 3.13, 2 Cor. 5.21 and 1 Tim. 2.6. Let us begin with the last since it sustains the theme of ransom.

According to 1 Tim. 2.6, 'there is one God and there is one mediator between God and man, the man Jesus Christ, ὁ δοὺς ἑαυτὸν ἀντίλυτρον ὑπὲρ πάντων, τὸ μαρτύριον καιροῖς ἰδίοις, 'who gave himself as a ransom for all for a testimony in its own times'. The phrases ὁ δοὺς ἑαυτόν and ὑπὲρ πάντων are already familiar to us and have been established as interpreting the death of Jesus Christ as a voluntary vicarious self-sacrifice. Our interest here, therefore, is the further amplification of this theme by the term ἀντίλυτρον.

Any casual reading of the verse cannot but recall Mk 10.45 where Jesus announces that he came to give his life as a λύτρον ἀντὶ πολλῶν, a ransom for many. Ἀντίλυτρον is the intensive form of λύτρον, i.e. the price of release[27] (see *Orphica Lithica* 593). It is 'a Hellenistically colored variant of that word of Jesus'.[28] The very intensive form used here militates against any attempt to read into λύτρον any allusions to the Suffering Servant[29] of Is. 53.10 where the Servant gave his life as an *āšām* For as Barrett[30] has convincingly shown, never once in the LXX is *lútron* used to render *'šm* or its cognates. Besides, there is a real difference in meaning between *'šm* and λύτρον; for the former basically relates to guilt, while the latter relates to the idea of equivalence or substitution. Nevertheless, Barrett suggests attractively that behind the phrase stands the idea of the self-sacrifice of the martyrs as a means of atonement for many (cf. 4 Macc. 6.27ff.; 17.22; 18.4). Thus 1 Tim. 2.6 is a further confirmation that διδόναι ἑαυτόν and ὑπέρ-formulae establish Jesus as a martyr whose death on the cross is a self-sacrifice which not only expresses his utter devotion and obedience to the will of God but also is a vicarious sacrifice which makes atonement for the sins of many.[31]

According to Gal. 3.13, 'Christ redeemed (ἐξηγόρασεν) us from the curse of the law, having become a curse for us (γενόμενος ὑπέρ ἡμῶν κατάρα)—for it is written, "Cursed be every one who hangs on a tree"'. This text stands in the context of a discussion of legalism and self-sufficiency as a basis for salvation. According to Paul, by the logic of their argument the legalists should admit that every one who relies on the works of the law must be under a curse because their own scriptures assert that 'Cursed be every one who does not abide by all the things written in the book of the law and do them' (Deut. 27.26). An assumed premise of the argument is that no man is able to keep the whole law. The logical conclusion of the argument of the legalists is that then men are in a hopeless situation and consigned to damnation. It is against that background that Paul offers another type of salvation, that through the cross.

The idea of ransom has been mentioned above. The term ἐξηγόρασεν used here is capable of two meanings: (a) to buy up or secure; (b) to redeem, deliver at some cost to the deliverer. The latter meaning is obviously demanded by the context.[32] The word, therefore, underlines the costliness of the rescue operation: it is at the cost of the life of Jesus himself, the vicarious sacrifice of a human being. The vicarious nature of that sacrifice is drawn out by the clause γενόμενος ὑπέρ ἡμῶν κατάρα.

There appears to be a word-play here on the term κατάρα (curse). Earlier the word was used in the sense of the judgment of God on the legalists for their failure to keep the Law they claimed to uphold. In contrast to that, Jesus is also seemingly under a curse because he experienced the crucifixion; for after all, according to Deut. 21.23, the cross is evidence that the crucified one is under God's judgment. Paul's version of Deut. 21.23 is interesting: Ἐπικατάρατος πᾶς ὁ κρεμάμενος ἐπὶ ξύλου, very different from the version in the LXX: κεκατεραμένος ὑπὸ θεοῦ πᾶς κρεμάμενος ἐπὶ ξύλου. The version in Paul looks at first sight like his own *ad hoc* rendering or a hazy recollection of the LXX.[33] However, there is the striking omission of ὑπὸ θεοῦ from the text in Paul's version that may not be fortuitous but deliberate, in order to cut the ground from under the legalists. Paul is concerned to argue that it is in the eyes of the so-called pious ones and the just ones that Jesus' crucifixion confirms him to have been an arch-sinner, and not in God's eyes.[34]

However, there is probably another issue involved. The Hebrew text of Deut. 21.23 reads *ky qllt 'lhym tlwy*. The text is ambiguous in the sense that *'lhym* in the context may be either subjective or objective. Consequently, throughout Jewish history two interpretations of the text emerged. First is the LXX translation: 'he who hangs is accursed in the sight of God'. The second interpretation is that of Jewish writers like Aquila, Theodotion, Symmachus, and the Targum of Jonathan who interpret it as 'he who hangs is a contempt of God, a reproach/insult to God'. This latter objective interpretation of *'lhym* may be the result of the persecutions of the Jews which made it difficult for them to believe that the crucified giants of faith were under the curse of God.[35] We may surmise that Paul's omission of ὑπὸ θεοῦ may be a hint that he is following the positive reinterpretation of Deut. 21.23 occasioned by the experience of martyrdom. In other words, a martyrological interpretation of the crucifixion of Jesus forces him to omit ὑπὸ θεοῦ.

Gal. 3.13 then argues that the death of Christ is like the payment of ransom. It is a vicarious sacrifice, which ransoms men from the judgment of God. Paul is here handling material already in use in the Church's apologetic.[36]

Similar to Gal. 3.13 is 2 Cor. 5.21. There Paul is discussing his work as an ambassador of Christ with a ministry of reconciliation, a reconciliation achieved through the death of Christ on the cross. In this regard he writes of Jesus: τὸν μὴ γνόντα ἁμαρτίαν ὑπὲρ ἡμῶν ἁμαρτίαν ἐποίησεν, 'so that we might become the righteousness of God through him'. τὸν μὴ γνόντα ἁμαρτίαν is *abstractum pro concreto* and establishes the sinlessness of Jesus. But though sinless, ἁμαρτίαν ἐποίησεν, literally 'he made sin'. In earlier scholarship, this was taken to mean the assimilation of Christ to Azazel, as in the Day of Atonement ritual (Lev. 16). However, that exegesis is unsatisfactory; because the scapegoat was not killed, the analogy breaks down woefully.[37] Nor should ἁμαρτία be interpreted to mean sin-offering, in view of the obvious contrast between sin and righteousness in this passage. The opposite of righteousness is sin and not sin-offering.[38] Therefore, we prefer the interpretation of Barrett that sin in this context is 'the guilt on account of which we are accused before the judgment of God . . . Paul does not say, for by definition it would not have been true, that Christ became a sinner, transgressing God's law; neither does he say, for it would have contradicted all experience . . . that every believer becomes immediately and automatically morally righteous, good as God is good. He says rather that Christ became sin; that is, he came to stand in that relation with God which normally is the result of sin, estranged from God and the object of his wrath.'[39] Christ, though himself sinless, was identified with sinful men in the consequences of their disobedience. And it is precisely because of this identification with the sinful men that his death can be said to be of some value for sinful men. Needless to say, this is a concrete application of the current Jewish idea that the merits of the righteous (e.g. martyrs) could be used for the benefit of the sinful.

Another indication of the martyrological interpretation of the death of Christ is αἷμα (blood). It is stated that redemption is through the blood of Christ (Rom. 3.25; 5.9; 1 Cor. 10.16; cf. 11.26; Col. 1.20; Eph. 1.7; 2.13). The 'blood' is, of course, synonymous with the cross of Christ. Hence the classic phrase of Col. 1.20: διὰ τοῦ αἵματος τοῦ σταυροῦ αὐτοῦ, i.e. through the blood of his cross. The juxtaposition of αἷμα and σταυρός is most striking and strange. For crucifixion was the least bloody of executions.[40]

It is often explained that blood symbolized life. For according to Lev. 17.14, 'the life of every creature is its blood'. Not only does blood symbolize life but it also can achieve atonement: 'The life of the flesh is in the blood; and I have given it for you upon the altar to make atonement for your souls; for it is the blood that makes atonement by reason of the life' (Lev. 17.11). Consequently, most scholars explain the 'blood of the cross' along the lines outlined above on the basis of Lev. 17.11 and 14).

This interpretation rightly captures something of the blood as symbolizing life. But it is inadequate because it totally ignores the scandalous nature of the cross. The cross taken by itself could not be given any salvific significance, except insofar as it was understood in martyrological terms. Thus the startling phrase 'the blood of the cross' requires us to understand 'blood' not only in terms of life but also as a reference to the historical and historic outpouring of Jesus' life on the shameful cross. The cross is thus seen as the epitome of life poured out[41] in obedience to the will of God. The *theologia gloriae* is held alongside a *theologia crucis*, the latter being a kind of corrective and reminder that the consummation is not yet achieved in its fulness. In short, Jesus was a martyr. And it is from this perspective that the 'blood of his cross' can be seen as achieving redemption: God reconciles (ἀποκαταλλάξαι) all things to himself, εἰρηνοποιήσας διὰ τοῦ αἵματος τοῦ σταυροῦ αὐτοῦ.

The εἰρηνοποιήσας clause stands in apposition to ἀποκαταλλάξαι and is, therefore, epexegetical of it. That clause is an exposition of atonement achieved through Jesus Christ's violent death on the cross. The concept of εἰρηνοποιήσας occurs elsewhere in the NT only at Eph. 2.15 in the phrase ποιῶν εἰρήνην. Its substantive, εἰρηνοποιός, occurs also at Mt. 5.9. In Colossians it expounds the crucifixion of Christ as a peace-offering. The Jews technically drew a distinction between a peace-offering and a sin-offering, though, as de Vaux has argued, in actual practice every sacrifice had an expiatory force. There is indeed some evidence that a martyr's death was at once a peace-offering which also made atonement for sin. Thus the fourth Servant song of Second Isaiah contains these words:

> he was wounded for our transgressions,
>   he was bruised for our iniquities;
> upon him was the chastisement (*mwsr*) that made us whole
>   (*slwmnw*),
> and with his stripes we are healed (Is. 53.5).

According to the Isaiah passage God caused the Servant to make himself vicariously guilty by taking on himself men's transgressions and offences and suffering the vengeance deserved by them. The aim of the chastisement was to attain peace, a state of salvation brought about through healing. That voluntary suffering unto death was a submission to God's justice and so became healing. The chastisement is inflicted out of love (cf. Prov. 3.11) but it is also punitive (Prov. 7.22; Jer. 30.14). Similarly, according to 3 Macc. 2.19, 20, the sufferings of the Jews under Ptolemy Philopater not only were a punishment for sins (3 Macc. 2.13, 17, 19; 6.10) but also resulted in the making of peace with God. The same idea is expounded at 4 Macc. 18.4. It seems, therefore, that the martyr-theology explains the unusual phenomenon of the death of Christ by conceiving it as both a sin-offering and a peace-offering, which technically are two different sacrifices, though in practice they flow into each other. Thus the 'blood of the cross' achieves peace and atonement by virtue of the martyr-like violent and shameful pouring out of the life of Jesus on the cross. The martyr's death achieves cosmic unity and harmony, even though it was itself a violent experience. The cross of Christ representing the martyr's death is the place where reconciliation is accomplished.

Another illuminating example of the martyrological understanding of αἷμα is 1 Cor. 10.16: τὸ ποτήριον τῆς εὐλογίας ὃ εὐλογοῦμεν οὐχὶ κοινωνία ἐστὶν τοῦ αἵματος τοῦ Χριστοῦ. This passage is to be studied along with 1 Cor. 11.25: τοῦτο τὸ ποτήριον ἡ καινὴ διαθήκη ἐστὶν ἐν τῷ ἐμῷ αἵματι.

Let us note first that whatever Paul is presenting here is a tradition of the Church. For, as he puts it at 11.23, παρέλαβον ἀπὸ τοῦ Κυρίου, ὃ καὶ παρέδωκα ὑμῖν, ὅτι . . . Thus 1 Cor. 10.16f. and 1 Cor. 11.25 must be understood against the background of the eucharistic theology of the Church and its understanding of the Last Supper. Secondly, there are Paschal overtones to the story: the phrase τὸ ποτήριον τῆς εὐλογίας appears to be a translation of *ks šl brkh*, the technical term for the third cup of wine over which grace was said after the meal.[42] Τῆς εὐλογίας is a genitive of quality. The phrase means that the wine in the cup is expressly consecrated by prayer to the sacred use of the Lord's Supper.

We now turn to an exegesis of the two passages. The first item is the reference to the ποτήριον,[43] the cup. The 'cup' obviously refers to the cup of wine which was used at the Eucharist and at the Passover. But that cup of wine was symbolic of the blood of Christ which had been shed on the cross (cf. Mk 14.24). Indeed, the language and ideas of 1 Cor. 11.25 recall that very verse. The former reads τὸ ποτήριον ἡ καινὴ διαθήκη ἐστὶν ἐν τῷ ἐμῷ αἵματι. The latter refers to the 'cup' as τὸ αἷμά μου τῆς διαθήκης τὸ ἐκχυννόμενον ὑπὲρ πολλῶν (Mk 14.24; cf. Mt. 26.28; Lk. 22.20). Indeed, the Lucan and Pauline phrases are identical. The cup, therefore, symbolizes the blood of Christ 'which is shed for you' (Lk. 22.20), while αἷμα refers to the tragic and violent outpouring of the life of Jesus in his death on the cross.

We are supported in our interpretation of the 'cup' as the tragic death of Jesus by earlier usage of the word. In addition to its literal meaning there are figurative uses which fall into two groups: (a) the cup of God's wrath[44] and (b) the cup of suffering, as, for example, in Mk 10.38; Mt. 20.22 (the martyrdom of James) and Mk 14.36; Mt. 26.39; Lk. 22.42 (the destined and imminent suffering and death of Jesus). These precede the reference to the cup at the Last Supper.

3. *The Scandal of the Cross of Glory*

'Materially, however, Jesus sees Himself confronted, not by a cruel destiny, but by the judgment of God . . . Hence one may suppose that there is an actual connection with the dominant concept in the Old Testament metaphor of the cup. According to this the cup-sayings express for Jesus more than for the Evangelists the fact that the approaching passion is not fate but judgment.'[45] In this regard the martyrological ideas are not far off; for Jewish martyrs discerned God's judgment in their execution. For example, the mother of the seven brethren who were put to death for their faith prayed thus: 'For we suffer because of our sins. And though the living Lord be angry with us a little while for our chastening and correction, yet shall he be at one again with his servants' (2 Macc. 7.33ff.; cf. 2 Macc. 6.12-17; 4 Macc. 10.10).[46] In view of this history, therefore, the cup may be supposed to have martyrological overtones as does the blood also.

Paul further expounds Jesus' death as having atoning efficacy. This is where we come back to 11.25: ἡ καινὴ διαθήκη ἐστὶν ἐν τῷ ἐμῷ αἵματι. The position of ἐστίν speaks against taking ἐν τῷ ἐμῷ αἵματι with διαθήκη. Therefore, ἐν is causal,[47] i.e. 'the cup is the new covenant in virtue of my blood'. Thus the martyrdom of Jesus establishes a new covenant; it is the sacrifice ratifying the covenant-relationship between God and the Church and establishing a new people of God (cf. Ex. 24.28; Jer. 31.31; Mk 14.24 and parallels). And covenant-relationship was possible because their sins were atoned for.[48]

The use of αἷμα in the context of the eucharistic rite of the Church compels us to understand it as referring to the martyrdom of Christ. Indeed, as 1 Cor. 11.26 puts it, 'as often as you eat this bread and drink this cup, you proclaim the Lord's death until he comes'. The eucharist, whatever else it is, celebrates the martyrdom of Christ— just as martyrs were celebrated in the liturgy[49] of the Jewish community at Hanukkah and Purim.

The third example of a martyrological interpretation of αἷμα is in Rom. 3.25. Recapitulating the gospel, Paul affirms that the sinner may be justified through faith in Jesus Christ ὃν προέθετο ὁ θεὸς ἱλαστήριον διὰ πίστεως ἐν τῷ αὐτοῦ αἵματι. Our first concern in this section is the meaning of αἷμα. Since elsewhere in the Pauline corpus, atonement is achieved through the cross of Christ, αἷμα here must refer to the death of Christ on the cross, i.e. the violent outpouring of his life in death. There is a further element here. In the

•

context Paul has been speaking of the sins of men on which God's wrath has been revealed. The essence of that sinfulness of Jew and Gentile alike is infidelity to the measure of revelation vouchsafed by God through either the Torah or natural revelation. In contrast to the sinfulness of men Paul introduces the death of Christ which brings about expiation of sin. In other words, that death of Christ is the supreme act of obedience to the will of God, which contrasts with the rebellious sinfulness of men. Here again, αἷμα designates the martyrdom of Christ. As such it occasions no surprise that faith accords that death a sacrificial meaning and salvific significance.

The operative word in the realm of the sacrificial interpretation of the death of Christ is ἱλαστήριον, because the reference to αἷμα is explicative of ἱλαστήριον. That word is derived from the root ἱλάσκεσθαι which means either to propitiate or to expiate. In the passage under study, since God is the subject of the action involving ἱλαστήριον, the only possible meaning is expiation.[50] Therefore, the devotion of Jesus even unto death has to do with the process of God taking the initiative to expiate sins. The violent death of Jesus is conceived of as an expiatory sacrifice.

The form ἱλαστήριον is either a noun or an adjective. As a noun ἱλαστηριον was the Greek translation of *kprt*, the lid of the Ark, otherwise known as the Mercy Seat (*propitiatorium operculum*), where blood was sprinkled on the Day of Atonement to atone for the sins of the Jewish nation.[51] Some scholars[52] have accordingly explained ἱλαστήριον of Rom. 3 as the Mercy Seat. In other words, Christ has become for the world what the lid of the Ark of the Covenant was for Israel. Christ is the place where atonement is made or sought.

However, this explanation of ἱλαστήριον is far from satisfactory for a number of reasons: first, ἱλαστήριον, as it occurs in Romans, does not have the definite article which it always has in the LXX when it refers to the Ark. Second, nowhere in Paul, nor for that matter in the entire New Testament, is Jesus portrayed as the antitype of the Ark of the Covenant. Third, the comparison with the Ark woefully breaks down because Jesus died and the Ark does not. The real comparison is either with the High Priest who makes the sacrifice or with the sacrificial victim rather than with the lid of the Ark. Fourth, the use of προέθετο appears to exclude the interpretation because the Ark was not in the public view. The emphasis on display is further drawn out by the additional phrase εἰς ἔνδειξιν. Finally, the contrast

3. The Scandal of the Cross of Glory

between νυνί in v. 21, an adverb of time,[53] and χωρὶς νόμου indicates that whatever Christ did was in antithesis to the OT revelation and, therefore, his concern was not with the temple cultus. For these reasons, it is unlikely that ἱλαστήριον is here used in the sense of the Mercy Seat. More probable, therefore, is the adjectival use of ἱλαστήριον.

The adjectival use of ἱλαστήριον[54] is not found in classical Greek and is rare in ecclesiastical Greek. But the adjectival use would mean Christ's death is that which expiates or is an expiatory sacrifice. So ἱλαστήριον brings us back to the sacrificial interpretation of the death of Christ as a sin-offering. In this connexion the concept of the atoning efficacy of a martyr's death comes into its own. Our exegesis of αἷμα brought us to the realm of martyr-theology, to the idea of a righteous man dying for others, to achieve their redemption. The classic statement of this quality of a martyr's death is 4 Macc. 17.21-24 where the death of the seven Maccabaean martyrs was described as ἱλαστήριον and ἀντίψυχον, i.e. a vicarious atoning offering. On that passage Grimm long ago rightly commented: 'dass diese Martyrien nicht allein wegen ihrer inneren ethischen Qualität, sondern auch wegen ihres hoch erspriesslichen äusseren Erfolges für die Theokratie von Gott als stellvetretende Sühnopfer angenommen worden sagen'.[55]

Scholarly study of προτιθέναι has settled for one or other of two possible interpretations: God set forth or God predestined Jesus to be the expiation of sin. In support of the former interpretation are the following points: first, εἰς ἔνδειξιν appears to define the purpose of προέθετο. And the phrase εἰς ἔνδειξιν takes us back to πεφανέρωται of Rom. 3.21, the cross being the public manifestation there referred to. This interpretation would be consistent with other NT passages, e.g. Gal. 3.1: 'Who has bewitched you, before whose eyes Jesus Christ was publicly portrayed as crucified?' (cf. also Jn 3.16ff.), as well as the use of προτιθέναι in Greek authors to designate the exhibition of dead bodies.[56] Secondly, it is argued that προτιθέναι used in the sense of 'purposed' is normally followed by the infinitive as at Rom. 1.13 and Eph. 1.9. The infinitive is lacking at Rom. 3.25. However, we should note that προτιθέναι need not be followed by an infinitive.

It is our position that both interpretations, 'set forth' and 'pre-destined', are possible. On balance the latter[57] is preferable because of the manuscript support (Origen, Ambrosiaster, Chrysostom, Oecumenius and Theophylact). Once προέθετο is explained as 'predestined', it becomes an answer to the scandal of the cross. The death of Jesus on the cross of shame did not take God by surprise but was in accordance with the predestined divine plan for the redemption of mankind. This was a normal part of NT passion apologetic,[58] as is evidenced by the use of Scripture passages to defend Christian tenets. The point of such apologetic was to emphasize the sovereignty of God, the Lord of history whose ways are unsearchable (cf. 1 Cor. 2.7).

We have so far examined two martyrological interpretations of the death of Jesus on the cross, which transformed the cross from a disaster into an instrument of salvation. We refer to the understanding of the cross as evidence of Jesus' voluntary self-offering to God and as a vicarious offering for others. We now turn to a third interpretation, namely that it is a part of a divine plan of salvation for the world (cf. Acts 4.29; Rom. 8.29; Eph. 1.5, 11). We have already touched on this when discussing προέθετο in Rom. 3.25. Now we turn to examine more precise statements of that perspective–1 Cor. 2.8, 1 Cor. 15.3 and Rom. 15.3.

According to 1 Cor. 2.8, 'None of the rulers of this age understood this (i.e. the wisdom of God); for if they had, they would not have crucified the Lord of Glory'. Throughout that section of 1 Cor. 2, there is a note of irony—men acting as though in their own right, not realizing that they were already instruments in the hands of God to work out his purposes. This takes up the apologetic tradition of the Church that God's plan was unfolding through the disastrous death of Jesus on the cross, whether men recognized it or not. That plan is described as θεοῦ σοφίαν ἐν μυστηρίῳ, τὴν ἀποκεκρυμμένην, ἣν προώρισεν ὁ θεὸς πρὸ τῶν αἰώνων εἰς δόξαν ἡμῶν (1 Cor. 2.7). The ἣν προώρισεν clause is an exposition of σοφίαν ἐν μυστηρίῳ; hence the issue is the meaning of the latter phrase.

According to some scholars σοφία and μυστήριον are to be explained along the lines of Gnosticism. Thus R. Bultmann wrote: 'The Gnostic idea that Christ's earthly garment of the flesh was the disguise in consequence of which the world-rulers failed to recognize him—for if they had recognized him they would not have brought about their own defeat by causing his crucifixion—lurks behind 1 Cor. 2.8'.[59] Similarly, W. Bousset[60] explained the failure of the cosmic powers to see the divine plan along the lines of Gnostic mythology in which God hid his identity in order to deceive the demons. Bousset's position is less radical than that of Bultmann because he agreed that there remained in the background other ideas approximating to gnosis; but he denied that such other ideas played a primary part. The exegesis of Bultmann and Bousset is untenable because it is very doubtful whether there is any idea of deception attaching to 1 Cor. 2.7f. Christ's identity did not belong to any teaching reserved for the τέλειοι. Indeed, according to the Greek text the cosmic powers simply did not know the plan of God; they did not realize the eternal dimension of the person of Christ.

We prefer to understand σοφία in its Jewish apocalyptic sense of 'Heilsgut', 'the most important and comprehensive eschatological blessing, or, in association with this, God's Law'.[61] Here was a divine plan unfolding from eternity. The cross did not take God by surprise; it was in his purpose from the start. Only in the light of the divine plan does the cross cease to be a scandal; it is a martyrdom in the eternal plan of God.

The failure of the persecutors to understand the mysterious dealings of God in contrast to the all-seeingness of God is found elsewhere in Jewish literature, e.g. 2 Macc. 6.30, where Eleazar at the point of death says: 'It is manifest unto the Lord, that hath the holy knowledge, that whereas I might have been delivered from death, I now endure sore pains in body by being beaten: but in soul am well content to suffer these things, because I fear him' (cf. Philo, *Flacc.* 164, 170; Wisd. 2.21f.) For our purposes there is a strikingly similar idea expressed in the first century AD Coptic document, the *Apocalypse of Adam*:

> . . . auch nicht werden sie den φωστηρ sehen. Dann werden sie das Fleisch des Menschen, über den der heilige Geist gekommen ist, strafen (κολάζειν).[62]

Whether there is any dependence of the Apocalypse on 1 Cor. 2 or not, it looks as though the idea enunciated here was a standard explanation of the so-called disaster of the cross. And that line of argument was standard in the martyr-theology, particularly of the apocalyptic genre (see Chapter 2 above).

Let us now consider the content of the θεοῦ σοφία. The unfolding of the divine plan had taken the form of the οἱ ἄρχοντες τοῦ αἰῶνος crucifying τὸν Κύριον τῆς δόξης. The phrase τὸν Κύριον τῆς δόξης, unique in the NT, except perhaps at James 2.1, clearly refers to Jesus Christ.[63] The phrase in its present context is probably drawing a deliberate contrast between the humiliation of the crucifixion and the glory of the post-resurrection Jesus. As Stauffer puts it, 'Kyrios takes on some colour from the theology of the passion'.[64] It is as though the phrase were a pithy expression of how Jesus entered into glory through suffering according to the divine plan.

Other *dramatis personae* are οἱ ἄρχοντες τοῦ αἰῶνος τούτου. The phrase yields two possible interpretations: first, the earthly rulers who had a hand in the crucifixion of Jesus, e.g. Annas, Caiaphas (high priest from AD 18 to 36), Herod (Lk. 23.6-12) and Pontius Pilate, the Roman prefect of Jerusalem who condemned Jesus to death by the cross. In support of this interpretation is the use of the aorist, ἐσταύρωσαν, throwing the emphasis on the historical facts.[65]

A second interpretation of οἱ ἄρχοντες τοῦ αἰῶνος τούτου identifies them as the cosmic powers.[66] Several arguments support this interpretation. First, according to 1 Cor. 2.6 οἱ ἄρχοντες are propagating some wisdom or teaching—which does not fit Pilate or Herod. Secondly, 'in the perspective of Paul's thought human rulers like Herod and Pilate do not play the part of "rulers of this aeon", but only of their servants'.[67] Thirdly, if, as Reitzenstein has argued,[68] ἄρχων is sometimes used of planetary deities and καταργεῖν (cf. v. 6) is a technical term for nullifying the astral influence of a supernatural power, then ἄρχοντες and καταργουμένων may be pointers in the direction of the astronomical interpretation. Fourthly, there is support from Church Fathers like Origen and Theodore of Mopsuestia[69] who interpreted οἱ ἄρχοντες of the cosmic powers. Finally, in the theology of Paul itself the victory of Christ is also represented as a victory over the cosmic powers (Col. 1.15; 2.15; Rom. 8.38; Eph. 6.12).

Without necessarily accepting the foregoing arguments *in toto*, it does not seem right to us to choose between the two interpretations. For in apocalyptic literature of intertestamental Judaism,[70] the struggles of the martyrs reflected a war in heaven itself. What happened on earth was because of what happened on the cosmic level. In other words, behind the *dramatis personae* stood the spiritual metaphysical authorities. This is a further aspect in which 1 Cor. 2.8 reflects the martyr theology.

Two more passages must be looked at: Rom. 15.3 and 1 Cor. 15.3. Let us start with Rom. 15.3, an aspect of which was taken up earlier in this chapter. Our concern now is the citation of Ps. 69.9 to support the claim that 'Christ did not please himself'. Paul seems to understand by that clause ὀνειδισμός (*ḥrph*), which appears a stock phrase for the sufferings of the martyrs.[71] In our context it refers to the sufferings and ultimately the death of Christ as evidence of his devotion to the will of God. But our interest for the moment is the use of Ps. 69.9 which was not only a martyrological proof-text but was used by the Church in its apologetic in order to show that the passion of Christ was part of the divine scheme for the salvation of the world. With that interpretation the cross ceases to be a scandal.

Much the same impression emerges from 1 Cor. 15.3 where Paul records the tradition that Χριστὸς ἀπέθανεν ὑπὲρ τῶν ἁμαρτιῶν ἡμῶν κατὰ τὰς γραφάς. The striking thing about this passage is the interest in both the historical facts and the theological interpretation of the event. The aorists ἀπέθανεν and ἐτάφη (v. 4) focus on the historical event of the crucifixion and the burial.[72] But the point of greatest interest to us is that all was κατὰ τὰς γραφάς.

The first issue is whether κατὰ τὰς γραφάς goes with ὑπὲρ τῶν ἁμαρτιῶν ἡμῶν[73] or with the death. The phrase more likely goes with the death for three reasons: first, the brief reference to his burial, i.e. ἐτάφη, throws the spotlight on the facts of the death and resurrection (cf. Rom. 6.4; Col. 2.12; Acts 13.29). Second, following the obvious parallelism between vv. 3 and 4, namely the references to the death and the resurrection, it is better to take κατὰ τὰς γραφάς with ἀπέθανεν just as κατὰ τὰς γραφάς in v. 4 goes with ἐγήργεται. Third, elsewhere in Paul there is a traditional antithesis between death and resurrection.[74] Thus it was the atoning death of Jesus Christ on the cross that was according to the Scriptures, i.e. in accordance with the divine plan and not fortuitous.

The next issue is the meaning of τὰς γραφάς. The plural αἱ γραφαί refers to the collection of individual books and several passages.[75] So αἱ γραφαί means in the first instance the broad principles of the religion of the Old Testament and the literature of the intertestamental period which attributes atoning efficacy to some deaths, particularly the deaths of martyrs.[76] In our context Paul is thinking of prophecies regarding the atoning death of Christ, the vicarious and atoning self-sacrifice. Indeed, in the teaching of Jesus himself this view had already been expressed in Mk 10.45[77] where the use of martyrological theology is unmistakable. In the second instance, the NT fastened on particular texts of Scripture in its passion apologetic like Pss. 22, 69, 118, Is. 53 and Deut. 21.22. Whether we think of individual texts or the broad principles of Judaism, the idea is the same: whatever happened to Jesus was part of the pre-ordained plan of God and not the disaster that it seemed at first sight. This, as we showed in Chapter 2, is part of martyrological apologetic.

Rom. 8.32 is also of interest to us: God τοῦ ἰδίου Ὑιοῦ οὐκ ἐφείσατο, ἀλλὰ ὑπὲρ ἡμῶν πάντων παρέδωκεν αὐτόν. Παραδιδόναι is well embedded in the Church's tradition of the Passion. But the sentence with God as subject indicates that the death of Christ was at the will of God. That point is emphasized by the obvious parallellism between the ἐφείσατο clause and the παρέδωκεν clause.

There is probably more in the sentence than a divine plan. The language of that verse recalls the sacrifice of Isaac[78] through Gen. 22.16f.: 'By myself I have sworn, says the Lord, because you have done this, *and have not withheld your son, your only son*, I will bless you . . . ' It may be that there is an Isaac typology behind the phrase τοῦ ἰδίου Ὑιοῦ οὐκ ἐφείσατο. If that surmise is accepted, then we have further confirmation of the martyrological understanding of the death of Christ. For Isaac was in later tradition regarded as a martyr.

In the Genesis account the significance of the attempt to sacrifice Isaac is the faith and obedience of Abraham, the patriarch, Isaac himself being a passive figure. However, in later traditions such as rabbinic literature the significance of the *'qdt yṣhq* (the binding of Isaac) is the voluntariness with which Isaac allowed himself to be sacrificed. Thus according to *Sifre* 32 on Deut. 6.5, R. Meir said, 'Thou shalt love the Lord . . . with all thy soul (life) like Isaac, who bound himself upon the altar'. Similarly, the Additional Service for the Jewish New Year includes the following prayer: 'Remember unto us, O Lord our God, the covenant and the loving-kindness and the oath which thou swarest unto Abraham our father on Mount Moriah; and may the binding with which Abraham our father bound his son Isaac on the altar appear before thee, how he overbore his compassion in order to perform thy will with a perfect heart'.[79] According to a prayer in *Lev. R.* 29.8, 'If the sons of Isaac walk in rebellion and wicked works, remember the binding of their father Isaac, and leave the throne of judgment and sit on the throne of mercy'. Thus, in Jewish tradition the binding of Isaac is the classic example of the redemptive efficacy of martyrdom.

In view of what is said subsequently about the eternal plan of God, it is interesting that in Targum Pseudo-Jonathan the ram offered in place of Isaac was a 'lamb' created between the evenings, that is to say, at twilight on the sixth day of creation; it had been prepared from the creation for the event and thus the event was seen as part of God's purpose from the dawn of creation itself.

If ὅς γε τοῦ ἰδίου υἱοῦ οὐκ ἐφείσατο echoes Gen. 22.16 (LXX), then we may with justification not only assume the Isaac typology but also infer the martyr theology associated with Isaac. Jesus like Isaac was a martyr whom his father did not spare but offered up as a vicarious sacrifice.

In our study of the passages dealing with the scandal of the cross, we have seen that Paul took the sting out of the scandal of the cross by reinterpreting through established martyrological themes: (a) that the death was in obedience to the will of God and out of zeal for the Lord; (b) that it was a vicarious sacrifice; and (c) that it was not an accident of history but in the fore-ordained plan of God for the redemption of the world.

Now, all the passages hitherto discussed specifically relate to the death of Christ. However, we wish now to turn to other passages in which Jesus is set forth as a martyr without dwelling on the salvific significance of his death. We refer to 1 Thess. 2.16 (cf. 1.6) and 1 Cor. 4.9-13.

After giving thanks for the faith of the Thessalonian Christians, Paul proceeds to announce that their faith was in imitation of the example of himself and of Christ. For our purposes the question is, How had Christ been an example to them? The key word μιμηταί and its cognate μιμεῖσθαι appear to have had ethical connotations[80] in both Greek and Judaeo-Christian traditions. Thus in Plato's *Theatetus* Socrates taught that the way of flight from evil was to become like God as much as is possible, by pursuing justice and piety through knowledge. In the Pauline literature the content of the imitation is varied. At 2 Thess. 3.7-9 it is imitation of how to work and support oneself. At Gal. 4.12 it is to emancipate oneself from the law, as Paul the Apostle had done although he had all the advantages of the law (cf. Phil. 3.4ff.). Elsewhere in Paul it is an imitation in humility (1 Cor. 4.14-21).

However, in the context of 1 Thessalonians the content of τὸ μιμεῖσθαι is defined as δεξάμενοι τὸν λόγον ἐν θλίψει πολλῇ μετὰ χαρᾶς πνεύματος ἁγίου. The internal construction of the sentence permits two interpretations of the δεξάμενοι clause: (a) it explains μιμηταί, i.e. 'in that you received the word with much affliction, with joy inspired by the Holy Spirit'; or (b) it supplies the antecedent fact and ground of the imitation, i.e. 'after that or inasmuch as you had received . . . ' The obvious parallelism between the two parts of the verse will be destroyed unless the δεξάμενοι clause is taken as a participle of identical action. Also, the use of the two aorists, ἐγενήθητε and δεξάμενοι, in the two parts of the sentence suggests that the two are co-extensive action and the latter explicative of the former. Therefore, it is preferable to read the δεξάμενοι clause as an explanation of imitation. Hence the content of the imitation is the fact of accepting affliction and persecution along with receiving the word of God. The point is the martyr spirit in which they accepted affliction with patience for the sake of God. Their endurance of affliction has proven them to be zealous of the Lord.

However, as Paul saw it, that experience was not unique to the Thessalonian church. Rather, they were walking in the footsteps of Paul himself—and of Jesus. The example of Paul in his patient endurance of affliction for the sake of the Gospel need not detain us here. But 1 Thess. 2.2 and 1 Cor. 11.23ff. are eloquent testimonies to them. Our present interest is the consideration of Christ as a proto-martyr. Elsewhere in Paul, at Rom. 15.3 and Phil. 2.5f., we have seen how Paul considered Jesus a martyr. On 1 Thess. 1.6 the comment of Cerfaux is worthy of quotation: 'Can this be understood without reference to the human, or rather superhuman courage of Jesus in his passion? Have we not here the first model which is set up for our imitation—a model which is really human? . . . By accepting death Christ has set us an example (see Rom. 15.3)'.[81] 1 Thess. 1.6, therefore, clearly sets Christ forth as a martyr, indeed, as the prototype of a martyr.

The theme is further developed at 1 Thess. 2.15. Once more treating the experience of persecution by the Thessalonian church, Paul reminds the Thessalonians that they are walking in the steps of the earliest Christians of Jerusalem and their experiences at the hands of their compatriots, τῶν καὶ τὸν Κύριον ἀποκτεινάντων Ἰησοῦν καὶ τοὺς προφήτας, καὶ ἡμᾶς ἐκδιωξάντων . . . Grammatically, τοὺς προφήτας may be taken as the object of either ἀποκτεινάντων or ἐκδιωξάντων. In support of taking it with ἐκδιωξάντων is that it is an anticlimax to refer first to Christ and then to the prophets. Indeed, elsewhere in the NT[82] the death of Christ is seen as the continuation and climax of the plight of the prophets (cf. Lk. 11.47-51; 13.33; 20.9-16). Historically speaking, of course, it will be more accurate to take προφήτας with ἐκδιωξάντων because few prophets actually were killed. But this argument carries little weight because the evidence is that it became a theme of martyrological tradition to have every prophet die a martyr like Isaiah and Jeremiah. On the other hand, viewed from the situation of the Thessalonian Church who were under attack, the comparison would be better suited to ἐκδιωξάντων. Indeed at Acts 17.5-10 the apostles were driven out of Thessalonica rather than killed.

However, we prefer to take προφήτας with ἀποκτεινάντων not only because it fulfils a martyrological topos, but also because to take it with ἐκδιωξάντων would be to weaken the argument. For that would probably have been expressed by οἵ καὶ with the finite verb (cf. Rom. 8.34; 16.7) instead of τῶν καὶ with the participle. The literal use of ἀποκτείνειν is very rare in Paul and is found only here and at Rom. 11.3 where it is a citation of 1 Kgs 19.10: τοὺς προφήτας σου ἀπέκτειναν. There as here, ἀποκτείνειν is used in reference to the prophets. Thus in our context the first καί is a correlative (cf. 1 Cor. 10.32). The idea is that Jews put to death the prophets, who therefore became martyrs at their hands. But however we take the words, the idea of persecution is expressed and becomes the content of the imitation.

Given this framework, Jesus is also set forth as a martyr. Blaming the Jews for the murder of Jesus was a standard Christian anti-Jewish polemic; so Mk 12.1-9; Lk. 24.20; Jn 19.11; Acts 2.23; 3.15; 4.10; 10.39; 13.27f.; Gospel of Peter 6-7; Ass. Is. 3.13; Justin, *Dialogue* 16.4. All these passages blamed the Jews for the death of Jesus and exonerated and exculpated the Roman authorities. Historically this is not quite true, for since crucifixion was a predominantly Roman form of execution and since the execution of Jesus was done by Roman soldiers (e.g. Mk 15.39), the Roman authorities must have had a hand in Jesus' execution.[83] But for apologetic reasons the earliest Christians laid the blame at the door of the Jews, as if to say, 'the Romans thought Jesus innocent and only the "wicked Jews" contrived his death'. The implication of this Christian propaganda was that Jesus died a martyr.

It appears that much later some Jews appropriated this view and accepted full responsibility for the death of Jesus. Thus b*Sanh.* 43a preserves a tradition from Ulla, a second generation Palestinian Amora, that 'On the eve of the Passover, Yeshu was hanged. Forty days before the execution a herald went forth and cried, He is going forth to be stoned because he has practised sorcery and enticed Israel to apostasy.' According to this tradition Yeshu, identified by many scholars with Jesus of Nazareth, was properly, legally and rightly killed by the Jewish authorities for leading Israel astray and for magic, two very serious charges in Jewish society. Another text from Agobard, the Christian bishop of Lyons in the ninth century AD refers to *ubi et petra in capite percussum* (Migne, *Patrologia Latina* 104.87, 88). Stoning indicates a Jewish mode of execution and, therefore, attributes Jesus' death to the Jews.

Our last passage is an indirect reference at 1 Cor. 4.11. Paul from vv. 9f. onward draws a contrast between the glories of the Corinthian Christians and the perpetual troubles and sufferings of the apostles. The apostles are like men condemned to death in the arena. In the present context 'all the misfortunes mentioned in 4.9-12 belong in reality to a martyr's situation except for the manual work which the Apostle . . . has voluntarily imposed upon himself'.[84] In the course of listing their woes he uses the term κολαφιζόμεθα. That word originally meant to 'hit with the fist' or 'buffet'. From that it acquired an extended meaning of 'maltreat'.[85] It is found neither in classical Greek nor in the LXX. But it occurs in a pagan letter of the Roman period and in the NT, where it is used of the experiences of Jesus at the passion (Mk 14.65 = Mt. 26.67). One wonders, therefore, whether the use of this unusual word is not meant to recall the buffeting of Christ through the buffeting of the apostles.[86] If so, here is further evidence that the life of the apostles is a clear reflection of Christ's suffering as a martyr.

We may now summarize our argument as follows. In the Pauline tradition Jesus is set forth directly and indirectly as a martyr. Passages like 1 Thess. 1.6 and 2.15 set him forth as the prototype of a martyr. The description of his death with the phrase τὸ δοῦναι ἑαυτόν highlights the point that the scandalous death on the cross was an expression of voluntary obedience and self-sacrifice to God. That phrase is a key element in any definition of the martyr—his suffering and his pursuit of the divine will. Further, the scandal of the cross is reinterpreted as a vicarious sacrifice by the additional phrase ὑπὲρ ἡμῶν and its synonyms or even by the use of αἷμα and ἱλαστήριον of the death of Christ. Furthermore, the scandal of the cross is explained as not a disaster but as part of the divine plan. All these elements are aspects of martyr-theology. The conclusion is, therefore, inevitable that a martyrological understanding of the cross transforms its shame into a thing of glory.

However, as we shall see later, the martyrdom of Christ is not seen purely in relation to his own death. It is often pressed into the service of exhortation to imitate the example of Christ (Rom. 15.13; Phil. 2.5ff.; 1 Thess. 2.14ff.) or into the service of expounding the salvation achieved through the costly death.

Chapter 4

THE MARTYRDOM OF CHRIST AND THE KERYGMA
OF THE APOSTLE PAUL

In this chapter we seek to argue that the martyrological interpretation of the death of Christ was pressed into the service of establishing other Christian claims in the realms of soteriology, Christology, ecclesiology, eschatology and ethics.

1. *The Martyrdom of Christ and Soteriology*

One of the most striking things about Paul's theology is his analysis of the human condition as sinful. What he says primarily of the Gentiles is extended to all men as haters of God:

> None is righteous, no, not one;
> no one understands, no one seeks God.
> All have turned aside, together they have gone wrong;
> no one does good, not even one . . .
> There is no fear of God before their eyes (Rom. 3.10-12, 18).

In short, 'all have sinned and fall short of the glory of God' (Rom. 3.23). This is the background against which Paul enunciates his teaching with regard to the coming together again of God and man, through God's initiative despite man's hostility towards God.

Various images are used to describe this coming together again of God and man—reconciliation, justification, redemption and sacrifice. Like all images, each metaphor is bound to be partial, each capturing an aspect of the coming together. Redemption is a metaphor from captivity. It highlights man's condition as one who is in bondage to the forces of evil—self-sufficiency, legalism and the cosmic powers. The most forceful description of that condition perhaps comes from Rom. 7.14-15, 18-19: 'I am carnal, sold under sin. I do not understand my own actions. For I do not do what I want, but I do the very thing that I hate . . . I can will what is right, but I cannot do it. For I do not do the good that I want, but the evil I do not want is what I do.' Man is a compulsive sinner, in bondage to sin. On the other hand, the death by crucifixion of Jesus in obedience to the will of God is in effect the payment by God of a ransom to buy back to himself man from his bondage to sin. Men 'are justified by his grace as a gift, through the redemption which is in Jesus Christ' (Rom. 3.24-25).

Another metaphor is reconciliation, the most personal of the images. It highlights the cessation of hostilities between God and man, the hostilities being on man's side. Col. 1.20 articulates this aspect: 'Through him (i.e. Christ), God was pleased to reconcile to himself all things, whether on earth or in heaven, making peace by the blood of his cross'. The clause 'making peace . . . ' is in apposition to 'to reconcile . . . ' and is therefore explicative of the latter. Justification, being a forensic metaphor, highlights the inexorable, righteous demands of God as Judge and King of the universe, although that metaphor is also tempered with the homely metaphor of God as Father. It is as Father and not a despotic, rigid King that God judges and takes action to restore man to fellowship with Himself. Rom. 5.1 articulates the thinking with regard to justification: 'being justified by faith, we have peace with God.' Justification and having peace are two ways of speaking of the reconciliation between God and man. Only justification underlines that whatever happens God is in himself δίκαιος (just and righteous) in all his ways.

In the brief comments on reconciliation, justification and redemption, an extraordinary phenomenon emerges. The chasm yawning between God and man has come about because of man's hostility to God—in short, his sin. And yet it is God who in himself is just and holy and therefore brooks no sin, who takes the initiative to reconcile man to himself. So the paradox is that God is at one and the same time just and righteous on the one hand, and the justifier of sinners on the other. It is to resolve this dilemma that the sacrificial image comes into its own.

The sacrificial metaphor, for our purposes, is perhaps the most important. For it manages to hold together the justice, righteousness and holiness of God, on the one hand, and the justification of sinful men by God, on the other. That justice of God is retained throughout the rescue operation at great cost, at cost no less than the life of Jesus who 'knew no sin and yet was made sin for us'. As Paul elsewhere puts it, 'you were bought with a price' (1 Cor. 7.23). And as we argued in Chapter 3, the giving up of that life on the cross was in obedience to the will of God and thus a martyr's death. So the martyr interpretation of the crucifixion of Jesus of Nazareth affirms, among other things, the costliness with which salvation was achieved.

The most articulate expression of this interpretation is the reference to the death of Christ as the shedding of 'blood', for example Rom. 3.23-26: 'since all have sinned . . . , they are justified by his grace as a gift, through the redemption which is in Christ Jesus, whom God put forward as an expiation by his blood, to be received by faith. This was to show God's righteousness, because in his divine forbearance he has passed over former sins; it was to prove at the present time that he himself is righteous and that he justifies him who has faith in Jesus.' For a detailed exegesis of this passage, see above, Chapter 3; we may note here that three of the key metaphors for salvation are used: justification, redemption and sacrifice are treated more or less as synonyms. But more important is the fact that the interest in Christ's martyrdom is because of what it achieves for believers, namely salvation.

In Chapter 3 we argued that 'blood' in this context means more than the OT understanding of it as life. Since in the context it is clearly synonymous with the cross of Christ or, as Col. 1.20 puts it, 'the blood of his cross', blood here means the costly expenditure of life in obedience to the will of God. That, as was argued above, means Jesus is a martyr. But it also means the salvific significance attached to that disastrous death is because it was reinterpreted as a martyr's death. The interest in the martyrdom of Christ is because it achieved reconciliation as a sacrifice or, as Rom. 3.25 puts it, a ἱλαστήριον (expiation)—a term which itself underlines the sacrificial interpretation of the death. Other passages that make the same point are Rom. 5.9; Col. 1.14, 20; Eph. 1.7; 2.13.

The references given so far focus on the blood of Christ, symbolizing the costly expenditure of life in obedience to the will of God. We have also mentioned the description of the death of Christ as ἱλαστήριον— which also underlines the sacrificial concept. But there is a third element which brings out the salvific interpretation of the martyrdom of Christ. We refer to the phrase ὑπὲρ ἡμῶν and its synonyms which often go with the statement of the historical fact, 'Christ died'. That, as we argued in Chapter 3, underlines the vicarious nature of the sacrifice made in the death on the cross. So that phrase also affirms that the death of Jesus on the cross, or rather his martyrdom, is a vicarious sacrifice to redeem men from alienation from God to fellowship with God.

What has been said so far tallies with the theology of Judaism where, as was outlined in Chapter 2, suffering and death, especially if it was of a martyr, made atonement for sin. Against the background of Paul's analysis of the human condition as sinful, the crucifixion of Christ in obedience to God became significant because of what it was believed to have done for the relationship between sinful man and God. The martyrdom of Christ is pressed into the service of Paul's teaching with regard to man's redemption from legalism, self-sufficiency and the cosmic powers into true fellowship with God.

Next door to the teaching on the salvific significance of the martyrdom of Christ is the teaching with regard to the Law. The salvific interpretation of the crucifixion of Jesus raises a whole question mark against the Law. For to attach salvific relevance to the crucifixion of Jesus was incompatible, *prima facie* at any rate, with the law's understanding of hanging as a curse from God (Deut. 21.23; cf. Gal. 3.13). And so, the question is raised of the relationship of Christ to the Law.

Paul seems to equivocate. On the one hand, 'the law is holy and the commandment is holy and just and good' (Rom. 7.12). The general scope and purpose and authority of the Law as an expression of the divine will are permanent and not in dispute. On the other hand, any understanding of the cross of Christ as a mark of ignominy and rejection by God was in the Church's view incorrect, though the Law would seem to have supported such a view. Consequently, Paul comes to argue that the martyrdom of Christ was the means of attaining freedom from the Law.

If Christ's death on the cross achieves salvation, then 'Christ is the end of the law, that everyone who has faith may be justified' (Rom. 10.4). Clearly the old way of achieving right relationship with God through obedience to the will of God expressed in the Torah has been superseded by the more meaningful and personal obedience of Christ to the will of God; God's favour can only be encountered through faith in what Christ achieved through the cross as the symbol of the love of God. Besides, since Paul is unable to write off the Law in its entirety, he comes to see it in comparison with Christ as merely 'our custodian until Christ came' (Gal. 3.24). The Law was, so to speak, the *pro tempore* instrument to make us look for Christ. Finally, the paradox of the cross raised the issue of whether it was possible to

achieve salvation by observing the Law. It was precisely because of
the martyrological interpretation of the cross that Paul looked to the
cross in faith for redemption, deserting his former attempt to achieve
redemption through the meticulous observance of the Law. The Law
is unimportant for salvation (Gal. 2.21). Thus the whole direction of
the debate about the Law in Pauline theology stems from the
martyrological interpretation of the crucifixion of Christ.

2. *The Martyrdom of Christ and Christology*

The second main area into the service of which the martyrdom of
Christ is pressed is that of Christology. In this context two Christological titles are of interest: *Son* and *Lord*.

Sonship of God was a concept that antedated Jesus Christ. It was
used of kings (Ps. 2.7), priests, the nation of the covenanted people of
God (Hos. 11.1) and of angels and supernatural figures (e.g. Dan.
3.25; Job 38.7). It did not primarily describe a metaphysical status;
rather it was a functional title.[1] Its crucial characteristic is obedience
to the will of God. Such obedience sometimes entails suffering.

Related to this is the statement of Rom. 8.32: 'He . . . did not spare
his own Son but gave him up for us all'. If, as we argued above, there
is an Isaac typology and through that a martyr theology, then the
Sonship of Jesus has as one of its elements Jesus' martyrdom. Better
still, his martyrdom confirms Jesus as the Son of God.

According to Rom. 1.3-4, Paul was an apostle set apart by God to
proclaim 'the gospel concerning his Son, who was descended from
David according to the flesh and designated Son of God in power
according to the spirit of holiness by his resurrection from the dead,
Jesus Christ our Lord'. This passage is striking for a number of
reasons, not least the fact that the death of Jesus on the cross, which
is the essence of his gospel, is not mentioned here. On the face of it,
Paul throws all the emphasis on the resurrection as the crucial event.
This would seem to receive confirmation in the proclamation of Jesus
as Son of God on the occasion of his resurrection which, so to speak,
inaugurates the life of glory.

However, the obvious exegesis is only a half-truth. It is important
to see the passage under consideration not in isolation but alongside
the other claims made about Jesus. The recurring theme in Paul's
letters is that the content of the Gospel is Christ crucified. One may,
therefore, surmise that the crucifixion and the resurrection are not

alternatives but two sides of the same coin. In any case, there can be no meaningful reference to resurrection without the assumption of the fact of the humiliation of death. Indeed, the passage itself mentions two conditions of existence: his life on earth and the post-resurrection life. According to E. Schweizer, 'his life on earth is depicted as the life of the Son of David. This may have been taken over from official Jewish theology. For this expects an Israelite king of the line of David to reign on earth as the Messiah. But surely the historical reality of Jesus' life in no way conforms to this expectation. Therefore we must ask at least if the expectation of the Davidic servant of God[2] has not had a decisive influence here. At all events the earthly existence of the Son of David has clearly been regarded as the lowly first stage which was fulfilled only by exaltation to the Sonship of God.'[3]

However, there are serious flaws in this exegesis. It is not exactly true that 'his life on earth is depicted as the life of the Son of David'. For the text also describes him even at that stage as God's Son (1.30). That is to say, throughout his whole life he was Son of God, and not only after the resurrection.[4] Secondly, Paul is demonstrably concerned to show the gradual unfolding of the true and full nature of Christ. Before his resurrection he was Son of God but in weakness; after his resurrection there was no mistake about it.[5] The sonship of Jesus during his life is presented also in Mark; for even before the centurion declared 'Truly this was the Son of God' (Mk 15.39), Jesus had been so declared by unclean spirits (Mk 3.11; 5.7), by the heavenly voice (Mk 1.11; 9.7), though the religious leaders of his day could not perceive it (Mk 14.61). Therefore, it is incorrect to regard the exaltation as 'the first beginning of Jesus' Sonship'.[6] The issue is the stages by which the full meaning of Jesus' sonship was realized. In his pre-resurrection days, his life did not seem to conform to the popular vision of the Son of God. His faithful prosecution of his mission was not enough for people to make them see the Son of God in him. His crucifixion would be added confirmation for them that Jesus could not be the Son of God, especially when seen against the background of Deut. 21.23. But to believers here was an irony: the humiliation of the incarnation and of the crucifixion witnessed to his sonship. Jesus' death on the cross which seemed to deny his sonship is ironically the strongest evidence of Jesus' singular dedication to the will of God. His martyrdom is the index of his sonship.

Moule has persuasively argued that it is 'unrealistic to put notions of sonship into successive compartments, as though we could segregate a more or less humanistic, merely messianic use from a transcendental and theological use developing at a later stage. The indications are, rather, that the words and practices of Jesus himself, together with the fact of the cross and of its sequel, presented the friends of Jesus, from the earliest days, with a highly complex, multivalent set of associations already adhering to the single word "Son."[7] The messianic king, God's Son, coincides in a remarkable way with the frail human figure, 'the Son of Man', whose vulnerable, martyr-like loyalty has brought him through death to this position of glory and dominion before the aged 'President of the Immortals'.[8] As Mark, too, sees it, there is a subtle linking of Son of God with Son of Man (e.g. Mk 14.36). To be Son of God is to be dedicated totally to the purposes of God, even the death on the Cross.

The other important Christological reference is *Lord*. Κύριος was used both in Graeco-Roman society and in Jewish society. In addition to its very secular use in Graeco-Roman society in the sense of 'master', it was also used to underline the divinity of the bearer. Nero was referred to either as Νέρων ὁ Κύριος or Νέρων Κύριος.[9] The term would therefore be well known and important in a place like Philippi which had its college of Augustiales, an order devoted to the worship of the divine Augustus. Thus we cannot escape the conjecture that the Christians of the East who heard Paul preach in the style of Phil. 2.9, 11 and 1 Cor. 8.5, 6 must have heard in the solemn confession that Jesus Christ is 'Lord' an implicit protest against other 'Lords' and against 'the Lord' as people were beginning to call the Roman Caesar. And Paul himself must have felt and intended this silent protest as much as Jude does when he calls Jesus Christ 'our only master and Lord' (Jude 4).[10]

On the other hand, the Jewish matrix of Christianity also used κύριος to translate *mr'* and *'dwn*, although it was also a possible translation for master. They were also familiar with the scriptural use of κύριος to represent the sacred name of God. However, because of the statement that 'every knee shall bow' at the mention of that name, it is natural to assume that Christ has become an object of worship. In other words, the operative meaning is that of κύριος in the sense of Adonai, underlining the divinity of God. Thus the predicate of God is used of Jesus, underlining Jesus' authority, exercised howbeit under God.

However there is a rider to this attribution of divinity to Jesus.

This is where we return to Phil. 2. The kenotic hymn says: διὸ καὶ ὁ Θεὸς αὐτὸν ὑπερύψωσεν ... καὶ πᾶσα γλῶσσα ἐξομολογήσηται ὅτι Κύριος Ἰησοῦς Χριστός. The introduction of this strophe with διό means this strophe is integrally linked with the preceding strophe, i.e. the exaltation of Jesus is the consequence of the whole life of obedience to the will of God, which was given its climactic and paradigmatic expression in the apparently disastrous death on the cross. In other words, Jesus entered into his glory as κύριος through his martyrdom, the most articulate expression of his obedience. The martyrdom appears, therefore, to be a substratum of the Christological title, Lord.

The same impression is given by the obvious contrast between δοῦλος and κύριος. We have in Chapter 3 argued against the exegesis of δοῦλος as the Servant of the Lord in Isaiah's prophecies, partly because the alleged parallels between the Servant Songs and Phil. 2 are far from clear and also because while 'bd in Isaiah is a title of honour, denoting a special relationship between God and the Servant,[11] δοῦλος in Phil. 2 is not a title and denotes 'the dishonour and limitations of the human body'.[12] This last point is what we wish to develop here.

The sharp contrast between δοῦλος and κύριος, between the dishonour and humiliation expressed by δοῦλος and the glory of God focussing on κύριος, almost compels us to understand δοῦλος as the common slave of the Roman Empire, one with no rights to himself. And there could be no better or more articulate expression of that status than the fact of the crucifixion which was reserved for slaves and lower classes generally. Hence the emphatic 'even the death on the cross', the drama of humility and obedience of God, and apparent powerlessness. Thus the man who began as a slave was exalted to become Lord through the humility and devotion to God of which the crucifixion was the paradigm.

Again, the use of ὑπερύψωσεν of the exaltation is also striking. That word is a *hapax legomenon* in the NT. According to W.D. Davies there is here an allusion to Is. 52.13: *yrwm wnś' wgbh m'd*, i.e. '(my servant) shall be exalted and extolled to be very high'. This is an unnecessary and incorrect assertion because, unlike Phil. 2, Is. 52.13 does not say that the exaltation is the result of the humiliation, whereas the pattern of humiliation and glorification is a theologoumenon of the early Church, expressing the death and exaltation which 'meant that he [Christ] was not only alive but sovereign'.[13] It is in the light of the theology of the exaltation of Christ in the early Church that we should seek to explain ὑπερύψωσεν.

It is still curious that an unusual word should now appear in a common theologoumenon of the Church. The only other occurrences of it in biblical Greek are Dan. 3.52f. and Ps. 96(97).9. A study of these references suggests that ὑπέρ is meant to intensify ὑψόω. In our context, then, ὑπερύψοω is probably meant to contrast with the utter degradation of the crucifixion of Jesus. He was treated as a slave by being subjected to crucifixion; but, as we have argued above, crucifixion is regarded by Paul as a martyrdom. Therefore, the theology of martyrdom by crucifixion appears to be a substratum of the concept of exaltation as Lord. As Moule puts it, 'What is the exaltation at the end of the passage but a variant of the coming with the clouds? Vindication after eclipse is here exactly as in Daniel 7.'[14] There can be no meaningful reference to vindication without reference to degradation and humiliation. Therefore, the death of Christ in obedience to the will of God, indeed his martyrdom, is a necessary substratum of the idea of his glorification.

A similar idea emerges from 1 Cor. 2.8: in the context of the curious and mysterious way in which God's purposes are fulfilled in this world, Paul wrote εἰ γὰρ ἔγνωσαν, οὐκ ἂν τὸν Κύριον τῆς δόξης ἐσταύρωσαν. In Chapter 3 we argued that a number of martyrological motifs are involved in this verse: the crucifixion did not take God by surprise but was part of his eschatological plan for the world in which he asserted his sovereignty over history, entailing martyrdom as part of a cosmic battle which ultimately issued in the victory of God, and of his martyrs. This is where we come to our Christology.

The striking thing about the passage is the juxtaposition of crucifixion and the phrase, 'Lord of glory'. The juxtaposition underlines the continuity of the crucified one with the 'Lord of glory' or the resurrected Lord. It is not two different persons, i.e. one who suffered a servile and accursed execution by the cross on the one hand, and the one whom we now know as Lord on the other hand. Rather it is the same person who was crucified and is now Lord of glory. In view of what has been said on Phil. 2, this juxtaposition may be making the same point, namely that the cosmic powers in their ignorance of the divine scheme of salvation subjected Jesus the Son of God to a servile and accursed execution and thereby ushered in the next stage of the divine drama, namely the lordship of Christ, which included lordship over the cosmic powers themselves. In this sense the martyrdom of Christ is a necessary stage of the drama which moves towards displaying the same crucified one as the sovereign Lord of history and the world and of things 'in heaven and on earth and under the earth' (Phil. 2.10). So once more the martyrdom of Jesus is a substratum of the affirmation of Jesus as Lord.

What then does the martyrological substratum contribute to the Christological affirmation? First, it is the clearest evidence of the sonship of Christ because the crucifixion of Christ was in obedience to the will of God and therefore a martyrdom. Second, a consequence of his living true sonship is his exaltation as Lord. Judaism in some of its traditions made similar claims for its heroes and martyrs. For example, Jewish Gnostics and apocalyptists claimed immortality for such heroes and martyrs as Adam, Enoch, Jeremiah, Baruch and Ezra. Some even entered heaven alive, e.g. Elijah (cf. Assumption of Elijah).[15] At a higher level the vindication involved sovereignty: martyrs were vindicated to be assessors with God at the judgment.[16]

3. *The Martyrdom of Christ and Ecclesiology*

Paul acquired his repute as Apostle to the Gentiles because he journeyed through the Orient preaching Christ to the Gentiles. According to Paul, the body of believers came into being as a result of preaching, proclamation and believing (Rom. 10.17). The content of that proclamation is Christ crucified (1 Cor. 1.23-24; 2.2; 1 Cor. 15.1ff.). We have argued in Chapter 3 that that proclamation made an affirmation of Jesus as a martyr and that the scandal of the cross was transformed into a thing of glory through a martyrological interpretation of it. Therefore, the message of the martyrdom of Christ was, in part at any rate, a founding message of the Church.

Now the early Church, as a worshipping community, expressed its worship in the words of the apostolic kerygma. That kerygma ended with the exhortation, 'repent and be baptized . . . and . . . receive the gift of the Holy Ghost' (Acts 2.38). Baptism is kerygmatic in the sense that it dramatizes the faith of the Church. Different metaphors are used for the rite: washing, birth (Rom. 6.5; 1 Cor. 4.15), divestiture of old humanity and investiture of new humanity (Col. 2.11, 15; 3.9-10; Rom. 6.3-4), or accountancy, whereby the transference of ownership to Christ is effected (e.g. 1 Cor. 10.2).[17] All these metaphors converge at one point, namely that baptism is "into Christ". Thus Paul asks, 'Do you not know that all of us who have been baptized into Christ Jesus were baptized into his death? We were buried therefore with him by baptism into death, so that as Christ was raised from the dead by the glory of the Father, we too might walk in newness of life' (Rom. 6.3-4; cf. 1 Cor. 12.13).

The striking thing about this quotation is its emphasis on the death of Jesus: we are baptized into the death of Christ. It further emphasizes that dimension by the reference to the burial with him. The death then is a crucial part of the kerygma which is dramatized by the rite of baptism.

In Chapter 3 we argued for the martyrological interpretation of the crucifixion of Christ which has made it a worthy atoning sacrifice. The self-surrender of Christ in obedience to God was a sacrifice which the baptism celebrates. 'By surrendering His Son in sacrifice for sinners, God offers in the place and in the favour of all men a sacrifice which abases them beneath the judgment of His condemnation and exalts by the power of His forgiving word'.[18] To say that baptism is into the death of Christ is to draw upon the theology of sacrifice in general and the sacrifice of the cross in particular.

Though we acknowledge the influence of general sacrificial notions in Judaism, it is important to remind ourselves that elsewhere Paul contrasts the sacrifice of the cross with the Sinaitic 'sacrifice'. We refer to 1 Cor. 10.2: 'all were baptized into Moses . . . ' Obviously baptism into Moses was not a Jewish concept; rather, it must have been coined by Paul himself on the analogy of baptism into Christ. The text of 1 Cor. 10.2-5 makes it clear that despite the analogy between baptism into Moses and baptism into Christ, there is yet a difference; for in the latter case there was salvation for many, if not all, but in the former case many were 'overthrown in the wilderness' because God was not pleased with them. Moses indeed was a deliverer and ruler, who brought Israel to birth, and instructed it in the divine law. But as it turned out, the law was not enough to ensure obedience. Unlike Moses, Christ completes the task by his death on the cross and his subsequent resurrection 'which are the culmination of His gospel and His example'.[19] The whole business of death as an expression and example in obedience to the will of the Father focuses on the interpretation of the death of Christ as a martyrdom. If the rite of baptism is into Christ's death, then whatever else baptism does, it celebrates the martyrdom of Christ. To that extent baptism is to Christians what some liturgies celebrating martyrs was to the Jews (see Chapter 2).

While baptism dramatizes the crucifixion of Christ for us, once for all, the other central rite of the Church, namely the Eucharist, repeatedly celebrates the death by the re-presentation of the cross and the resurrection of Christ. 'As often as you eat this bread and drink the cup, you proclaim the Lord's death until he come' (1 Cor. 11.26). The Eucharist of the Church is a repeated drama of the crucifixion of Christ.

Paul's comments on the Eucharist cannot be understood apart from the earliest community's practice of the rite and the historical tradition of 'the night when he [Jesus] was betrayed' (1 Cor. 11.23). Hence also the emphasis at 1 Cor. 11.23 on the fact that he was passing on to the Corinthians what he had himself already received.[20] In view of the martyrological ideas involved in the crucifixion, as we have argued in Chapter 3, the Eucharist may be said to celebrate the martyrdom of Jesus.

Furthermore, there are three details which confirm a martyrological emphasis. First is the note about the breaking of the bread (1 Cor. 11.24). The rite recalls not only the last meal Jesus and his disciples had together but also the violent death of Jesus on the cross in self-surrender to God who chose to offer deliverance to men through that event. Second is the cup. It does refer in the first instance to the cup of red wine at the meal. But as Jesus himself stated, the cup of red wine represented his 'blood . . . which is poured out for many' (Mk 14.24). In other words, it represents his impending violent death in total self-surrender to God. This note is further emphasized when in the garden of Gethsemane Jesus prayed for his Father to 'remove this cup' from him (Mk 14.36). Although in the Old Testament the cup was a metaphor for divine punishment and retribution, it is in this context specifically applicable to the impending suffering and death. The martyr associations of the word are self-evident.

The third of these martyrological details is what is said over the cup: 'This cup is the new covenant in my blood' (1 Cor. 11.25). 'Blood', as we have argued in Chapter 3, represents the costly expenditure of the life of Jesus on the cross in obedience to the will of God and, therefore, may be considered a shorthand term for the depiction of Jesus as a martyr. But that violent death was in fact a self-sacrifice by which a new covenant was established. Needless to say, this presupposes the Sinaitic covenant (Ex. 24.8) by which the Hebrews became the covenanted people of God. Now in Jesus the prophecy of Jeremiah that a new covenant is to be made (Jer. 31.31-

34) is realized. The old covenant has been abrogated and superseded by a veritable law on their hearts. What brings about the newness is that whereas the old covenant was sealed with the blood of sacrificial animals, the new covenant was sealed by the self-sacrifice of Jesus Christ. Since human sacrifice was abolished in Judaism, the only category of human sacrifice that could be acceptable was the sacrificial death of martyrs. By the martyr death of Jesus and thus his self-sacrifice, a new covenant is established to set up a new people of God. The martyrdom of Jesus signifies in the end the creation of a new people of God.

Similarly, the rite expresses the κοινωνία of that community (1 Cor. 10.16). Jourdan is convincing in his argument that Paul may have compressed three ideas into this one term: (i) the communion of Christians in Christ; (ii) a reminder of the death of Christ; and (iii) the messianic hope.[21] Since the martyrdom of Christ was a means of establishing a new people of God, the rite of Eucharist which recalls that martyrdom also becomes a means of securing the assembly of the people of God. The violent death of Christ in self-surrender to God established a κοινωνία or is a medium of this fellowship, realized through the partaking. Κοινωνία is subjectively realized in the devout response of the believer and objectively established by the divine institution of the ordinance itself.

4. *The Martyrdom of Christ and Eschatology*

In Chapter 2 we argued that in the theology of Judaism persecution and martyrdom often raised the question of eschatology: what is the relation of the martyrdom and persecution of the just to the goodness, justice and omnipotence of God which is affirmed by faith? And if all history is moving steadily to a τέλος, the Parousia of Christ, what is the fate of those who do not live to share the τέλος, because they have been done to death as martyrs? Or, what will be the fate of those who confessed the faith with much suffering? And what of the persecutor himself? All these and and other questions relate to eschatology. Against that background it is not surprising that the martyrdom of Christ should have eschatological consequences.

Our starting point should be the preaching of Paul. Paul's preaching was undertaken in the belief that the gospel was to be preached throughout the whole known world before the end came.[22] His gospel of the martyrdom of Christ which made atonement for sin was related to the eschaton by ensuring that all men had a chance to repent on account of that martyrdom, before God sat in judgment of the world.

An essential component of eschatology is its stress on the sovereignty of God. This is expressed, for our purposes, in two striking ways. First, the martyrdom of Christ was a dramatic way of showing the sovereignty of God because by it Jesus showed obedience to the will of the Father. It is the insistence that the apparent scandal of the cross of Christ had not taken God by surprise but was in fact the unfolding of the divine plan which governs the world of which he is the sovereign Lord. The clearest statement of this belief is Gal. 1.4: '[the Lord Jesus Christ], who gave himself for our sins to deliver us from the present evil age, according to the will of our God and Father'. In Chapter 3 it was argued that the phrase 'gave himself . . . ' interprets the death of Christ as a martyrdom which has salvific significance. But his death, the passage continues, was 'according to the will of God the Father'. The apparent disaster of the cross was really part of the divine plan and through that apparent disaster God further established his sovereignty as Lord of history and the world. The martyrdom of Christ forms an eschatological drama. And, as we saw in Chapter 2, explaining a martyrdom as being in the predestined plan of God is a standard martyrological motif.

The eschatological reference of the martyrdom of Christ is heightened by the additional clause that the martyrdom of Christ is ὅπως ἐξέληται ἡμᾶς ἐκ τοῦ αἰῶνος τοῦ ἐνεστῶτος πονηροῦ (Gal. 1.4b). The purpose (ὅπως) of the martyrdom of Christ was to rescue us.[23] But from what? The answer is the present age. The function of πονηροῦ requires us to digress a little.

There are two ways of reading πονηροῦ: as a tertiary predicate, i.e. 'out of the present age, evil as it is' (e.g. 1 Pet. 1.18); or as a genitive of possession, 'to rescue us from the age of the evil one who besets us'. In this second sense the meaning is not different from that in the Lord's Prayer, 'deliver us from the evil one'. It is not easy to choose between the two, though on balance we prefer the second exegesis.

However, for our purpose it is perhaps not necessary to resolve that problem. For, either way, the present phase of history is influenced by evil forces. That point is made elsewhere in Pauline literature, in Rom. 12.2; 1 Cor. 2.6; 3.18; 2 Cor. 4.4; Eph. 2.1f.; 5.16. Again, the idea of the present age has a corollary in the age to come. Thus the phrase τοῦ αἰῶνος τοῦ ἐνεστῶτος which is a *hapax legomenon* in the NT, is synonymous with the more familiar ὁ αἰὼν οὗτος which is this side of ὁ αἰὼν ὁ μέλλων (cf. Eph. 1.21; Mt. 12.32). In Jewish eschatological teaching we find the idea of two aeons, the present age (*h'wlm hzh*) and the age to come (*h'wlm hb'*).[24] The present time has no meaning unless it is related to the age to come and the Messianic age. The present time therefore has an eschatological dimension. The self-surrender redeems from the *tempus praesens* which is in the course of entrance (cf. 2 Macc. 1.16; Rom. 8.38; 1 Cor. 3.22). It is the age which is full of sorrow because of the *dolores Messiae* (cf. 1 Cor. 7.26) and is in the highest degree immoral (cf. 2 Thess. 2.3ff.) and marked by violence.

It is hardly surprising, then, that the theme of the martyrdom of Christ takes on an eschatological colouring. It is the turning point in the history of the world. The sovereignty of God is expressed in Christological terms. Earlier in this chapter, we argued that Paul insisted not only on the continuity of the crucified one with the Lord of the Church but also that the martyrdom of Christ was a necessary stage to the lordship of Christ (Phil. 2.5ff. and 1 Cor. 2.8). That lordship expresses the sovereignty of Christ and through that the sovereignty of God. Thus the lordship of Christ is not only a christological statement but also an eschatological statement.

One last point about the eschatological overtones of the martyrdom of Christ is the idea that that death of Christ is part of the cosmic battle which in Jewish theology was an eschatological woe, preceding the End. In the theology of Paul, the death of Christ delivers from the cosmic powers to whom men by sin were in captivity (Eph. 6.12; Col. 2.14-15; Rom. 8.38). That deliverance was achieved because the cross was the Armageddon at which the last battle was fought between Christ and the cosmic powers who were routed. And so, in 1 Cor. 2.8, the cosmic powers, not understanding the eschatological plan of God, 'crucified the Lord of glory' and thereby achieved their own defeat.

The study of the relationship between the martyrdom of Christ and eschatology would be incomplete without some reference to the *crux interpretum*, 1 Thess. 2.14-16. In praising the Thessalonian Christians for their faith well-demonstrated by their heroic endurance of persecution from the Jews, Paul announced that they were in good company because Christ was done to death by the Jews as they had done to death other messengers of God such as the prophets. The juxtaposition of the death of Christ and that of the prophets is a standard martyrological motif,[25] and an anti-Jewish polemic. The martyrological implications of this were considered in Chapter 3.

However, for the present purpose the important point is the comment on the persecutions of Christ and the prophets. In engaging in persecution the Jews were Θεῷ μὴ ἀρεσκόντων, καὶ πᾶσιν ἀνθρώποις ἐναντίων. The first clause is a litotes which is capable of two interpretations: first, the Jews lived not to please God and that would be well demonstrated by their alleged destruction of the messengers of God (cf. Rom. 8.8; 2 Cor. 5.9); second, as a consequence of their obstinacy shown in their murder of Christ and the prophets before him, the Jews were hateful to God. The latter appears to be preferable because the other interpretation would be an anticlimax after the hostile things said about the Jews. But we consider that the two interpretations can and should be held together because to show oneself not pleasing to God is *de facto* to be rejected by him. Insofar as the Jews persecuted the messengers of God, they did not support the cause of God and, by the same token, were rejected by God. This already links the martyrdom of Christ and the eschatological rejection of the Jews.

And so we come to the phrase εἰς τὸ ἀναπληρῶσαι αὐτῶν τὰς ἁμαρτίας πάντοτε. The articular infinitive expresses either purpose or the conceived result. In our context the purpose and the result coalesce. Logically it may denote purpose, for what is in result is to Paul also in purpose.[26] The charges Paul has levelled against the Jews—killing Christ, killing the prophets, persecuting the earliest Christians—were in God's plan to have the effect of filling up their sins. That is, of course, a Jewish theologoumenon which the Christian Church took over, namely that there is a full score of sins to be filled before the eschaton.[27] Thus the persecution and martyrdom of Christ, the prophets, the apostles, the Judaeo-Christians and Gentile Christians were severally and individually part of the unfolding of the eschatological drama. The force of εἰς τὸ, therefore, is to emphasize that the process is going on in every period of time. In other words, the martyrdom of Christ should not be treated as an isolated event but seen in the perspective of the entire purposes of God for the world of which he is the sovereign Lord.

Having described the culpability of the Jews for the martyrdom of Christ, Paul pronounces the judgement that ἔφθασεν δὲ ἐπ' αὐτοὺς ἡ ὀργὴ εἰς τέλος. ἡ ὀργή is, of course, an eschatological concept; it is the divine wrath which is through and through a process which, though already revealed, in disasters and punishments (cf. Rom. 1.18-32; 13.4, 5), has yet to come to its consummation (1 Thess. 1.10; Rom. 5.9; 11.22). But what is the relation of the wrath of God to the martyrdom of Christ?

According to our passage that wrath ἔφθασεν. Φθάνειν is either transitive 'to anticipate' or intransitive 'to arrive at the intended end'; and in view of the fact that there is an ἐπί clause after it, the intransitive use of φθάνειν is preferable here. This, coupled with the eschatological nature of ἡ ὀργή, leads us to read ἔφθασεν as a constative aorist. In other words, we are here reading another version of the point made by the ἀναπληρῶσαι clause. The consummation has not yet come. The force of εἰς τέλος is to counterbalance πάντοτε in v. 16b and is therefore synonymous with εἰς τὸ αἰῶνα, i.e. for ever or finally.

But what does it mean to say the eschatological wrath has come upon the Jews? Some scholars have sought to explain it through some historical event which spelt disaster for the Jews. For example, Bammel[28] posits the expulsion of the Jews by Claudius as the historical setting for our verse, ἡ ὀργή being the expulsion of the Jews from Rome—an event which Paul saw as a step in the historical drama. While we agree that ἡ ὀργή is an eschatological process, we consider it unnecessary to draw in the expulsion of the Jews for three reasons. First, the ἔφθασεν clause (2.16c) comes at the climax of a series of charges in 2.14, 15, 16a, 16b. These present us with quite an adequate explanation from within the text and context, as may be gathered from our exegesis of the ἀναπληρῶσαι clause. Second, since the expulsion order of Claudius affected both Jews and Christians, it would be a bad example for Paul to use in his polemic against the Jews. For not only could the Jews retort, 'but you too were expelled', but also Paul would open himself up to the charge of dishonest argumentation, precisely what he was fighting against at 1 Thess 2.1ff. Third, the expulsion of the Jews affected only the Jews in Rome and there is no evidence that it assumed any significance in the provinces such as would warrant its being taken as a catastrophe affecting the Jews as a nation.

We propose an explanation from within the context itself. In so far as the Jews have opposed God's will and have done so in rejecting and killing Christ and the prophets, they *de facto* have come under the cloud of God's wrath or aversion to evil.[29] As long as the Jews persecuted Christ and other devotees of God, remaining in the spiritual condition of rebellion to God, the wrath of God was final. This view is apparently known within the Qumran community. For example, CD 1.19-21 reads: 'They chose insolence, justified the wicked and condemned the just and broke the covenant, transgressed against the law, threatened the life of the just and all who walked uprightly they held in abomination; they persecuted them with the sword and delighted in quarrelling with the people, but the wrath of God was kindled (*wyḥr 'p 'l*)' (Vermes, 158; Lohse, 66). See also Ps. 103.9; Sibyll. Or. 3.174, 280, 556, 601; 2 Macc. 7.17, 19, 31, 35-37; Ass. Mos. 9.7; 1QS 2.15; 9.17; Josephus, *Bell.* 6.110.

5. *The Martyrdom of Christ and Ethics*

In our study of ecclesiology we argued that the death of Christ interpreted as a martyrdom was the foundation message of the Church. Upon being influenced by the message of the cross, men were baptized into Christ. To be 'in Christ' means to have Christ as the *Vorbild*,[30] to 'be conformed to his death' (Phil. 3.10; cf. Rom. 8.29). And what does this mean?

Ignoring for the moment what it means for Christians, let us see it in relation to Christ. The key to it is the sonship of Christ, who is the only true son and through whom Christians became sons by adoption. The cross was the clearest illustration of Jesus' sonship because it was embraced in obedience to the will of God, as an expression of the humility of Christ (Phil. 2.5ff.). It was at one and the same time an expression of Jesus' love for God and God's love to men through Christ's death (Rom. 5.8; Rom. 8.35; 1 Cor. 5.14; Gal. 2.20). Christ's death becomes the example par excellence of obedience, humility and divine love. Since no other mortal demonstrated the obedience, humility and love of God to the degree Jesus did, Jesus alone is the example for Christians. And for the same reason a Christian is called to suffer, if need be, in imitation of Christ: that is, in patient endurance and with gladness (1 Thess. 1.6; 2.14ff.). The call to men to be sons by adoption carries with it the obligation to live the kind of life of which the cross of Christ was the most articulate expression, namely humility and obedience to the will of God and love of God.

Obviously the ethical dimension of the martyrdom of Christ has been too briefly treated here. But it will come up for discussion again when we consider the persecution of the Church in a subsequent chapter. In this chapter we have tried to argue and demonstrate that although Paul set forth Jesus of Nazareth as a martyr, there was no preoccupation with the fact of the martyrdom but rather with the meaning and significance of that martyrdom. Consequently, the martyrdom of Christ is pressed into the service of soteriology, christology, ecclesiology, eschatology and ethics. The emphasis is not so much on the fact of the martyrdom of Christ but rather on the implications of that fact for the relationship of God to his creation.

Chapter 5

PERSECUTION AND THE APOSTLE

Paul was persecuted by Jew and Gentile alike, subjected to mob violence, lynch justice and juridical punishment in consequence of his missionary activities in the Roman empire. As he himself summarized it when his credentials as an apostle were challenged at Corinth, 'Are they servants of Christ? I am a better one . . . with far greater labours, far more imprisonments, with countles beatings . . . Five times I have received at the hands of the Jews the forty lashes less one. Three times I have been beaten with rods; once I was stoned . . . in danger from my own people, danger from Gentiles, danger in the city, danger in the wilderness . . . At Damascus, the governor under King Aretas guarded the city of Damascus in order to seize me, but I was let down in a basket through a window in the wall, and escaped his hands' (2 Cor. 11.23-33). Some of his letters were written while incarcerated—Philippians, Colossians (which we assume to be Pauline), Philemon. How, then, did Paul understand the nature of his sufferings?

1. *His suffering of persecution as evidence of zeal for the Lord*

The passage from 2 Cor. 11 cited above stands in the section answering fools according to their folly. He tells of his qualifications as an apostle: his Jewish qualifications, which he shares on equal terms with the Jerusalem apostles, and his Christian qualifications as a pioneer missionary who patiently experienced much affliction in the course of his ministry. The persecutions he endured authenticated his vocation as a servant of Christ (2 Cor. 11.23), an apostle. His argument simply put is as follows: no one could so happily accept direct physical violence, physical dangers and treachery unless he had been genuinely called by God to that apostolic vocation. Thus his endurance of sufferings proclaim him a genuine apostle of Christ. Furthermore, 'it is in these circumstances (not in the enjoyment of mystical vision) that Paul's union with Christ is expressed'.[1]

Paul interpreted the persecutions he underwent as evidence that he was a devotee of Christ and of God. Further articulation of this view is Gal. 6.17: τοῦ λοιποῦ κόπους μοι μηδεὶς παρεχέτω· ἐγὼ γὰρ τὰ στίγματα τοῦ Ἰησοῦ ἐν τῷ σώματί μου βαστάζω, i.e. henceforth let no man give me trouble because I bear in my body the *stigmata* of Jesus. It has been suggested[2] that the verse should be read in the light of Gal. 6.12-16, namely that the στίγματα should be read as a contrast to the circumcision of the Jews. However, that exegesis is unacceptable; for 6.16 'peace and mercy be upon all who walk by this rule . . . ' reads well as the benediction closing the section starting from v. 11, while v. 18 'the grace of our Lord Jesus Christ be with your spirit . . . ' reads well as the benediction closing the whole epistle. Therefore, it is better to read vv. 17-18 as a separate paragraph. Further, it has been well remarked that 'in its paltriness [such an exegesis] is alien to the lofty self-consciousness which these words breathe'.[3]

Now what does Paul mean by τὰ στίγματα τοῦ Ἰησοῦ? Στίγματα is a *hapax legomenon* in the NT. Elsewhere in the Greek Bible it occurs only at Cant. 1.11 and the Greek Hexapla of Judges 5.30. It is based on the metaphor of slavery, slaves being branded to show ownership. But there was also a specifically cultic and religious tattooing which indicated that the person was the possession of the deity and therefore under his protection. For example, Herodotus tells the story of how a runaway slave took refuge in the temple of Heracles and had the marks of the god on him, thereby becoming inviolate (Herodotus 2.113).[4] So whatever the τὰ στίγματα may be, they are evidence that Paul belongs to Jesus and is a devotee of Jesus.

According to Deissmann[5] they are protective marks or magical amulets. His evidence is a reading from a scroll that 'I bear the corpse of Osiris . . . Should anyone trouble me, I shall use it against him.' In that text βαστάζειν means to carry an amulet. However, not only does Deissmann fail to produce evidence that the amulets are called στίγματα in the papyri but also 'it is not probable that the apostle would compare his Christian experience to the doings of sorcery'.[6] Indeed, to have done so would have been to play into the hands of his opponents.

E. Dinkler,[7] on the other hand, argues that the στίγματα are 'eine korpörliche Signierung mit dem Zeichen Χ(ριστος)' made at his baptism. However, there is no other evidence adduced for this practice in the early Church. Furthermore, nowhere else does Paul see his baptism as something special which marked him personally off from other Christians, as Dinkler's theory would require us to suppose. Nor is the plural τὰ στίγματα explained on Dinkler's thesis.

E. Hirsch[8] explains the phrase against the background of the Damascus road incident, where vision allegedly left Paul with a bodily weakness thereafter. However, τὰ στίγματα seems to us to be a most unnatural way to refer to bodily weakness; and again, the theory does not account for the use of the plural.

The most convincing interpretation of the τὰ στίγματα seems to be the scars which he received as a result of the persecutions that accompanied his apostolic ministry.[9] The phrase ἐν τῷ σώματί μου standing immediately after τὰ στίγματα confirms that they are physical scars. In the context of the Galatian church, there is the concrete example of the scars he received as a result of the stoning at Lystra (Acts 14.6-21), an incident which certainly left an indelible mark upon Paul's memory[10] (Gal. 4.13; 2 Tim. 3.10, 11; 2 Cor. 11.25). This being our identification of τὰ στίγματα, it becomes clear that his sufferings or the scars that came from the stoning on his apostolic ministry were seen by Paul as authenticating his devotion to God and possibly his apostleship which had been challenged in Galatia. If for the Jews circumcision was a mark of their being owned by God, for Paul the permanent marks of the persecutions he underwent branded him as the apostle of Christ.

Before we leave the passage, we must address ourselves to the qualification of τὰ στίγματα by τοῦ Ἰησοῦ. A. Schweitzer and A. Wikenhauser,[11] while not ruling out the idea of the scars, seek to explain it through the Christ-mysticism, that is, the suffering is 'the having-died of Christ' which was appropriated by Paul at his baptism. But, this theory is unnecessary because there is no reason for introducing the idea of baptism here and nowhere else does Paul appeal to his baptism to buttress his apostleship. Furthermore, the use of τοῦ Ἰησοῦ primarily refers us back to the historical Jesus, since the mysticism is normally expressed with either Χριστός or Κύριος. It seems to us, therefore, that τοῦ Ἰησοῦ may be a deliberate attempt to recall the sufferings of Christ as the protomartyr for Christians. If so, then Paul's scars are evidence of his imitation of

Christ, which give power to his ministry and authenticate his devotion to God and Christ. Thus Gal. 6.17 seems to us to affirm that the persecution and scars that came upon Paul as a result of his apostolic ministry were interpreted as evidence of his devotion to or zeal for the Lord, which is a martyrological motif, as well as a sign or proof of his apostleship.

2 Cor. 6.4-10 and 2 Cor. 11.16ff. make the point that Paul's sufferings were evidence of his devotion to God and his apostleship. In ch. 6 he claims that as an apostle it is fitting and normal that he should have troubles, persecutions included (2 Cor. 6.4-5): 'At every opportunity we give proof of ourselves as ministers of God by great constancy in tribulations (θλίψεις), hardships (ἀνάγκαι), agonies (στενοχωρίαι), under blows, imprisonments, in the midst of riots . . . ' (2 Cor. 6.4-5). Three words used have to do with sufferings: θλίψεις occurs several times in the letters of Paul (2 Cor. 1.4, 8; 2.4; 4.17; 7.4; 8.2, 13). Ἀνάγκη generally means 'necessity' (e.g. Rom. 13.5); but the context here as at 2 Cor. 12.10 demands the meaning 'suffering', or possibly 'torture'. It means the affliction experienced by the apostle.[12] This sense of the word follows its uses in the OT, especially the apocalyptic uses, as well as in Josephus and in the rabbis, where the constraint 'does not lie in the natural condition produced by the dualism of spirit and matter, but in the afflictions and oppressions caused and interpreted as divine visitations either of the people or of individuals in the form of persecution, enmity . . . '

Στενοχωρία (e.g. 2 Cor. 12.10; Rom. 8.35) is the revelation of God's wrath. The line of difference between στενοχωρία and θλῖψις is difficult to draw as, for instance, in Rom. 2.8. 'The two relate to the present and future experiences on earth, but they also carry a reference to the Last Judgment'.[13] Paul's afflictions as well as his whole life are set out as a description of the afflictions of the servant of God.

Thus, these three words at 2 Cor. 6.4-5 are general terms for Paul's experience of faring ill. In the following verse he gives concrete examples of such ill-faring: being beaten, imprisoned, or mobbed in violent disorders. Despite such experiences, he is not crushed, because he is convinced that in them he commends himself as God's servant. His persecution and suffering are a *sine qua non* of being zealous for the Lord and a messenger of God. The apostle is the successor of the prophets of old who came into much suffering as a result of their witness to God among a stiffnecked people.[12]

Col. 4.3 is another articulation of the same idea. Paul asks for their prayers so that he may boldly proclaim 'the mystery of Christ, on account of which I am in prison'. The 'mystery of Christ' is, of course, the Christian message of salvation (cf. Col. 1.26; 2.2). For the sake of that Gospel he as an apostle must endure the suffering and imprisonment that is the lot of all the messengers of Jesus Christ (cf. Eph. 6.19f.). Paul may have been imprisoned on a charge arising from his apostolic work—for instance, preaching the abolition of the distinction between Jew and Greek. On the other hand, it is not impossible that Paul is here concerned with the purpose rather than the cause of the imprisonment, namely that his imprisonment was an opportunity offered him by God for the purpose of preaching the Gospel (cf. Phil. 1.16).

Equally striking is Col. 4.18: μνημονεύετέ μου τῶν δεσμῶν, which appears somewhat unexpectedly in a section of greetings. According to some scholars, Paul drew attention to his fetters because his handwriting was very poor as a result of having his hands chained. However, as J.B. Lightfoot suggested, by drawing attention to his fetters he may be saying, 'My fetters authenticate my apostleship and, therefore, you must listen to me even though you do not know me in person'.

On the basis of Gal. 6.17 and 2 Cor. 6.4-10 (cf. 2 Cor. 11.16ff.; Col. 4.3, 18), therefore, we argue that the apostle Paul saw in his sufferings and persecution the evidence of being a devotee of Christ and the authentication of his apostleship and his apostolic authority.

Related to the zealot-theme is his conception of his sufferings as a means of proclaiming Christ in order to make converts. In this connection Phil. 1.12-13 is most interesting: his incarceration has made for progress or furtherance of the gospel ὥστε τοὺς δεσμούς μου φανεροὺς ἐν Χριστῷ γενέσθαι ... Our interest is in the words ἐν Χριστῷ. Some scholars[15] take them with τοὺς δεσμούς, thus making 'in Christ' a definition of his custody—custody which has come about as a result of devotion to Christ. However, plausible as this interpretation is, it does not do justice to the fact that ἐν Χριστῷ is placed between φανεροὺς and its verb γενέσθαι. ἐν Χριστῷ seems to qualify φανεροὺς,[16] and as such may have either of two meanings: (a) his custody has by the grace of Christ (cf. 1 Cor. 6.2) become the talk of the praetorium instead of restraining the gospel as the imprisonment was intended to do. Or (b) his imprisonment is *in the presence of Christ*. That is, he is continuing the forensic metaphor to say that although he has been judged by the world a criminal (hence his custody), yet in the presence of Christ who is in control of the situation, his incarceration is part of the inscrutable purpose of Christ. Thus according to Phil. 1.12-13, his preventive custody, far from being a fettering of the gospel, has given publicity to the apostle and his message.

Another example of the zealot-theme being applied to the persecution of Paul is Phil. 1.20: awaiting judgment and unsure of the outcome, he argues that whatever may transpire ὡς πάντοτε καὶ νῦν μεγαλυνθήσεται Χριστὸς ἐν τῷ σώματί μου, εἴτε διὰ ζωῆς εἴτε διὰ θανάτου. Θάνατος in the context clearly speculates on the possibility of a death sentence being passed on him. Thus a possible martyrdom of the apostle is read as a glorification of Christ in the apostle's person. The martyrdom would be a *hallul-ha-shem* which, as we argued in Chapter 2, is an aspect of the zealot-theme. Indeed 1QH 2.24f. offers much that is similar to our passage: *'l npšy b'bwr hkbdkh bmšpṭ rš'y whgbyrkh by ngd bny 'dm ky bḥsdkh 'mdy*, 'They (violent men) assail my life, that thou mayest manifest thyself in glory by the judgment of the wicked and show thy might in my favour before the children of men: for my assurance (springs) from thy mercy'.[17] The use of *hkbdkh* is worthy of note. Its root *kbd* is close in meaning to *gdl* which is behind μεγαλυνθήσεται (= *ytgdl*). Not only is there linguistic similarity but also the general idea of God's greatness being manifested in a man and God's mercy are associated in both passages. Phil. 1.20 appears, therefore, to contain a standard martyrological motif: sufferings and a possible martyrdom serve to sanctify the name of Christ and, therefore, to prove devotion to Christ.

Paul's sufferings for the sake of the gospel are interpreted as authenticating his discipleship, apostleship and apostolic authority. They are also seen as an example to other Christians to endure much affliction in the pursuit of their commission to preach and live the gospel (cf. 1 Thess. 2.14; 1.16).

2. The Persecution of the Apostle a Part of the Cosmic Battle

The best example of this theme is 1 Thess. 2.18. After having been persecuted out of Thessalonica, Paul made more than one abortive attempt to return, but failed because 'Satan prevented us'. This presumably refers to some historical event.

According to some scholars it is 'the exigencies of the mission at the time being'.[18] This exegesis is unsatisfactory because under no circumstances can the mission be looked upon as the work of Satan. For Paul's own strategy was to sow the seeds at one centre for a time and then move on. In any case, as he says at 1 Thess. 3.1ff., despite his enforced departure he kept contact with the Thessalonians through his assistants.

Other scholars[19] identify the occasion as a malady similar to that mentioned in 2 Cor. 12.7. This too is unsatisfactory because 'there is no evidence that the affliction was such that Timothy and Silvanus shared it'.[20]

We prefer to interpret 1 Thess. 2.18 through Acts 17.5f.: Jason, as a result of the uproar, was hauled before the magistrates λαβόντες τὸ ἱκανόν (Acts 17.9). That phrase is a Latinism, 'satis accipere', to take security. The issue now is to identify the nature of the security. According to Ramsay[21] it consisted in Jason giving a pledge to keep Paul out of Thessalonica. But if indeed that was a court sentence, then it is difficult to see how Paul could so soon after the episode try to return, in full knowledge of the consequence for both himself and Jason.

An alternative translation, 'a bail for their appearance when called for trial',[22] leaves us with two possibilities. First, as long as the case was not called and the attitude of the magistrates to his mission remained undefined, Paul could not return to a public ministry. That temporary ban on his missionary activities in Thessalonica Paul considered the work of Satan. Second, since the Jews had had a hand in the situation, fomenting the trouble which cut Paul's ministry short, their action was the work of Satan, on which God's wrath is later pronounced. Whatever the historical detail, the opposition to Paul's active ministry at Thessalonica that led to his enforced departure and continued absence from Thessalonica was interpreted as the work of Satan. This is the martyrological motif which interprets persecution and martyrdom as part of the cosmic battle between the forces of God and the forces of evil.[23]

Another relevant text is 1 Cor. 15.32. In the context of the resurrection of Christ and of believers 1 Cor. 15.30-32 speak of the dangers that never were absent from his apostolic ministry. One example of the danger is put thus: εἰ κατὰ ἄνθρωπον ἐθηριομάχησα ἐν Ἐφέσῳ, τί μοι τὸ ὄφελος; Weiss[24] read this as an unfulfilled conditional clause: 'If after the manner of men I had fought beasts at

Ephesus, what would it profit me?' While this is syntactically possible, one would have expected an ἄν in the apodosis as at John 11.21, Acts 18.14. It is less likely 'weil man der realen Beispielen kein fingiertes folgen lassen wird'.[25] In any case, κατὰ ἄνθρωπον can hardly have any proper meaning on Weiss's thesis.[26] Further, 1 Cor. 4.11 had already hinted at stormy times at Ephesus. For these reasons we prefer to read it as a simple conditional clause. The question then is the meaning of ἐθηριομάχησα. One possibility is a literal interpretation, namely that Paul was condemned to fight beasts in the arena but miraculously escaped. This interpretation has the support of Ambrosiaster, Theodoret of Cyprus, Erasmus, Luther, and Calvin. But unless this were a violation of the *Lex Julia de vi*, such as did occasionally occur, such an interpretation would require us to posit the loss of Paul's Roman citizenship which he claimed later at Caesarea. The silence of 2 Cor. 11.23ff., Acts and 1 Clement on a condemnation to the arena also makes this interpretation most unlikely.

On a figurative interpretation the fight with beasts at Ephesus is a struggle with brutal men, regarded as part of a cosmic battle. This interpretation has the support of Tertullian (*de Resurrectione* 48), Chrysostom, Theophylact, Oecumenius, Pelagius. There is evidence that brutal men are depicted as beasts.[27] It remains to identify that struggle. The most obvious reference, to the tumult at Ephesus (Acts 19.23ff.), is dubious because it is not clear whether 1 Corinthians was written before or after the tumult. And in any case, although the tumult was over Paul's missionary activities, Paul himself was not directly involved. Gaius and Aristarchus were those hauled before the theatre. It is in fact virtually impossible to identify any particular struggle.

J.W. Hunkin,[28] following the figurative sense, argued that Paul was using the image to portray himself as a 'bestiarius hardened by long training'. There is some archaeological evidence[29] from Corinth that a theatre was decorated with life-sized figures engaged in fighting beasts. The inscription underneath reads, 'The lion recognizes the man under the bull as his saviour and likes him'. On this view, Paul would appear to be referring to his taming violent and hostile Corinthians. This interpretation, though plausible, is ultimately unsatisfactory because it puts the emphasis on a game rather than on the danger which 1 Corinthians seems to emphasize.

On the other hand, as we argued in Chapter 2, the persecutor was sometimes described as a beast, in order to class him with Satan, and to interpret the persecution as part of the cosmic struggle. In other words, whatever the incident or events which Paul regarded as a form of persecution, it was also interpreted by Paul as part of the cosmic battle between the forces of God and the forces of Satan.[30]

3. *The Apostle's Persecution and Eschatology*

Our study of 1 Cor. 15.32 has brought us to a further conclusion. Paul relates his endurance of whatever the travail was at Corinth to the resurrection. His endurance of persecution and suffering was rooted in his eschatological perspective, namely his conviction that he would be raised at the last, following the example of Christ who died and was raised by God.

A similar point is made at Phil. 1.23, written at a difficult time when Paul's future was most uncertain. He was awaiting judgment after a period of protective custody resulting from his missionary activities. It is in that context that Phil. 1.23 comes to be written: violent execution at the orders of the judge can be a witness to Christ. He writes: 'My desire is to depart and be with Christ'. In the context we have outlined above, τὸ ἀναλῦσαι has a martyrological connotation, namely a violent death. On the face of it, his very positive attitude to death might recall the Greek idea that death is gain (for example Plato, *Apol.* 40D: θαυμάσιον κέρδος ἂν εἴη ὁ θάνατος; cf. Josephus, *Bell.* 7.358). However, the Greek idea has no place here. In the Greek concept death is the true life, but in Pauline theology both life and death are valued as vehicles of divine revelation. For Paul a decision by the court to execute him would not be a disaster, because he then would die as a martyr. And according to martyrological theology, a martyr's death is transformed by the eschatological hope. To that extent Paul was employing Jewish martyrological theology, typically stated by *Sifre Deut.* 307: *lmhr yhyh ḥlqy 'm 'lw l'wlm hb'*, 'tomorrow will be my share with these (sufferings) for the world to come'. Similarly, in 4 BC two rabbis, Judas, son of Sepphoraeus, and Matthias, son of Margaius, exhorted their disciples to pull down the golden eagle set up in the temple by Herod the Great, saying that 'It was a noble deed to die for the law of one's country; for the souls of those who come to such an end attained immortality and an eternally abiding sense of felicity' (Josephus, *Bell.* 1.650). And when the disciples pulled it down and they were about to be done to death, they explained their great joy that 'after our deaths, we shall enjoy greater felicity' (see also 1.653). Similarly, because of the eschatological hope described as 'going to be with Christ', presumably in Paradise, a possible martyrdom holds no terror for Paul.

Our final passage on this topic is Col. 1.24. This notorious verse is sandwiched between two sections dealing with the redemptive work of Christ, of which Paul was the apostle and missionary. Col. 1.13-22 deals with the redemptive work of Christ. 1.23 announces Paul as the minister to proclaim that work of Christ. Then in 1.25 the author returns to Paul's role in the divine plan for the redemption of the world. So the kerygma is the context of the difficult passage of Col. 1.24. Now, as we argued in Chapter 4, Paul's missionary efforts were in part to prepare for the eschaton, and so it should occasion no surprise that Col. 1.24 should have eschatological implications.

Our verse shows a climactic parallelism between its two parts, which may be laid out as follows:

χαίρω	ἐν τοῖς παθήμασιν[31]	ὑπὲρ ὑμῶν
ἀνταναπληρῶ τὰ ὑστερήματα	τῶν θλίψεων τοῦ Χριστοῦ	ὑπὲρ τοῦ σώματος αὐτοῦ

The importance of the parallelism for the interpretation of the passage will become evident later.

Πάθημα is used in two senses in the letters of Paul: first, it sometimes means 'passion' (e.g. Gal. 5.24; Rom. 7.5); second, it means 'sufferings' (e.g. Rom. 8.18; 2 Cor. 1.5-7; Phil. 3.10; 2 Tim. 3.11). In view of the context as well as the parallelism of the verse, παθήματα can only have the sense of 'sufferings'. Besides, the plural παθήμασιν rules out the sense of 'passion' which would be properly expressed by the singular. The phrase therefore refers to the sufferings of the apostles which had been a part of their ministry and to which reference is made at 2 Cor. 1.5-7; 11.16-33; Phil. 3.10.[32]

The sufferings of the apostle are said to be ὑπὲρ ὑμῶν. ὑπέρ with the genitive sometimes means 'in place of'. That meaning is inapplicable because Paul does not even know his readers by sight; he has only heard of their faith (Col. 1.4). Nor does he seem to have made contact with them hitherto. So ὑπὲρ ὑμῶν can only mean 'for your sake' or 'on behalf of you'. That translation excludes any ideas of vicarious suffering, as will be made clear when we consider ἀνταναπληρῶ. The point of the phrase is to draw out the fact that as the apostle to the Gentiles all his missionary efforts and their concomitant sufferings such as his current custody are for the sake of the Gentile churches.

Why does Paul rejoice in his afflictions? The attitude of joy in the face of outrage was taught by the Stoics who said that it was a sign of virtue to adopt fortitude and accept cheerfully untoward fortune. According to Seneca, *nihil aeque magnam apud nos admirationem occupet quam homo fortiter miser.*[33] Indeed, to bear pain with loftiness of spirit is held out as an example to others (cf. Seneca, *Ad Polybium* 5.4). Further, Stoics were exhorted to be thankful for sufferings.[34]

However, there is a difference between Paul and the Stoa; for whereas for the Stoics it is a question of accepting fate, what is fixed (Seneca, *Ad Marciam* 21.4), there is no inflexible logic where Paul is concerned. For Paul, what happens may be taken to be a part of God's overall activity in the world. Further, whereas according to the Stoics divinity is reason, the world principle (Cicero, *Tusc.* 2.21.47), Paul believes in an objective, personal God from whom everything comes and to whose glory everything is. Therefore, his joy in the face of suffering is a way of affirming that God is in control of the situation.

The attitude of joy despite sufferings is an established martyr's attitude: 'Gladly do we give our bodily members to be mutilated for the cause of God. But God will speedily pursue after thee; for thou cuttest out the tongue that sang songs of praise unto him' (4 Macc. 10.20-21; cf. 4 Macc. 1.18-23; 3 Macc. 4.1; Josephus, *Ant.* 2.299; 1 Thess. 1.6; 2 Cor. 1.5-7; 6.10; 7.4; 13.9; Phil. 1.29; 3.10; 1 Pet. 4.13; Acts 5.41). The eschatological overtones of joy in the midst of affliction is confirmed for us by the fact that in Paul's theology joy is a fruit of the Spirit (Gal. 5.22; cf. Rom. 12.12). 'Christian rejoicing, which endures through affliction, is rooted in the Christian hope of what God will do, and at all times the Christian looks beyond his immediate environment to God in prayer.'[35] Joy alongside other qualities is a natural product of a vital relation between the Christian and the Spirit. Joy refers to a quality with a religious basis and is grounded in conscious relationship to God (Rom. 14.17; 15.13; Phil. 1.4, 25). 'In Paul it [χαρά] is bound up with his work as an apostle. It is χαρὰ τῆς πιστεῶς, Phil. 1.25, fruit of the Spirit, Gal. 5.22. There is

thus reference to the eschatological and paradoxical element in it . . .
The eschatological significance may also be seen in the connexion
with ἐλπίς, Rom. 12.12; 15.13 . . . The material relation between the
two is brought out in Rom. 5.1ff. with the help of the opposite
concept of θλῖψις.'[36] It could even be said that joy in affliction is
evidence that the Spirit is given at such times in order to give
utterance and cheerfulness, and to put the sufferer in the council
chamber of God, thereby enabling him to understand the full import
of the suffering in the eschatological plan of God.

Another reason[37] which the apostle gives for joy in affliction is
that ἀνταναπληρῶ . . . τὰ ὑστερήματα. Given the parallelism of the
passage ἀνταναπληρῶ counterbalances τὰ ὑστερήματα which thus
becomes attracted into the former. Ἀνταναπληρῶ is a *hapax
legomenon* in the Bible. Outside the New Testament it is very rare:
we find it in Demosthenes, *Oratio de Classibus* 14.17; Dio Cassius,
Historiarum Romanarum quae supersunt 44, 48; Apollonius Dyscolus,
De Constructione Orationis; Ptolemaeus Μαθηματικὴ σύνταξις 6.9;
Clement of Alexandria, *Stromateis* 7.12; Epicurus, *Epistle* 1.11; but
in all these cases the meaning of ἀνταναπληρῶ is in dispute. We
propose, therefore, to work from the relation of ἀνταναπληρῶ to τὰ
ὑστερήματα. It is not without significance that Paul avoids the
commoner ἀναπληρῶ. In the Pauline writings, the word has four
meanings: (a) to be full, 1 Cor. 14.16; (b) to fill up, 1 Thess. 2.16; (c)
to complete or fill up a deficiency, 1 Cor. 16.7; Phil. 2.30; (d) to fulfil
a prophecy or law, Gal. 6.2. The choice of the unusual form suggests
that he desires to stress the ἀντί prefix. That would be in obvious
contrast to τὰ ὑστερήματα. Ἀντί sometimes means 'instead of'. That
sense is ruled out because of the once-for-all-ness of Christ's saving
death.[38] So we prefer to understand ἀντί to mean 'in turn' as in such
phrases as ἀντανακλωμένη (Wisd. 17.19), ἀνταπατᾶν (i.e. to deceive
in turn; Josephus, *Ant.* 5.308), ἀνταποδιδόναι (i.e. to give back in
turn, Jos. *Ant.* 19.358). Thus Paul's sufferings fill up[39] in turn what
is lacking in the θλίψεις τοῦ Χριστοῦ.

According to Schneider,[40] αἱ θλίψεις τοῦ Χριστοῦ refer to the
historic sufferings of Christ on the cross. But although θλῖψις and
πάθημα are sometimes synonymous (cf. Eph. 3.13; 2 Cor. 1.5; Phil.
3.10), θλῖψις is never used in the Pauline literature of the afflictions
of Christ on the cross. Indeed, as Staab[41] convincingly argued, the
redemptive act of Christ is normally expressed in the Pauline
literature with 'blood', 'cross', 'death', etc. Moreover, the phrase ἐν

τῇ σαρκί μου[42] (i.e. in my person) makes it clear that it is Paul's own physical sufferings which constitute the θλίψεις τοῦ Χριστοῦ. The sufferings of the apostle, now focused on his incarceration, are identical with the sufferings of Christ in the sense that they were endured in the cause of Christ (cf. Acts 9.5; 22.7; Gal. 6.17; 2 Cor. 1.5; Phil. 3.10). Thus τοῦ Χριστοῦ is an objective genitive. It is a 'characterising genitive'.[43]

According to other scholars αἱ θλίψεις τοῦ Χριστοῦ refers to the Messianic Woes, i.e. the period of apostasy, persecution and confusion through which the Messianic age is born.[44] But the singular suffering of the apostle Paul cannot be equated with the Messianic Woes which were expected to be widespread. Besides, there is no evidence of urgency and excitement in the situation, as should occur if the thought were that of Messianic Woes. The Hebrew for Messianic Woes is *ḥblw šl mšyḥ* (= Aramaic: *ḥblyh dmšyḥ*). The normal Greek translation of *ḥblym* is ὠδῖνες and nowhere do we find ὠδῖνες and θλῖψις nor their Hebrew equivalents, *ḥblym* and *zr* respectively, to be synonymous or interchangeable. Finally, the idea of Messianic Woes is a very apocalyptic concept whereas, Col. 1.24 stands in a very unapocalyptic context. Thus, the apocalyptic theme of Messianic Woes is out of place here.[45]

Another interpretation[46] takes αἱ θλίψεις τοῦ Χριστοῦ as a reference to a mystical union with Christ's passion. This too is unconvincing because 'Mysticism is not bound by the measure of time and it permits the mystic to become absorbed into his object. The apostle, however, understands himself as a "servant of Christ", as an obedient servant who must render service to his Lord. It also would remain incomprehensible how—in view of such an intimate communion of suffering—there could still be mention of a measure of afflictions which lacked something for its fulfilment.'[47] Again, as Lohmeyer puts it, 'the expression "what is lacking in Christ's suffering" remains unexplained, if one presupposes such a mysticism of suffering. In a "mystical suffering in accordance with Christ" either the entire suffering of Christ is present and "what is lacking" is never perceptible, or else the person's suffering of faith remains separate from the exemplary sufferings of Christ. In the latter case the suffering would remain intrinsically incomplete as long as death or the parousia does not forbearingly adjust all these earthly deficiencies. And certainly one could not speak of "completing" (the sufferings).'[48]

It is evident that no explanation of αἱ θλίψεις τοῦ Χριστοῦ which ignores τὰ ὑστερήματα will do justice to the subject in hand. Furthermore, the interpretation must take seriously the eschatological implications of the verse. The most convincing thesis is the Jewish idea that there is a full score of sins to be completed before the end of the world (cf. Dan. 8.23; 9.24; Pseudo-Philo 26.13; *Gospel of Peter* 17; 4 Esd. 10.6; b.*Sotah* 9a). The persecutions and the sufferings which the Apostle undergoes in pursuing his call as apostle to the Gentiles in their own way fill up the full score of sins to be completed before the end of the world. Paul's sufferings thus stand in the eternal plans of God to bring near the eschaton.

To sum up: persecutions and sufferings were a *sine qua non* of Paul's apostolic ministry. Indeed, it could be said that the more he was persecuted the more he demonstrated his zeal for the Lord and through that authenticated his apostolic authority. For that same reason he became an example to other Christians. Moreover, his own sufferings constitute a part of the cosmic battle between the forces of God and the forces of Satan. Finally, his sufferings are put in an eschatological frame of reference; for not only is his endurance of persecution rooted in the eschatological hope but also his persecution is seen as part of the filling up of the full score of sins predestined to precede the coming of the Parousia. One striking point is the absence of any ideas of vicarious atoning efficacy attaching to his sufferings because that had been achieved once for all by the martyrdom of Christ. Paul is a confessor and may yet be a martyr. But Christ is the martyr *par excellence* and whatever Paul experiences is in imitation of Christ.

Chapter 6

PERSECUTION AND THE CHURCH

In the preceding Chapter attention was drawn to the fact that the apostle Paul was perhaps the most persecuted apostle of Christ Jesus. But there is another side to the story, namely that when Paul, then Saul, appears on the scene, he is a persecutor of the Church, one who wrought much havoc on the Church in order to destroy it. As he himself puts it, 'as to zeal a persecutor of the church' (Phil. 3.6; Gal. 1.13, 23; 1 Cor. 15.9). Well may it be said that Saul had meted out to him what he himself in the past meted out to the followers of Christ. His conversion did not mean the end of persecution for the Church. Several of the books of the NT presuppose persecution, and Paul's own letters to Thessalonica, for example, were written to encourage a church which was under persecution. In this chapter we address ourselves to the interpretation given to the sufferings and persecution of the Christian congregations in general.

1. *Persecution of Christian Congregations a* sine qua non *of Zeal for the Lord*

Paul interprets the persecutions that were met by the various congregations in consequence of embracing the Christian message as a *sine qua non* of being in Christ. The most eloquent testimony to this theology is 1 Thess. 3.1-4, where, after his enforced departure from Thessalonica, Paul sent Timothy to encourage the Thessalonian Christians to remain constant in the faith, despite the persecutions that had come upon them. Standing firm in the faith in such a time would be proof of their zeal for the Lord.[1]

The zealot-theme is made more directly apparent by the grounds for the exhortation: αὐτοὶ γὰρ οἴδατε ὅτι εἰς τοῦτο κείμεθα. And, indeed, the apostle had forewarned them of the suffering that should come upon them in consequence of embracing his message. The phrase κείμεθα εἰς is equivalent to τεθείμεθα εἰς, to be set, appointed or destined (cf. Lk. 2.34; Phil. 1.16).[2] It was in the destiny of followers of Christ to meet with persecution.

If this is an affirmation of the zealot-theme, it is also an affirmation of the eschatological theme. For as we argued in Chapter 2, the zeal of the martyr was rooted in a conviction about the transcendent omnipotence of God as the sovereign Lord of history. That point is also made by the phrase κείμεθα εἰς which is parallel to μέλλομεν followed by the present infinitive (cf. 1 Thess. 3.4; Rom. 8.13, 18; Gal. 3.23). The two phrases underline that the sufferings are by divine appointment and therefore belong to the unfolding of the divine plan for the world.

Equally interesting for our present purpose is Phil. 1.29-30: 'it has been granted to you that for the sake of Christ you should not only believe in him but also suffer for his sake, engaged in the same conflict which you saw and now hear to be mine'. Whatever disabilities the Philippian Christians had come under were ὑπὲρ Χριστοῦ (Phil. 1.29). The sufferings of the Philippian church were evidence that they were devoted to the Lord Christ: 'it is a struggle after the likeness of Christ's own passion'.[3] Again that claim is prefaced with the phrase ὑμῖν ἐχαρίσθη. The passive is an indirect way of referring to God as the subject of the activity. So it is God who in his grace and inscrutable purposes gave them the privilege of believing Christ as well as suffering for Christ; the persecution and suffering that have come upon them are in the divine plan for those who are zealous for him.

Paul approaches the zealot-theme through another metaphor, that of 'proving'. 2 Thess. 1.5 reads: 'this [their heroic endurance of the persecutions] is evidence of the righteous judgment of God, that you may be made worthy of the kingdom of God, for which you are suffering'. Their persecutions are for the sake of God's kingdom and, therefore, they are zealots of God and his kingdom. The Greek for 'that you may be . . .' is εἰς τὸ καταξιωθῆναι ὑμᾶς τῆς βασιλείας τοῦ Θεοῦ. The εἰς τὸ introduces the purpose of God in bringing about the persecution. καταξιωθῆναι, a *hapax legomenon* in Pauline literature, emphasizes the purifying nature of the persecution with a view to making them worthy of God's kingdom. The persecutions are regarded as a 'chastisement of love', giving the persecuted Christians a chance to prove themselves fit for the kingdom. Their suffering and persecution prove them zealots of Christ.

There is a third metaphor used to express the zealot-theme, namely the *imitatio Christi*. In our exegesis of Phil. 2.5ff., we argued that the martyrdom of Christ on the cross is set forth as a model for the Christian to follow. In that context the imitation is seen in ethical terms just as in Graeco-Roman and Jewish thought. For example, Plato's *Theaetetus* recalls Socrates' teaching that the way to flee from evil is to become as much like God as possible. Imitation of God for him was to become just and pious through knowledge. Similarly, in the Judaeo-Christian tradition the call to be as perfect as God is primarily an ethical concept.[4]

However, in the theology of Paul the *imitatio Christi* is not only ethical but also can be literal. Consequently, Paul interprets the persecutions which came on the Thessalonian church as being in imitation of Christ (1 Thess. 1.6; 2.14f.). So, too, is their patient endurance of sufferings. Altogether they show by their patient endurance of persecution that they are true devotees of Christ whose example they are following.

There is one last metaphor which we wish to include under the zealot-theme, namely the athletic, which occurs at Phil. 1.27: whatever the future held in store for him personally, Paul's concern was to exhort them to stand firm in the faith, συναθλοῦντες τῇ πίστει τοῦ εὐαγγελίου. The word συναθλοῦντες occurs only here and at Phil. 4.3 in the NT and is a metaphor of wrestling with complex obstacles, among which persecution would be one. Indeed, that metaphor is a stock martyrological motif (4 Macc. 6.10; 9.23; 11.20; 13.15; 17.12ff.; Wisd. 10.2; 2 Tim. 2.5; 4.7; Ignatius, *Ad Polyc.* 6.1) and underlines the zealot-theme. Whatever persecution was to come upon the Philippian Christians was part of the wrestling match between the forces of Christ and the forces of Satan for the mastery of the souls of men.

Finally, we must draw attention to a corollary of the *imitatio Christi*. In so far as by *imitatio Christi*, the Thessalonian Christians had followed the example of the zeal of Christ, they too, become examples of zeal for Christ to other congregations and Christians such as those of Macedonia and Achaia (1 Thess. 1.6-8).

Thus in addressing himself to the persecution of Christian congregations, Paul made use of the stock martyrological theology that persecution can be and is evidence of the zeal of the persecuted for their Lord. This is expressed in various ways. However, whereas in Jewish theology the object of the zeal was God, in the Pauline theology the object of the zeal was the Lord Jesus Christ—the one peculiarly Christian twist in what is otherwise an established martyr theology.

2. *Persecution of Christians and the Cosmic Battle*

In our exegesis of 1 Thess. 2.18 we saw that the inability of Paul to return to see his church was the work of Satan and therefore part of the cosmic battle—a stock martyrological tenet. It is only a short step to seeing the plight of the Thessalonian church as the work of Satan. That point is specifically made at 1 Thess. 3.5. When Paul sent Timothy from Athens to look after the Thessalonians, it was because he was concerned μὴ πῶς ἐπείρασεν ὑμᾶς ὁ πειράζων καὶ εἰς κενὸν γένηται ὁ κόπος ἡμῶν. The phrase ὁ πειράζων is of course a name for Satan.[5] The content of Satan's activity in this connexion is to use persecution to lure the Christians away from the faith which Paul by his missionary endeavour had built at Thessalonica. In other words, the persecution that faced the Thessalonian Christians was part of the cosmic battle between the forces of the devil and the forces of God. The concern of Paul that the Thessalonians might succumb to the tricks of Satan stems from the seriousness with which apostasy was viewed in Judaism, expressed in such terms as 'the profanation of the Holy Name'.

In our discussion of 1 Thess. 3.3 earlier in this Chapter, it was argued that the use of σαίνεσθαι might have a veiled allusion to the activity of Satan as the deceiver. But for the moment we wish to direct our attention to the description of the opponents as ἀντικείμενοι. Obviously that word refers to some historical personalities who by their opposition to the faith have become the opponents or enemies of Christ. One of the names of Satan, is, of course, ἀντικείμενος (2 Thess. 2.4; 1 Tim. 5.14; Wisd. 2.4; Pseudo-Philo 60.3). May it be that the opponents of the faith are described as ἀντικείμενοι in order to underline that they are instruments or agents of the devil? If the surmise is accepted, then the crisis at Philippi was interpreted by Paul as part of the cosmic battle between the forces of Satan and the forces of God.

3. *Persecution of Christians and Eschatology*

Earlier in this Chapter we argued that in Pauline theology, as in

Jewish theology, the zealot-theme was rooted in eschatology. Throughout, it is emphasized that the plight of the faithful devotees of Christ had not taken God by surprise, even though *prima facie* it looked scandalous that the faithful devotees of the sovereign and righteous Lord of history should suffer at the hands of unbelievers. Paul resolves that dilemma in the eschatological affirmation that the suffering and persecution had been in the inscrutable purposes of God for the world. It was argued that the use of κείμεθα εἰς at 1 Thess. 3.4 and ὑμῖν ἐχαρίσθη underlined the unfolding of a divine plan.

The faithful endurance of persecution is rooted in the hope of the ultimate vindication by God of those who are faithful to him. Again we already touched on this with regard to 2 Thess. 1.5 where the persecutions made them worthy of the kingdom. The faithful endurance of persecution almost assured one of a place in the kingdom of God. 'If God judges righteously then those who have suffered in persecution will be thought worthy . . . of the kingdom of God (the eschatological community of the redeemed at the parousia . . .) and will in fact become members of it . . . God judges righteously with the intention that those who have suffered while righteous may be received into his kingdom; this is the actual result of his judgment, and it is stated in his decree of judgment'.[6] The persecuted will have peace; the persecutors will be punished. This assurance is not based on legalism such as characterized some sections of Judaism. Rather, it is because by that endurance which showed zeal and obedience to the Lord one was conformed to the image and likeness of Christ and, therefore, was in Christ assured of the glory which is Christ's. Because faithful endurance proves that one is in Christ, the martyr almost automatically shares in the glory reserved for the sons of God through Christ. In this connexion we turn to a study of Rom. 8.17ff.

In this passage, Paul begins to make reference to the sufferings of Christians which are to be contrasted with the future glory. Hitherto he had been talking of the receipt of the Holy Spirit to make them sons of God, which in turn makes them heirs of God with Christ. And then comes the clause εἴπερ συνπάσχομεν ἵνα καὶ συνδοξασθῶμεν . . . (v. 17). Συνπάσχομεν has been interpreted as a reference to the dying of the Christian with Christ in baptism and so refers to the mortification of the flesh.[7] However, such an interpretation ignores the fact that συνπάσχομεν is present tense, and therefore refers to a current situation. Also, it is very doubtful that πάσχειν is ever used of the mortification of the flesh. Moreover, πάσχειν in the theology of Paul as in the rest of the NT has martyrological overtones. Consequently, we seek to presuppose a situation of persecution and suffering behind Rom. 8.17ff. The references to 'tribulation, distress, persecution . . . sword' at Rom. 8.35 makes it not impossible that Rom. 8.17ff. was written against the background of some persecution and suffering whether as a fact of history or as an expectation.

From Rom. 8.16ff. there are a number of compounds formed with συν—συμμαρτυρεῖν, συγκληρονόμος, συμπάσχομεν, συνδοξάζειν, συστενάζειν, συνωδίνειν, συνεργεῖν and σύμμορφος. These occurrences do not seem to recall primarily the ideas of mysticism. The συν-part seems only to underline the idea of fellowship in a literal sense. For example, συγκληρονόμος which in Greek usually means 'fellow-heir' in a literal sense[8] appears to mean in the NT 'he who receives, or will receive, something along with another'[9] (cf. Heb. 11.9; 1 Pet. 3.7). Συμπάσχομεν is perhaps to be interpreted in the sense that Christ is with the Christian both in his suffering and in his eventual glorification. To attack a Christian is to attack the deity of whom the Christian is a devotee. Grundmann rightly explains it thus: 'With Rom. 8.17—συμπάσχομεν—one is thus to think of Christ's suffering even to the point of martyrdom, which is endured in prospect of resurrection from the dead'.[10] Συνδοξάζειν means to give and have a share in the divine δόξα (cf. Mt. 13.43; Col. 3.4).[11] Following the example of Christ the protomartyr, who entered into glory through suffering, it is necessary for Christians to experience suffering in order to enter the glory prepared for his faithful devotees.

That glory belongs to the age to come, while the suffering belongs to the ὁ νῦν καιρός, the present passing age. The two-fold scheme presupposes the rabbinic theology of *h'wlm hzh* and *h'wlm hb'* as well as the apocalyptic distinction between the present time of stress and a future of vindication.[12] Such language describes cosmic history. So the suffering is placed in a cosmic setting. The suffering is a *sine qua non* of a world which itself is groaning and it ushers in the new and golden age.

While the faithful can expect glory in Christ, the persecutor can expect damnation and punishment because as a persecutor he would have allied himself with Satan (2 Thess. 1.6). The point about punishments and rewards is that the day of judgment involves retribution. The faithful such as the martyrs will have ἄνεσις, i.e. rest or refreshment (cf. 2 Cor. 2.13; 7.5; 8.13), while the wicked such as the persecutors will have θλῖψις which is defined as ὄλεθρος αἰώνιος, i.e. death or extinction, spiritual death or separation from God (4 Macc. 10.15; Enoch 90.7; Test. Dan. 10; Ps. Sol. 2.35). Such language used of the fate of the persecutor highlights the sure ultimate defeat of all the forces of evil that oppose the purposes of God the sovereign Lord of the world.

Earlier we argued that the faithful martyrs could expect a share in the glory of Christ. That was to some extent a half-comfort. It only raised for the persecuted the fate of those who died as martyrs before the Day of the Lord when the glory of Christ would be revealed. This brings us to a closer study of 1 Thess. 4.13ff.

The martyrs are variously described—οἱ νεκροί (4.16), or οἱ κοιμώμενοι (a euphemism for the dead, 4.13). This last is made explicit as a reference to the martyred Christians by a fuller description, namely οἱ κοιμηθέντες διὰ τοῦ Ἰησοῦ (4.14), those who are dead as Christians. οἱ κοιμώμενοι is a present participle and has the support of ℵ, A, B, etc. That textual support is better than that of the perfect participle κεκοιμημένοι which is read by D and G. Besides, the perfect is an obvious accommodation to the aorist at 4.14, 15. But if the present participle is the better reading, then there is a reference to the continued and protracted persecution of Christians at Thessalonica which was taking the lives of some Christians.

The phrase οἱ κοιμηθέντες διὰ τοῦ Ἰησοῦ calls for further comment. The construction of 4.14 makes it possible to take διὰ τοῦ Ἰησοῦ either with what goes before, κοιμηθέντες, or with what follows, ἄξει. The latter approach is supported by Theodore of Mopsuestia, Moffatt, Adeney and the RSV. However, that exegesis is less desirable and satisfactory than the former construction because the phrase in question is an obvious parallel with νεκροὶ ἐν Χριστῷ at 5.16. As Frame puts it, 'it is the logical though not the grammatical equivalent of οἱ κοιμηθέντες ἐν Χριστῷ in 1 Cor. 15.18'.[13] Moreover, 'The whole balance of the sentence is against [the latter reading]. It harmonises less well with the phrase in the next verse, the dead in Christ, and introduces an element of redundancy. There is no need for the additional phrase "with him".'[14] Finally, the former reading is grammatically better[15] (cf. 4 Macc. 16.25; Rev. 6.9; 20.4). So we take our stand with Ephraim, Chrysostom, Calvin, Lightfoot, Milligan, von Dobschütz, Dibelius and Frame to read οἱ κοιμηθέντες διὰ τοῦ Χριστοῦ.

What, then, is the force of the διά phrase? It has sometimes been taken as an expression of the Christ mysticism of St Paul. But whereas the reference to death in the context of Pauline mysticism is primarily to a moral and spiritual death, here κοιμηθέντες refers to biological death. Indeed, nowhere in Pauline theology is death in the metaphorical sense described with κοιμᾶσθαι. Also, it is not Paul's custom to use διά to describe his mysticism. That is expressed with either with ἐν or σύν. Again, the use of the personal name, Jesus, argues against any idea of mysticism in this context.

The other interpretation is that διά expresses attendant circumstances;[16] in other words, our phrase οἱ κοιμηθέντες διὰ τοῦ Ἰησοῦ refers to the Christians who died in their zeal for Jesus as was demonstrated by their patient endurance of persecution, before the Parousia of Christ.[17] The attendant circumstances of the death were the persecutions raging in the church of Thessalonica. In that situation there has been a natural excitement and interest in the Parousia.

The dead martyrs stand in contrast to ἡμεῖς οἱ ζῶντες οἱ περιλειπόμενοι. The appositional relation of περιλειπόμενοι to οἱ ζῶντες, coupled with the phrase εἰς τὴν παρουσίαν (4.15) which defines the temporal limits, indicates that the concern is with the Christians who survive the persecutions,[18] the confessors so to speak.

According to Paul confessors have no advantage over martyrs and vice versa, so far as the Parousia goes. Both groups would meet the Lord Jesus (4.17) at the Parousia when God vindicates his moral character by giving all mankind their deserts. The vindication is described in very glowing apocalyptic terms. Παρουσία originally described the actual physical presence of a person (cf. 2 Cor. 10.10; Phil. 1.26), but it came to be used in a technical sense as well, to mean the pageantry of public ceremonies. The citizens of a city went out of the city to meet a visiting emperor, prince, governor or potentate. Such a visit was called the Parousia.[19] This technical language the Christians borrowed to describe what in the OT was known as the Day of the Lord. It underlined the future presence of Christ their Lord in his kingly glory (1 Thess. 2.19; 3.13; 5.23; 1 Cor. 15.23). Both the confessors and martyrs would be in the triumphal procession of the sovereign Lord of history, Jesus, sharing eternal felicity with their Lord. Such language is all symbolic and figurative.

There is one last item to deal with before we leave 1 Thess. 4. In mentioning οἱ περιλειπόμενοι, Paul identifies himself with them—ἡμεῖς οἱ ζῶντες οἱ περιλειπόμενοι (vv. 15, 17). In 1 Thess. ἡμεῖς occurs forty-three times and twenty-two times in 2 Thess. In 1 Thess. the first person plural occurs in some form of the verb forty-five times, of which twenty are participial. In 2 Thess. there are seventeen cases of the first person plural in some form of the verb, of which only one is participial. The first person singular occurs only at 1 Thess. 2.5 and 3.17. The first person plural frequently designates the plural of majesty and humility; but in the verses now under review ἡμεῖς appears to have a literal sense, identifying Paul with those who will survive to the Parousia. After all, he like them had been under persecution, even if in a different situation (1 Thess. 2.18; 1.6; 2.14-16).

This identification of Paul with those who would survive the persecutions to live to the Parousia presupposes that Paul expected the Parousia in his own generation. The expectation is based on a strand of Jewish theology which saw persecution as an eschatological woe, a catastrophic supernatural intervention heralding the times of bliss and doom.[20] Thus in 1 Thessalonians Paul appears to be interpreting the persecutions currently facing the Thessalonian Church as an eschatological woe, heralding the Parousia.

Paul's speculation about the timing of the Parousia is later modified in 2 Thess. 2. Apparently, assuming that the current persecutions were a Messianic Woe, some had gone further to suggest that the day of judgment had arrived (2 Thess. 2.2). So Paul wrote back to the Thessalonians to say that the conclusion did not follow from his reading of the situation as a Messianic Woe. Only God knew the precise timing of the arrival of the Parousia. Indeed, Paul envisaged a worsening of the situation before the Parousia. But all the same the persecution continued to be seen as a manifestation of the ἀποστασία heralding the Parousia. So far as the confessors are concerned, theirs was not to compute the timing of the Parousia but to continue in faithfulness, ὑπομονὴ καὶ ἐλπίς.

In the theology of Paul, the Spirit is the earnest of the eschaton. Therefore one would *prima facie* suspect that treating the persecutions as an eschatological woe would have some reference to the Holy Spirit at some point. And this in fact does happen. Paul's exhortation to congregations under attack is that they manifest joy (Phil. 1.20; 1 Thess. 2.2), patience (1 Thess. 1.3; 2 Thess. 1.4; 3.5), and faithfulness, which according to Gal. 5.22 are 'fruit of the Spirit'. For example, Paul could boast of the 'steadfastness and faithfulness in all your persecutions and in the affliction which you [i.e. the church of Thessalonica] are enduring' (2 Thess. 2.4; cf. 1 Thess. 1.6). That operation of the Holy Spirit in the persecuted people of God was sealing them off for the day of Christ. So the Holy Spirit is an eschatological agent, active in times of persecution as the Spirit of true witness and emboldenment in persecution situations.

Before we leave the subject of persecutions and the Church, we should consider 1 Cor. 13 and Paul's own understanding of what he had formerly done to the Christians. Faithful and patient endurance of persecution has been praised. But that can soon be misconstrued as an encouragement to death. And so we come to the problem discussed in Chapter 2, namely the difficulty of drawing sharp lines between martyrdom and suicide. It is in this connexion that we now address ourselves to 1 Cor. 13.3: ἐὰν παραδῶ τὸ σῶμά μου ἵνα καυθήσομαι, ἀγάπην δὲ μὴ ἔχω, οὐδὲν ὠφελοῦμαι. The phrase παραδιδόναι σῶμα is equivalent to παραδιδόναι ἑαυτόν and διδόναι ἑαυτόν and means 'to devote oneself to service'. However, in view of ἵνα καυθήσομαι, the idea is that of sacrificing oneself in a death by burning.

According to Preuschen[21] the phrase alludes to the practice of branding slaves with a hot iron, a reference to a habit of some Christians giving themselves into slavery so as to offer the price of their person to the poor. However, the practice is nowhere attested before 1 Clem. 55.5 which is some forty years later than 1 Corinthians. The clause ἵνα καυθήσομαι also argues against it because 'giving my body to be burnt' is not a natural expression for branding. Indeed, one would have expected the object εἰς δεσμά or εἰς δουλείαν rather than ἵνα καυθήσομαι.

On the other hand, a literal understanding of καυθήσομαι makes perfectly good sense. There are two possibilities: self-immolation such as those of Calanus the Indian gymnosophist who burnt himself in the reign of Alexander the Great (Cicero, *Tusculan Disputations* 2.53); Zamarkos (Dio Cassius, *Hist.* 54.9);[22] martyrdom by fire (e.g. Dan. 3.28; 2 Macc. 7.5ff.).[23] Here is a case of the difficulty of distinguishing between martyrdom and suicide. But Paul is quite clear on this: the sacrifice of one's life is nothing *per se*; it assumes significance only if it is a manifestation of ἀγάπη. Paul 'finds the enthusiasm of the martyr suspect if it simply expressed the charismatic endowment which can be, even though it does not have to be, an outlet for human hybris'.[24] Martyrdom is valuable only when it is subsumed under genuine love of God.

This chapter will be incomplete unless we address ourselves to Paul's own interpretations of his former persecution of the Church—Gal. 1.13; 1 Cor. 15.9-10; Phil. 3.6; 1 Tim. 1.13. When he was in Judaism, a religion of faith and custom, Paul beyond measure ἐδίωκον τὴν ἐκκλησίαν τοῦ Θεοῦ καὶ ἐπόρθουν αὐτήν (Gal. 1.13). The imperfects ἐδίωκον and ἐπόρθουν indicate the long continuance of the course of action Paul took against the Church. According to Baeck[25] διώκειν translates the Aramaic *yny*, 'to harry, taunt', the usual word for arguing maliciously and spitefully. However, in view of the link with ἐπόρθουν, διώκειν is best translated 'persecute'. Πορθεῖν is originally a military term (cf. Homer, *Iliad* 4.308; 1.162; Euripides, *Phoen.* 564f.). It appears the military overtones were never really lost and this may account for the fact that G reads ἐπολέμουν instead of ἐπόρθουν.[26] Because of the military background of the word, it is tempting to suggest that Paul saw his persecution of the Christians as a religious and holy war. That of course is a martyrological motif (cf. 4 Macc. 9.23; 11.8; 16.14).

Paul's reference to his former life as a persecutor of the Church is to underline that the great role he now plays as an apostle was a matter of the grace of God. Thus the contrast between his life as a persecutor of the Church and his role as an apostle serves to illustrate the central teaching of the grace of God (cf. 1 Cor. 15.9-10).

Paul seems to use this contrast to draw sharp lines between Judaism and Christianity. At Gal. 1.12 he uses the word Ιουδαισμός. His use of it 'is significant of the apostle's conception of the relation between his former and his present faith, indicating that he held the latter, and had presented it to the Galatians, not as a type of Judaism, but as an independent religion distinct from that of the Jews'.[27]

Finally, Paul claims at Phil. 3.6 that it was out of ζῆλος that he used to persecute the Church. The word in this context is an expression of intense irony: he seems to exalt his pre-conversion active persecution of the Christians as apostates and heretics. And yet in actual fact he condemns it. In Galatians it is because he was ζηλωτής, an ardent supporter of the traditions of the fathers. In Philippians it is out of zeal for the Law which appeared to be contradicted by the proclamation of the Christians that the crucified one was also Lord. It was zeal of sorts, misguided zeal perhaps, the contrast of the zeal of the martyrs and confessors. Persecution occurs as a manifestation of conflicting zeals.

In this chapter we have been examining Paul's interpretation of the persecution of the Church. The persecuted churches also are zealous for the Lord, and their zeal is rooted in their eschatological hopes. But at no point is atoning efficacy attached to it, because the climactic sacrifice was made by the martyrdom of Christ on the cross.

NOTES TO CHAPTER 1

1. A. Deissman, *Light from the Ancient East*, London (1910), 112. Pauly–Wissowa, *Real-encyclopädie*, II, 638-40.

2. Livy, *Hist.* 8.20.

3. L. Friedlander, *Roman Life and Manners under the Empire*, II, London (1913), 76ff.

4. *Ibid.*, 44.

5. J. Marquardt, *Römische Staatsverwaltung*, III², Leipzig (1878), 559; T. Mommsen, *Römisches Strafrecht*, Leipzig (1899), 925f.

6. *zqyp* = ὡρθωμένος means 'lifted up'. But it acquired a technical sense, 'be crucified' (cf. Est. 7.10). See G. Kittel, '*zqyp* (ὑψωθῆναι) = gekreuzigt worden', *ZNW* 35 (1936), 282-85; C.F. Keil, *Ezra, Nehemiah and Esther*, Edinburgh (1873), 88.

7. The usual words for this impalement were *tlh* or *tl'*; Gk. κρεμάζειν, κρεμᾶν and κρεμμάνυμαι (cf. Lam. 5.12). But as Est. 7.9, 10 suggest, σταυροῦν seems to have been used interchangeably with κρεμάζειν. The more usual Greek word is ἀνασκολοπίζειν, e.g. Herodotus 1.128; Philo, *Flacc.* 84.

8. Thus the Peshitta and the Targum of Deut. 21.23 read *ṣlb*, which in all Aramaic dialects appears to have been the special word for hanging/crucifixion (cf. Kittel, *op. cit.*, 284). *Ṣlb* appears to be interchangeable with *zqyp*'; cf. Targum to 1 Chron. 10.10 which reads *zqyp*' instead of *ṣlb*. So too the Targum to Est. 9.13.

9. Pauly–Wissowa; *Dig.* 42.19; 38.2; Ulpian, *Dig.* 48.13, 6; Paulus, *Sent.* 23, 1; Callistratus, *Dig.* 48.19, 28, 15; Josephus, *Ant.* 20.129; Josephus, *Bell.* 2.253; Seneca, *Ep.* 17.5; Cicero, *In Verr.* 5.64; Juvenal 8.187.

10. See Pauly–Wissowa under *Crux*, *Lex porcia* and *Lex Sempronia*; Mommsen, *Strafrecht*, 921; J. Blinzler, 'Kreuzigung', in *Lexikon für Theologie und Kirche*, 622.

11. Blinzler, *op. cit.*; Mommsen, *op. cit.*, 918-21; M. Goguel, *The Birth of Christianity*, London (1953), 534ff.

12. E. Schürer, *A History of the Jewish People in the Time of Jesus Christ*, Edinburgh (1910), 61-65.

13. J.B. Lightfoot, *St. Paul's Epistle to the Galatians*, London (1890), 152f.

14. Mommsen, *op. cit.*, 923f.; J.E. Sandys, *A Companion to Latin Studies*, Cambridge (1921), 299.

15. A.H.M. Jones, *Studies in Roman Government and Law*, Oxford (1960), 61.

16. *Hastings Dictionary of the Bible*, IV, 299.

120   *Persecution & Martyrdom in Paul*

17. *Encyclopaedia Biblica*, III, 2901; *Hastings Dictionary of the Bible*, II, 972.

18. Burning men alive appears to have been a common mode of execution among the Assyrians and Babylonians. According to a cuneiform inscription from Western Asia, King Assurbanipal of Assyria avenged himself on his rebellious brother, Samas-sumukin, viceroy of Babylon (c. 648 BC) by condemning him to be burnt alive (S. Birch, *Records of the Past*, London (1874-81), I, 77; IX, 56); cf. also C.J. Ball, *Apocrypha*, II, London (1892), 362.

19. Ball, *op. cit.*, 304; b.*Ab. Zara* 3a; L. Ginzberg, *The Legends of the Jews*, IV, Philadelphia, 328f.

20. A.H. Greenidge, *The Legal Procedure of Cicero's Time*, Oxford (1901), 323; Mommsen, *op. cit.*, 48, 960; W.W. Buckland in *Cambridge Ancient History*, XI, 843.

21. Greenidge, *op. cit.*, 333; Mommsen, *op. cit.*, 300, 960.

22. Paulus, *Sent.* 26.1: 'Lege Julia de vi publica damnatur, qui aliqua potestate praeditus civem Romanum antea ad populum provocantem, nunc imperatorem appellantem necaverit necarive iusserit torserit verberaverit condemnaverit inve publica vincula duci iusserit'; cf. *Dig.* 48.6.7; Pauly–Wissowa, 2204; Mommsen, *Strafrecht*, 663; Mommsen, 'Die Rechtsverhältnisse des Apostels Paulus', *ZNW* 1 (1901), 188.

23. H.L. Strack, *Jesus, die Häretiker und die Christen*, Berlin (1910), 64-67.

24. I. Elbogen, *Der jüdische Gottesdienst in seiner geschichtliche Entwicklung*, Berlin (1905), 36-38. The writings of Justin Martyr presuppose the twelfth petition: for example, he writes in his *Dialogue with Trypho*: 'You [i.e. the Jews] have slain the Just One and His Prophets before Him; and you reject (ἀθεῖτε) those who hope in Him and in Him who sent Him—God the Almighty and Maker of all things—cursing in your synagogues those who believe on Christ' (Justin, *Dial.* 16.4; cf. 47.4; 43.4; 108.3; 137.2).

25. *Jewish Encyclopaedia*, V, 285; *Hastings Dictionary of the Bible*, I, 800f.

26. *Jewish Encyclopaedia*, V, 286.

27. For a very full account see H.L. Strack and P. Billerbeck, *Kommentar zum Neuen Testament*, V, Munich (1926), 293-333; J. Juster, *Les Juifs dans l'empire romain*, II, Paris (1914), 159-61; Schürer, *op. cit.*, II.ii.59-62.

28. Buckland in *Cambridge Ancient History*, XI, 843; Mommsen, *Strafrecht*, 964f.

29. G. la Piana, 'Foreign Groups in Rome during the First Centuries of the Empire', *HTR* 20 (1927), 291; Josephus, *Ant.* 18.65f.; Tacitus, *Ann.* 2.85.

30. P. Orosius, *Historia adversus Paganos* (ed. C. Zangemeister, *C.S.E.L.*, V, 451, vii.6, 15-16; Suetonius, *Vita Claudii* 25.4.

31. H.M. Gwatkin, *Selections from Early Christian Writers*, London (1893), 11.

32. S.R. Driver, *Deuteronomy*, Edinburgh (1902), 279f.

33. Juster, *op. cit.*, II, 161.

34. *Encyclopaedia Biblica*, III, 2722.

35. *Jewish Encyclopaedia*, XI, 569f.; Mishnah *Makkoth* 3.12-13.

36. *Ibid.*

37. Mommsen, *Strafrecht*, 90; W.M. Ramsay, *St. Paul the Traveller and the Roman Citizen*, London (1895), 106-107.

38. A.N. Sherwin-White, *Roman Society and Roman Law in the New Testament*, Oxford (1963), 27.

39. Mommsen, *Strafrecht*, 984; F. de Zulueta in *Cambridge Ancient History*, IX, 874.

40. Cicero, *In Verrem* 5.62, 66; Josephus, *Bell.* 2.308; Schürer, *op. cit.*, II.ii.278f.; Mommsen, *Strafrecht*, 47, 329, 663.

41. There is a related law which pronounced instant death on all Gentiles who entered the inner confines of the temple—Philo, *Legatio* 212; Josephus, *Bell.* 1.152, 246, 341; 4.182; 5.193; 6.260; *Ap.* 2.82.

42. Schürer, II.i.187-90; Blinzler, *op. cit.*, 176.

43. See also E.R. Goodenough, *The Jurisprudence of the Jewish Courts in Egypt*, New Haven (1929), 33f.

NOTES TO CHAPTER 2

1. C.F.D. Moule, *The Birth of the New Testament*, London (1962), 105. See also E. Güttgemanns, *Der leidende Apostel und sein Herr*, Göttingen (1966), 12.

2. D.S. Russell, *The Method and Message of Apocalyptic*, London (1964); H.H. Rowley, *The Relevance of Apocalyptic*, London (revised edn, 1963).

3. A. Schlatter, *Der Märtyrer in den Anfängen der Kirche*, Gütersloh (1915), 13f. A. Schweitzer, *The Quest of the Historical Jesus*, London (1910); M. Hengel, *Judentum und Hellenismus* (Wissenschaftliche Untersuchungen zum Neuen Testament, 10), Tübingen (1969), 22ff.

4. C.G. Montefiore and H. Loewe, *A Rabbinic Anthology*, London (1938), 259. See also C.J. Ball, *Holy Bible with Commentary*, London (1888), II, 305-307.

5. Ball, *op. cit.*, 344.

6. L.H. Brockington, *A Critical Introduction to the Apocrypha*, London (1961), 110.

7. Brockington, *op. cit.*, 123.

8. S. Tracy, *3 Maccabees and Pseudo-Aristeas*, Yale Classical Studies, New Haven (1928), I, 247.

9. E. Schürer, *History of the Jews in the Time of Jesus*, Edinburgh (1890), II-III, 218; O. Eissfeldt, *The Old Testament*, Oxford (1966), 582.

10. R.B. Townshend, *4 Maccabees* in R.H. Charles, *Pseudepigrapha*, Oxford (1915), II, 654; M. Hadas, *III and 4 Maccabees*, New York (1953); J. Jeremias, *Heiligengräber im Jesu Umwelt*, Göttingen (1958), 49-50; Jeremias,

122   *Persecution & Martyrdom in Paul*

'Das Lösegeld für Viele', *Judaica* 3-4 (1947-48), 255, 262.

11. Hadas, *op. cit.*, 107ff.

12. H.W. Surkau, *Martyrien in jüdäischer und frühchristlicher Zeit*, Göttingen (1938), 29.

13. Eissfeldt, *op. cit.*, 619; J.B. Frey in L. Pirot (ed.), *Supplément au Dictionnaire de la Bible*, I, col. 367; Rowley, *Relevance of Apocalyptic*, 59. Strictly speaking Enoch 1–104 should be split into the following: (a) 6–36—the origins of evil; (b) 93.1-10; 91.12-17—the apocalypse of weeks; (c) 91–104—persecution. It might be noted that ch. 32 is absent from the Qumran texts.

14. 1 Macc. 13.25f.; 4 Macc. 17.8-10; Jerome, *Onomasticon* 133.17f. (Klostermann); W. Maas, 'Die Maccabäer als christliche Heilige', *MGWJ* 44 (1900), 145-56; J. Obermann, 'The Sepulchre of the Maccabaean Martyrs', *JBL* 50 (1931), 250-65; J. Jeremias, *ZNW* 40 (1940), 254f.; Jeremias, *Heiligengräber*, 18-23; E. Bammel, 'Zum jüdischen Märtyrerkult', *ThLZ* 78 (1953), 119-26; C.H. Kraeling, 'The Jewish Community at Antioch', *JBL* 51 (1932), 130-60.

15. B.W. Bacon, 'The Festival of Lives Given for the Nation in Jewish and Christian Faith', *HJ* 15 (1916-17); D. Daube, 'The Last Chapter of Esther', *JQR* 37 (1946), 139-47; Y. Vainstein, *The Cycle of the Jewish Year*, Jerusalem (undated), 129f., 135f.

16. We do well to remember that the cult of the Maccabaean martyrs was not an isolated case. In the prayers for fast days, there is a litany which celebrates the biblical prophets and their deliverance from persecution, danger or martyrdom—Mishnah *Ta'anith* 2.4ff.; H. Danby, *The Mishnah*, Oxford (1933), 196; H. Adler, *Synagogue Service Day of Atonement*, New York (1928), 54f.

17. G. Downey, *A History of Antioch in Syria*, Princeton (1961), ch. 11.

18. Brockington, *op. cit.*, 75; W.O.E. Oesterley, *Ecclesiasticus*, Cambridge (1912), xx-xxi.

19. J. Geyer, *The Wisdom of Solomon*, London (1963), 17. But see J.A.F. Gregg, *The Wisdom of Solomon*, Cambridge (1909), x-xiii, who dates it second century BC.

20. G.B. Gray, *Psalms of Solomon*, in *Pseudepigrapha*, ed. R.H. Charles, II, 628; Rowley, *Relevance*, 78.

21. J.T. Milik, *Ten Years of Discovery in the Wilderness of Judea*, London (1959), 19; G. Vermes, *Discovery in the Judean Desert*, New York (1956), 31-33; F.M. Cross, *The Ancient Library of Qumran*, London (1958), 89; A. Dupont-Sommer, *The Dead Sea Scrolls*, Oxford (1952), 57, which dates CD between 45 and 40 BC.

22. R.H. Charles, *The Assumption of Moses*, London (1897), xii-xiii; W.J. Farrar, *The Assumption of Moses*, London (1918), 9; C. Lattey, 'The Messianic Expectation in the Assumption of Moses', *CBQ* (1942), 21ff.; Rowley, *Relevance*, 107. But see S. Zeitlin, in *JQR* 38 (1947-48), 35, who

dates it about AD 150.

23. R.H. Charles, *Ascension of Isaiah*, London (1917), xi; A. Dillmann, *Ascensio Isaiae, aethiopice et latine*, Leipzig (1877), ix-xiii; Eissfeldt, *op. cit.*, 609; D. Flusser, 'The Apocryphal Book of Ascensio Isaiae and the Dead Sea Sect', *IEJ* 3 (1953), 30-47. The last author ascribes it to the Qumran community.

24. H.W. Surkau, *Martyrien*; H. Strathmann, μάρτυς, μαρτυρία, in *TDNT*, IV, 474-514. The nearest to our modern understanding of μάρτυς is Rev. 2.13 where it is used of Antipas who died. But that is unique.

25. E. Barker, *From Alexander the Great to Constantine*, Oxford (1956). H. Bengtson, *Griechische Geschichte von den Anfängen bis die römische Kaiserzeit* (Handbuch der Altertumswissenschaft, 3 Abt. 4 Teil), 3rd edn, Munich (1965), 326ff.; W.W. Tarn, *Alexander the Great*, New York (1948-50), I, 10ff., 40ff.; F.-M. Abel, *Histoire de la Palestine depuis la conquête d'Alexandre jusqu'à l'invasion arabe*, Études bibliques, Paris (1952), I, 22-87.

26. E. Bickermann, *Der Gott der Makkabäer*, Berlin (1939), 137.

27. W.W. Tarn, *Hellenistic Civilisation*, London (1950), 186; E. Bevan, *Jerusalem under the High Priests*, London (1958), 82.

28. Bickermann, *op. cit.*, 18, 66; Bevan, *op. cit.*, 81f.

29. D. Rössler, *Gesetz und Geschichte*, Neukirchen (1960); G. von Rad, *Der heilige Krieg im alten Israel*, Göttingen (³1959).

30. Bevan, *op. cit.*, 92.

31. W. Bousset, *The Anti-Christ Legend*, London (1896), esp. ch. 8; S.R. Driver, 'Abomination of Desolation', *HDB*, I, 12ff.; H. Gunkel, *Schöpfung und Chaos*, Göttingen (1895).

32. G.H. Box, *Judaism in the Greek Period*, Oxford (1932), 33.

33. L. Cerfaux and J. Tondriau, *Le Culte des souverains dans la civilisation gréco-romaine*, Tournai (1957); L.R. Taylor, *The Divinity of the Roman Emperor*, Middletown, Conn. (1931), chs. 1 and 2; S.H. Hooke (ed.), *Myth, Ritual and Kingship*, Oxford (1958).

34. M. Hengel, *Die Zeloten*, Leiden (1961), 153 (2nd edn. [1976], 154); O. Betz, 'Die Donnersöhne', *RQ* 3 (1961-62), 41ff.

35. Hengel, *loc. cit.*; G.F. Moore, *Judaism*, Cambridge (1962), III, 165 n. 253; Jeremias, Ελείας, *TDNT*, II, 928-41; C.F. Keil, *The Books of Kings*, Edinburgh (1877), 256.

36. A. Büchler, *Studies in Sin and Atonement in the Rabbinic Literature of the First Century*, London (1928), 1, 5, 25.

37. See also W. Robertson Smith, *Religion of the Semites*, London (1927), 291f., 596.

38. L. Ginzberg, *The Legends of the Jews*, Philadelphia (1911-38), VI, 399 n. 42.

39. Martyrdom of Isaiah; b.*Yebamoth* 49b; *Sanh.* 103b; j.*Sanh.* 28c; *Targ. Is.* 66.1; Heb. 11.37 (cf. 2 Kgs 27.26); Josephus, *Ant.* 10.3.7; Justin, *Dialogue* 120; *Vitae Prophetarum* 80; Origen, *On Mt.* 10.18.

40. In Mandaean sources and Jewish Kabbalistic circles Abel was considered a prophet; e.g. *Yalkut Reuben* Gen. 44; Ginzberg, *op. cit.*, V, 149 n. 152; C.H. Kraeling, *Anthropos and Son of Man*, New York (1927), 163.

41. H.L. Strack and P. Billerbeck, *Kommentar zum Neuen Testament*, Munich (1922), I, 643; H.A. Fischel, 'Martyr and Prophet', *JQR* 36 (1946-47), 271 n. 25.

42. *Vit. Proph.*, 38, 52; cf. Ginzberg, *op. cit.*, VI, 357 n. 28; *Vit. Proph.* 92; Origen, *On Mt.* 10.18.

43. *Lev. R.* 27; *Lam. R.* 3.15; *Tanh.* ed. Buber, *Emor.* 12; J.J. Stamm, *Das Leiden ... Unschuldigen in Babylon und Israel*, Zürich (1946).

44. Fischel, *JQR* 36 (1946-47), 366.

45. 1 Kgs 19.10 (esp. in the LXX); Ps. 69.6, 13; Dan. 3.6; Bel and the Dragon 5, 25, 41; Song of the Three Children 22, 68; Ass. Mos. 10.7; Ass. Is. 5.9, 10; Ecclus 2.18: 'we will fall into the *hands of the Lord*, and not into the hands of men; for as his majesty is, so is his mercy'. The phrase 'hand of God' denotes God's power (cf. 2 Sam. 24.14; 1 Kgs 18.46) and his eternal purposes (cf. Ezek. 1.3; 3.14).

46. J.A. Sawhill, *The Use of Athletic Metaphors in the Biblical Homilies of St. John Chrysostom*, Princeton (1928); Surkau, *op. cit.*, 17.

47. 1 Macc. 2.33-48; 4 Macc. 11.3; Mart. Is. 5.4-5, 8; cf. b.*Yebamoth* 49b; Philo, *Leg.* 117, 233f.; *Quod Omn.* 114, 118; Josephus, *Bell.* 1.148-150, 647f.; *Ant.* 11.70; 12.274-77; 14.149. It may also be that the phrase διδόναι ἑαυτόν in martyrological contexts also underlines the suicidal overtones of martyrdom.

48. Josephus, *Bell.* 7.320ff., esp. 325, 351, 389; *Bell.* 1.150-151. b.*Git.* 57b, preserving a tradition from the third generation Amora, Rabbi Ammi, which is nevertheless a tradition going back to the time of Vespasian, tells the story of how some Jewish maidens and youths jumped into the sea, rather than allow themselves to be employed in a life of shame (Montefiore and Loewe, *op. cit.*, 255).

49. b.*Yoma* 85b; *Ab. Zar.* 18a (Hanina b. Teradion).

50. *Tanch. B. Masse'e* 81a (translation of Montefiore and Loewe, *op. cit.*, 258).

51. b.*Sanh.* 74a; *Ab. Zar.* 24b; *JE*, VIII, 353f.

52. Montefiore and Loewe, 259.

53. Ginzberg, *Legends*, I, 198ff.

54. *Tanchuma*, ed. Buber, Lek Leka 2; see Moore, *Judaism*, II, 106.

55. Montefiore and Loewe, *op. cit.*, 253f.

56. *Ibid.*, 261. See also *Midr. Ps.* 18.7; 16.3; *Pesikta* 87a.

57. *Mid. Teh.* II.7 (text of Wurschau 33); cf. *Gen. R.* 65 at 27.27 (translation by Montefiore and Loewe, 267). See also German translation of *Mid. Teh.* by A. Wünsche (1892), 140f., and English translation by W. Braude, I, 166f.

58. E. Stauffer, *Jerusalem und Rom*, Bern (1957), 129, 163 n. 8; E. Stauffer, 'Der gekreuzigte Thoralehrer', *ZRGG* 8 (1956), 250ff.

59. *Sifre Deut.*, Wa'ethanan 32, f. 73b (cf. Horowitz and Finkelstein, 56; Montefiore and Loewe, *op. cit.*, 544, 540-55). See also W. Wichmann, *Die Leidenstheologie: eine Form der Leidensdeutung im Spätjudentum*, Stuttgart (1930), ch. 8; E. Lohmeyer, 'Die Idee des Martyriums in Judentum und Urchristentum', *ZSystTh* 5 (1927), 231-49, esp. 240.

60. Song of the Three Children, 5, 6, 7; 1 Macc. 2.49; 2 Macc. 6.12, 16; 7.33; 4 Macc. 4.21 (δικὴ); 10.10; Enoch 91.5; Jer. 11.20; 15.19; 20.7-9, 12; Is. 53.4; Ps. 69.5, 26; Est. 14.6.

61. R.C. Trench, *Synonyms of the New Testament*, London (⁶1961), 279ff. See also Ps. Sol. 2.3; 3.4; 5.6; 7.9; 8.2, 22, 29; 1QS 8.4; 1QH 1.3; 3-19; 1QM 17.1, 9.

62. A. Büchler, *Studies in Sin and Atonement*, Oxford (1928), 152-53; F. Rosenthal, *Vier apokryphische Bücher*, Leipzig (1885), 98.

63. Several terms are used. The key ones are *srp* = πυρόω; *thr* = καθαρίζειν; *kpr* = καθαρίζειν, ἰλάσκεσθαι; '*šm* = λυτρόω; ἁγιάζειν.

64. Surkau, *op. cit.*; E. Lohse, *Märtyrer und Gottesknecht*, Göttingen (1955), 104-109; J.J. Stamm, *Erlösen und Vergeben im AT*, Bern (1940), 68f.

65. Is. 26.17; 66.8; Jer. 22.23; Hos. 13.13; Mic. 4.9f.; b.*Sanh.* 98b; *Shabb.* 118; *Mekhilta Ex.* 16.29 (59a): Rabbi Eliezer (c. 90 AD) said, 'If you observe the Sabbath [properly] you shall be preserved from three punishments before the woes of the Messiah and before the days of Gog and the age of the great Assize'. See also Strack–Billerbeck, *Kommentar*, I, 950f. See also Dan. 8.23; 9.24; 11.33; 12.1; 2 Macc. 6.12-17, esp. v. 14; Jub. 14.16; Mk 13.7f.; Mt. 23.32; 24.6; Lk. 21.9; 1 Thess. 2.16; 2 Thess. 2; Heb. 11.40; Rev. 6.11.

66. Other such references are Dan. 11.33f.; 12.1; Pseudo-Philo, *Liber Antiquitatum Biblicarum* 26.13: Et erit cum impleta fuerint peccata populi mei, et ceperint inimici potentari domui ipsorum, accipiam ego lapides istos (And it will be when the sins of my people are filled up, and their enemies have the mastery over their house, I will take these stones . . .); 36.1; 41.1; 47.9; Gospel of Peter 17; Apoc. of Esdras 10.6; b.*Sotah* 9a; Ass. Mos. 7–10.

67. R. Martin-Achard, *From Death to Life*, Edinburgh (1960).

68. Dan. 12.1-4; 2 Macc. 7.17, 19, 31, 35, 36; 4 Macc. 9.9; 10.11, 15, 21; 11.3, 23; 17.21; 18.5, 22; Jer. 26.15.

69. Montefiore and Loewe, *op. cit.*, 263. In some of the more hellenized writings it appears to be understood in terms of the more hellenistic idea of δίκη (vengeance) or δράσαντι παθεῖν (Josephus, *Bell.* 3.346). Wickedness carries within itself its own judgment (cf. 4 Macc. 9.32).

70. Cited by S.R. Driver, *Daniel*, Cambridge (1900), 91. A similar idea is found in a non-biblical writer like Plato who in his *Apology* (end) mentions that Minos and others, who were righteous in their lives, give judgment at 'the other place'.

71. See also Enoch 103.3-4; 104.3. It looks as if in Enoch the martyrs appear as accusers of the wicked persecutors.

72. C.L. Grimm, *Kurzgefasstes exegetisches Handbuch zu den Apokryphen*

126   *Persecution & Martyrdom in Paul*

des Alten Testaments, Leipzig (1857), 60f.; E. Kautzsch, *Die Apokryphen und Pseudepigraphen des alten Testaments*, Tübingen (1900), 48ff.

73. K. Siegfried, *HDB*, IV, 930.

74. Ecclus 44.1–50.21; Wisd. 10.1ff.; 4 Macc. 16.20ff.; 18.11ff.; CD 2.16f.; Heb. 11; 1 Clem. 4.1ff.; 9.1ff; 55.1ff. This genre was apparently shared with Stoic diatribe; cf. O. Michel, *Der Brief an die Hebräer*, Göttingen (1949) 244f.; H. Thyen, *Der Stil der jüdisch-hellenistischen Homilie*, Göttingen (1955), 40ff. For further examples of martyrs being examples to posterity, see 2 Macc. 6.28, 31; 4 Macc. 1.2, 7ff., 30; 6.7, 19, 31-34; 7.12, 18; 9.5, 6, 23; 10.2; 11.12; 13.9; 16.3, 20, 21; 18.13; Ecclus 2.10; 44.20; 48.25; 49.27; Philo, *Quod Omn.* 105f.; Josephus, *Ap.* 2.219, 232-235; *Bell.* 7.251; *Martyrdom of Jose b. Joezer*; E. Lohmeyer, *ZSystTh* 5 (1927), 231-33.

75. J. Jeremias, *Heiligengräber*, 18-23, 67-72 (Zechariah's tomb at Kidron); Schlatter, *Der Märtyrer*, 23-29; J. Obermann, *op. cit.*, 250-65.

76. E. Bammel, 'Zum jüdischen Märtyrkult', *ThLZ* (1953), 119-26; B.W. Bacon, 'The Festival of Lives Given for the Nation in Jewish and Christian Faith', *HJ* 15 (1916-17), 119-26.

77. b.*Ta'an.* 30a; cf. Mishnah, *Sopherim* 18.5, 7; J. Obermann, *op. cit.*

78. H.-J. Kraus, *Worship in Israel*, Oxford (1966), 88-92; Bacon, *op. cit.*

79. Mishnah, *Ta'an.* 2.4ff.; Danby, *Mishnah*, 196; H. Adler, *Synagogue Service Day of Atonement*, New York (1928), 54ff.

80. Dan. 12.1-2; 2 Macc. 6.26; 7.9, 11, 14, 23, 29, 36; 12.43-45. It is not as simple a matter as saying resurrection language is used only in Jewish writings while immortality is found only in the hellenized Jewish works.

81. E.W. Heaton, *The Book of Daniel*, London (1956), 236f.; G. Vermes, *The Dead Sea Scrolls in English*, Harmondsworth (1960), 23ff.

82. N. Porteous, *The Book of Daniel*, London (1965), 168.

83. P. Volz, *Jüdische Eschatologie von Daniel bis Akiba*, Tübingen (1903), has argued that the concept of the resurrection of the dead is within a context bearing upon the final consummation of human history. However, there is trenchant criticism of his position by W. Baumgartner, 'Ein Vierteljahrhundert Danielforschung', *TR* (1939), 59, 83, 125f., and 201-208.

84. A. Dupont-Sommer, 'De l'immortalité astrale dans la "Sagesse de Solomon"', *Revue des Études grecques* 72 (1949), 80-87; E. Jacob, *Theology of the Old Testament*, London (1958), 54f.

85. 1 Kgs 22.26; Ass. Mos. 10.1; Mart. Is. 1.8-9; 2.4-5, 8; 3.11; 4.2-3; 5.1; 7.9-10; 1QS 1.17-18; 3.23; Dan. 7.2ff.; Enoch 89f. W. Bousset and H. Gressman, *Religion des Judentums im späthellenistischen Zeitalter*, 3rd edn, Tübingen (1926), 331f.; Volz, *Eschatologie*, 86ff.; H.W. Huppenbauer, 'Belial in den Qumrantexten', *TZ* 15 (1959), 81-89.

NOTES TO CHAPTER 3

1. G. Bertram, μωρία in *TDNT*, IV, 832-47.
2. See Chapter 1.
3. E. Bammel, 'Crucifixion as a Punishment in Palestine', ch. xiv in *The Trial of Jesus*, ed. E. Bammel, 164.
4. G. Stählin, Σκάνδαλον, *TDNT*, VII, 399ff.
5. J. Héring, 'Messie juif et Messie chrétien', *RHPR* 5-6 (1938).
6. Polybius 8.18.11: 'So Bolis said he would give himself (δώσειν ... ἑαυτόν) to the matter'; cf. 10.6.10. With this may go 1 Macc. 6.44 where commenting on Eleazar Avaran's heroic attempt to kill the king of the opposing enemy, 1 Macc. writes that Eleazar ἔδωκεν ἑαυτὸν τοῦ σῶσαι τὸν λαὸν αὐτοῦ. 1 Macc. 11.23; 14.29; 2 Macc. 6.28; 7.9; 3 Macc. 2.31; 6.6; Ecclus 29.15: ἔδωκεν γὰρ τὴν ψυχὴν αὐτοῦ ὑπὲρ σοῦ.
7. See Strack–Billerbeck, *Kommentar*, II, 537, 540.
8. H. Schlier, *Galaterbrief*, Göttingen (¹²1962), 32.
9. See also C.K. Barrett, 'The Background of Mark 10.45', in *New Testament Essays. Studies in Memory of T.W. Manson*, Manchester (1959), 1-18; E. Lohse, *Märtyrer und Gottesknecht*, Göttingen (1955), 94-110.
10. Strack–Billerbeck, *Kommentar*, II, 410.
11. C.H. Dodd, *According to the Scriptures*, London (1952), 57-59; B. Lindars, *New Testament Apologetic*, London (1961), 99f.
12. W.D. Davies, *Paul and Rabbinic Judaism*, London (1948), 274.
13. E. Ellis, *St. Paul's Use of the Old Testament*, Edinburgh (1957). However, Lindars has also argued that 'the wide variety of non-septuagintal phrases indicates that the biblical work has been done at the earliest possible period, very probably by Jesus himself' (*New Testament Apologetic*, 78-79). Even so, one cannot be sure that it was not a general interpretation of the death of Christ as a vicarious suffering rather than specifically tied to Is. 53.
14. J. Jeremias, παῖς, *TDNT*, V, 708; 'Zur Gedankenführung in den paulinischen Briefen', in *Studia Paulina*, Haarlem (1953), 154.
15. F. Brown, S. Driver and A. Briggs, *Hebrew and English Lexicon*, Oxford (1907, repr. 1968), 788.
16. J. Jeremias, παῖς, *TDNT*, V, 636ff.
17. L. Krinetzki, 'Der Einfluss von Is. 52.13–53.12 Par auf Phil. 2.6-11', *TQ* 139 (1959), 180f.; K. Rengstorf, *TDNT*, II, 264-84.
18. M.D. Hooker, *Jesus and the Servant*, London, (1959), 120.
19. The singular ἀνθρώπου is read by p⁴⁶, Marcion, Origen and Cyprian. However, the singular is the secondary reading because the plural ἀνθρώπων is the more difficult reading. Further, the singular appears to be a conscious recall of the Son of Man.
20. O. Michel, *Prophet und Märtyrer*, Gütersloh (1932), 11-12, 21.
21. Davies, *op. cit.*, 263.
22. 1 Cor. 1.13; 15.3; Rom. 8.3. See also F. Blass, *Grammar of NT Greek*,

128   *Persecution & Martyrdom in Paul*

London (1898), 134-35.

23. C.F.D. Moule, *An Idiom Book of New Testament Greek*, Cambridge (1959²), 63; Moule, *The Origin of Christology*, Cambridge (1977), 118f.

24. H. Riesenfeld, ὑπέρ, *TDNT*, VIII, 508-509.

25. R. de Vaux, *Studies in Old Testament Sacrifice*, Cardiff (1964), 91; E. Stauffer, *New Testament Theology*, London (1963), 132.

26. G. Wiencke, *Paulus über Jesus Tod*, Gütersloh (1939), 67; W. Eichrodt, *Theology of the Old Testament*, London (1961), 165 n. 2.

27. Büchsel, λύτρον, ἀντίλυτρον, *TDNT*, V, 340-49.

28. J. Jeremias, 'Das Lösegeld für Viele (Mk. 10.45)', *Judaica* 3 (1948), 249-64.

29. R.H. Fuller, *The Mission and Achievement of Jesus*, London (1954), 57.

30. Barrett, 'The Background of Mark 10.45', 5-6.

31. We are wondering about the difference between 'for many' and 'for all'. It seems to us that the latter makes a very universalistic claim than the former. See also Moule, *Origin of Christology*, 119.

32. L. Morris, *The Apostolic Preaching of the Cross*, London (1965), 55ff.; Büchsel, ἀγοράζειν, *TDNT*, I, 125; Cerfaux, *Christology of St. Paul*, 135.

33. Justin Martyr quotes it in a form identical with Paul's version (*Dialogue* 89.2). But it is easier to believe that he was quoting from Paul than using an independent source.

34. H.W. Schmidt, 'Das Kreuz Christi bei Paulus', *ZSysTh* 21 (1950-52), 148.

35. Lightfoot, *Galatians*, 152f.

36. Lindars, *New Testament Apologetic*, 135.

37. See also A. Schlatter, 'Ist Jesus ein Sündenbock?', in *Kampfende Kirche*, fasc. 22, n.d.

38. See also Bachmann, *Der zweite Brief des Paulus an die Korinther*, in *loc.*.

39. Barrett, *The Second Epistle to the Corinthians*, 180.

40. Wiencke, *op. cit.*, 59.

41. L. Morris, 'The Biblical Use of the Term Blood', *JTS* 3-4 (1952-53), 216-27; J. Behm, αἷμα, *TDNT*, I, 174.

42. Strack–Billerbeck, *Kommentar*, IV, 628, 630f.; J. Jeremias, *Eucharistic Words of Jesus*, London (1966), 87.

43. It is striking that the cup is mentioned before the bread. This may be just sheer convenience because he is going to dwell much longer on the bread as it fits the issue of meat offered to idols. On the other hand, it may be an attempt to throw the focus on the violent death of Christ.

44. L. Goppelt, ποτήριον, *TDNT*, VI, 149-52.

45. *Op. cit.*, 152-53; N. Brox, *Zeuge und Märtyrer*, München (1961), 161; J. Schmid, *Das Evangelium nach Markus* (RNT) (1954²), 200.

46. Löhse, *Märtyrer und Gottesknecht*, 73ff. After biblical times, Polycarp, bishop of Smyrna (AD 69-155) uses 'cup' as a symbol of martyrdom: 'I bless

thee in that thou hast deemed me worthy that I might take a portion among the martyrs in the cup of my Christ' (*Mart. Polyc.* 14.2).

47. G. Dalman, *Jesus-Jeschua*, Leipzig (1922), 147.

48. The Passover rite was apotropaic and had nothing to do with atoning sacrifices. Nevertheless, the operative idea was that of deliverance of a sort. But what is uppermost for the Church was the reinterpretation in the light of the Last Supper.

49. It is interesting that the word ἀνάμνησις is used at 1 Cor. 11.25. The word is a sacrificial term. In our context it is a sacrificial memorial by which the martyrdom of Christ is made real; cf. M. Thurian, *The Eucharistic Memorial*, London (1960), i.

50. B. Weiss, *Die paulinischen Briefe und der Hebräerbrief*, Leipzig (1902), 45; A. Deissmann, *Bible Studies*, Edinburgh (1961), 124-35 (esp. 129); C.H. Dodd, *The Bible and the Greeks*, London (1935), 82-95.

51. E.g. Ex. 25.18, 19, 20; 31.7; 37.6; Heb. 9.5; Philo, *Vit. Mos.*.

52. F.J. Leenhardt, *The Epistle to the Romans* (Eng. tr. by H. Knight), London (1961); W. Lüthi, *The Letter to the Romans* (Eng. tr. by K. Schoeneberger), Edinburgh (1861), 43; J. de Valdes, *St. Paul's Epistle to the Romans* (Eng. tr. by J.T. Betts), London (1883); Strack–Billerbeck, *Kommentar*, III, 165f.; Büchsel *TDNT*, III, 321f.; T.W. Manson, *JTS* 46 (1945), 1-10.

53. According to Meyer νυνί is used dialectically as at Rom. 7.17, 1 Cor. 5.11, 13.13. On purely linguistic considerations this is a possibility. However, the context which contrasts between two relations, i.e. dependence on the Law and independence of the Law, makes it more likely to be an adverb of time. The use of νυνί with a temporal force is also embedded in Pauline tradition as at Gal. 3.23; 4.3, 4; Rom. 7.5; 16.25, 26 and Col. 1.23, 26.

54. When it has been decided that ἱλαστήριον is used adjectivally, there is yet the issue of whether it is the accusative masculine, i.e. the expiator or atoner, or accusative neuter, i.e. that which expiates. The masculine use appears to have the support of the Old Latin MSS which read 'propitiatorem'. We prefer the neuter to the masculine because the masculine use is not found elsewhere; cf. Büchsel, *TDNT*, III, 319.

55. C.L.W. Grimm, *Kurzgefasstes exegetisches Handbuch zu den Apokryphen des Alten Testaments*, Leipzig (1857), 303. Other examples of atoning efficacy attaching to the death of martyrs are 3 Macc. 2.19, 20, Ps. Sol. 8.20, Dan. 9.24; Song of Three Children 17; Wisd. 3.6.

56. Herodotus 3.148; 6.21; Plato, *Phaedo* 115E; Thucydides 2.34.1. προτίθεναι in the active voice sometimes may mean 'to sacrifice' (cf. Arndt–Gingrich). But we do not as yet have any evidence of the middle voice used in this sense.

57. C. Bruston, 'Les consequences du vrai sens de ἱλαστήριον', *ZNW* (1906), 77-81; Leenhardt, *in loc.*; H. Lietzmann, *Römerbrief*, Tübingen (1919²), *in loc.*; C.F.D. Moule, *An Idiom Book of New Testament Greek*, Cambridge (1959²); C.J. Vaughan, *The Epistle to the Romans*, London

(1870), *in loc.*; H.J. Schoeps, *Paul*, London (1961), 146.

58. J.S. Pobee, 'Mark 15.39. The Cry of the Centurion—A Cry of Defeat', in *The Trial of Jesus: Cambridge Studies in Honour of Professor C.F.D. Moule*, London (1969), 91ff.; B. Lindars, *New Testament Apologetic*, London (1961).

59. R. Bultmann, *Theology of the N.T.*, London (1952), I, 175.

60. W. Bousset, *Hauptprobleme der Gnosis*, Göttingen (1907), 242; W. Bousset, 'Zur Hadesfahrt Christi', *ZNW* 19 (1919-20), 50-66, esp. 64; W. Bousset, *Kyrios Christos*, Göttingen (1921²), 191.

61. U. Wilckens, σοφία, *TDNT*, VII, 520 n. 382.

62. A. Böhlig and P. Labib (ed.), *Apocalypse of Adam*, Halle (1963), 77 lines 14-18. (Translation: 'Nor shall they see the φωστήρ, i.e. the one who brings life. Then they will punish the flesh of the man, on whom the Holy Spirit has come'.)

63. Some scholars, explaining κύριος of the historic Jesus, interpret τῆς δόξης as an epithet rooted in the fact that Christ is the wisdom of God (cf. Prov. 8). So F. Hahn, *Christologische Hoheitstitel*, Göttingen (1963), 91f. The critical material on James 2.1 is interesting though slight. τῆς δόξης in James 2.1 is placed before τοῦ κυρίου by 614, Syriac and Sahidic texts. It is omitted by 33, 429 and one MS of the Sahidic.

64. E. Stauffer, *Theology*, 116; A. Robertson and A. Plummer, *1 Corinthians*, Edinburgh (1958²), *in loc.*.

65. This interpretation is supported by Tertullian, *Ad Marc.* 6, where it is denied that the ἄρχοντες are spiritual beings because of the ignorance on their part. It may also be of interest that in the OT the political enemies of the king were described as evil demons; see S. Mowinckel, *Psalmenstudien*, I, Oslo (1921), 69; Robertson and Plummer, *op. cit.*, 39-40.

66. J. Héring, *The First Epistle of St. Paul to the Corinthians* (Eng. tr. by A.W. Heathcote and P.J. Allcock), London (1962), *in loc.*; H. Lietzmann–W.G. Kümmel, *An die Korinther I und II*, Tübingen (1949), 12; M. Dibelius, *Die Geisterwelt in Glauben des Paulus*, Göttingen (1909), 89f.; R. Leivestad, *Christ the Conqueror*, London (1954), 106; H. Schlier, *Principalities and Powers in the NT*, Edinburgh (1961), 45ff.; V. Taylor, *The Atonement in the NT*, London (1958³), 63, 81.

67. Leivestad, *ibid.*.

68. R. Reitzenstein, *Poimandres*, Leipzig (1904), 270f., 353.

69. Origen, *De Principiis* 3.3.2 (MPG XI.315AB); Origen, *Contra Celsum* 8.5; K. Staab, *Paulus-Kommentare aus der griechischen Kirche*, Münster (1933), 174. But see A.T. Hanson, *The New Testament Interpretation of Scripture*, London (1980).

70. Dan. 10.13, 20; 12.1; Est. 7.6; 9.2; Russell, *Method and Message of Apocalyptic*, ch. 9; G.B. Caird, *Principalities and Powers*, Oxford (1956), 16-17; C.D. Morrison, *The Powers That Be*, London (1960), 6; G. Delling, ἄρχων, *TDNT*, I, 488f.; Michel, *Prophet und Märtyrer*, 10; Surkau, *op. cit.*, 90.

71. Dan. 9.16; 12.2; 1 Macc. 1.58; Ps. Sol. 2.19; cf. I Tim. 3.7; Heb. 10.33; 11.26; 13.13. Verb ὀνειδίζειν = *ḥrp*—Ps 44.16; 2 Macc. 7.24; 3 Macc. 7.8; Mt. 5.11 = Lk. 6.22; Mk 15.32 = Mt. 27.44; 1 Pet. 4.14. A. Harnack, 'Das ursprungliche Motiv der Abfassung von Märtyrer und Heilungsakten in der Kirche', *SBA* (1910), 101; M. Brückner, *Die Entstehung der paulinische Christologie* (1903), 133.

72. It is sometimes argued that Χριστός without the definite article means that the concern is with the title rather than the proper name. Thus R. Fuller has argued that Χριστός in this context is a title because the anarthrous titular use is established in Semitic speech—*The Foundations of NT Christology*, London (1965), 160; F. Hahn, *Christologische Hoheitstitel*, 208 n. 6; Strack–Billerbeck, *Kommentar*, I, 66. Others have argued that the Semitic equivalent of χριστός, messiah, cannot be used as a proper name; so e.g. N.A. Dahl, 'Die Messianität Jesu bei Paulus', *Studia Paulina*, 83-95; also Dahl in *Der historische Jesus und der kerygmatische Christus*, ed. H. Ristow and K. Matthiae, Berlin (1961), 161; J. Jeremias, 'Artikelloses χριστός', *ZNW* 57 (1966), 211-15; B. Klappert, 'Zur Frage des semitischen oder griechischen Urtextes von I Kor. X.3-5', *NTS* 13 (1967), 168-73. However, in this context with the specific reference to the death of Jesus, we believe it is a proper name; cf. Rom. 5.6, 8; 1 Cor. 8.11; Gal. 2.21; and see E. Schweitzer, 'Two NT Creeds Compared', *Current Issues in NT Interpretation*, ed. W. Klassen and G.F. Snyder, London (1962), 167; L. Cerfaux, *Christ in the Theology of St. Paul*, London (1959), 491; O. Cullmann, *Christology of the NT*, London (1963), 133-34.

73. E.g. Jeremias, *Servant*, 89; Jeremias. *Eucharistic Words*, 103 n. 1; Lindars, *New Testament Apologetic*, 60; Cerfaux, *Christ*, 25.

74. J. Nelis, 'L'Antithese littéraire Zoe-Thanatos dans les Épîtres pauliniennes', *ETL* 20 (1943), 22ff.

75. Schrenk, γραφή, *TDNT*, I, 751-52.

76. Strack–Billerbeck, *Kommentar*, I, 275.

77. J. Jeremias, 'Das Lösegeld für Viele', *Judaica* 3-4 (1947-48), 249-64. Jeremias has suggested that the atoning efficacy of the death may be based on Is. 53 and therefore is to be explained through the Suffering Servant. However, E. Lohse has demostrated that the idea of vicarious atonement by death was current in Palestinian Judaism and not exclusively Is. 53 (*Märtyrer und Gottesknecht*, Göttingen [1955], 64-110).

78. Earlier in this letter to the Romans, there has been a parallelism between Isaac and Jesus at Rom. 4.24. Rom. 8.32 is, therefore, taking up after a typology that was not developed in the earlier reference. See Barrett, *Romans, in loc.*.

79. For further examples, see Moore, *Judaism*, I, 539f.; H. Johansson, *Paracletoi*, 168ff.; C.K. Barrett, *From First Adam to Last*, London (1962), 27f.; I. Maybaum, *The Sacrifice of Isaac*, London (1959); N.A. Dahl, 'The Atonement—an Adequate Reward for the Akedah', in *Neotestamentica et*

Semitica, ed. E.E. Ellis and M. Wilcox, Edinburgh (1969), 15-29; G. Vermes, *Scripture and Tradition in Judaism*, London (1961).
80.   Xenophon, *Mem.* 1.63: οἱ διδάσκαλοι τοὺς μαθητὰς μιμητὰς ἑαυτῶν ἀποδεικνύουσιν; *Letter of Aristeas*, 188, 210, 281; 4 Macc. 9.23; Mt. 5.48; 1 Cor. 4.16; 9.1; Phil. 3.17-20; Eph. 5.1-11. See also M. Buber, *Israel and the World*, New York (1948), 66f.; J. Schoeps, *Aus frühchristlicher Zeit. Religionsgeschichtliche Untersuchungen*, Tübingen (1950), ch. 13; Michaelis, μιμέομαι, *TDNT*, IV, 661ff.
81.   L. Cerfaux, *Christ in the Theology of St. Paul*, London (1959), 182-83.
82.   H.A. Fischel, 'Martyr and Prophet', *JQR* 36 (1946-47), 271f.
83.   Pobee, *loc. cit.*.
84.   Héring, *1 Corinthians*, 68.
85.   K. Schmidt, κολαφίζειν in *TWNT*, III, 818; Strack–Billerbeck on Mt. 26.37 (*taqa'*).
86.   K.L. Schmidt, ῾Ιησοῦς Χριστὸς κολαφιζόμενος und die "colaphisation" der Juden', in *Aux Sources de la tradition chrétienne* (Mélanges offerts à M. Goguel), Neuenberg (1950), 217-18.

NOTES TO CHAPTER 4

1.   E. Schweizer, *Lordship and Discipleship*, London (1960), 25; O. Cullmann, *The Christology of the New Testament*, 272ff.
2.   *Op. cit.*, 59.
3.   Schweizer does not limit the concept of Servant of God to Isaiah's servant. 'Jesus was called Servant of God because every righteous one who took on himself suffering and humiliation for God's sake was so called' (51).
4.   This exegesis has the problem of facing up to the fact that Son of God is described as Son of David. 'Son of David' is a Messianic title. But there is no clear instance to support the view that in pre-Christian times 'Son of God' was a title for Messiah (Lohse, υἱός, *TDNT*, VIII, 361). Perhaps it is not fortuitous that Paul does not exactly use the term 'Son of David' but speaks of being descended from David.
5.   Τοῦ ὁρισθέντος υἱοῦ Θεοῦ. It is an issue whether to take ἐν δυνάμει with ὁρισθέντος or with υἱοῦ Θεοῦ. In the former sense, it may be translated 'declared with might to be the Son of God'. The glorification is an act of power. However, there is an obvious antithesis between the successive conditions experienced by the Son of God.
6.   Schweizer, *ibid.*
7.   Moule, *The Origins of Christology*, 30-31.
8.   *Ibid.*, 26.
9.   See M. Meyer, *Griechische Texte*, cited in A. Deissmann, *Light from the Ancient East*, London (1927[4]), 355.

10. J.S. Reid, *The Municipalities of the Roman Empire*, Cambridge (1913), 509.

11. Krinetzki, *op. cit.*, 180-88; K.H. Rengstorf, δοῦλος, *TDNT*, II, 261-80.

12. M.D. Hooker, *op. cit.*, 120.

13. A.M. Ramsey, 'What was the Ascension?', *BSNTS* 2 (1951; reprint 1963), 47.

14. C.F.D. Moule, 'From Defendant to Judge and Deliverer: an Enquiry into the Use and Limitation of the Theme of Vindication in the N.T.', *BSNTS* 1-3 (1950-52; reprint 1963), 40-53.

15. Ass. Elijah; 4 Esdras 14.9; Gen. R. 21.5; Strack–Billerbeck, IV, 'Exkursus zu Elijah', and II, 334ff.

16. See Chapter 2. Also in Greek legends heroes such as Dionysos, Zagreus, Orpheus, Codrus, Remus, Hippolytus of Troizen, Glaucus, Dirce, Arion and Ino became divine through a 'Passio' (cf. Fischel, *op. cit.*, 381). There is also in history a tendency for sympathetic feelings aroused by martyrdom to apotheosize the martyr. Thus, for example, 'feelings around that one [i.e. Julius Caesar] had been betrayed soon were transformed into worship and Caesar became a god' (L.R. Taylor, *The Divinity of the Roman Emperor*, Connecticut [1931], 242).

17. Oepke, βάπτω, *TDNT*, I, 537.

18. Leenhardt, *op. cit.*, 154.

19. *Ibid.*

20. Paul's account here is the oldest Christian document about the Lord's Supper. But it is also a record of the traditions of the Church.

21. Jourdan, 'Koinonia in 1 Corinthians 10.16', *JBL* 67 (1948), 111ff.

22. J. Munck, *Paul and the Salvation of Mankind*, London (1959).

23. The sense of 'rescue' rather than 'remove' is preferable in this context; cf. Acts 7.10, 34; 12.11, 23; 23.27; 26.17.

24. Strack–Billerbeck, IV, 799f.; Sasse, αἰών, *TDNT*, I, 206; II, 543-44; Bousset, *Religion*, 243.

25. H.J. Schoeps, *Aus frühchristlicher Zeit*, 126-43.

26. J.E. Frame, *Epistles of Paul to the Thessalonians*, Edinburgh (5th Impression 1960), 113.

27. Dan. 8.23; 9.1, 24; 11.36; 12.1; 2 Macc. 6.12-17; 7.37; Jub. 14.16. The authenticity of the ἀναπληρῶσαι clause and the ἔφθασεν clause has been challenged by some scholars. But we follow A. Jülicher that the first two clauses of v. 16 bear in the highest degree the Pauline stamp. In form, the same is true of the abrupt conclusion in 16c, for which a quotation from some Jewish apocryphon has been quite superfluously suggested. As a matter of fact, both verses read like 'echoes from an angry indictment lately flung in the face of his persecutors by Paul' (*Introduction to the N.T.*, London [1904], 60).

28. E. Bammel, 'Judenverfolgung und Naherwartung zur Eschatologie des ersten Thessalonischerbriefs', *ZThK* 56 (1959), 294-315.

29. Vermes, *op. cit.*, 98; Lohse, *op. cit.*, 66.
30. E. Larsson, *Christus als Vorbild*, Uppsala (1962).

NOTES TO CHAPTER 5

1. C.K. Barrett, *The Second Letter of Paul to the Corinthians*, London (1973), 300; Dibelius, *2 Corinthians*, 96.
2. O. Michel, *Prophet und Märtyrer*, 33-34.
3. E. de Witt Burton, *Galatians*, Edinburgh (1921), 359. H.A.W. Meyer, *The Epistle to the Galatians* (ET) 5th edn, Edinburgh (1888), 353.
4.. See also Is. 44.5; 2 Macc. 2.29; Ps. Sol. 15.8, 10; Philo, *de Spec. Leg.* 58; Rev. 13.16, 17; 14.9ff.; O. Betz, στίγμα, *TDNT*, VII, 658-64.
5. A. Deissmann, *Bible Studies*, 358-60.
6. W.F. Adeney, *Thessalonians and Galatians*, Edinburgh (Century Bible, n.d.), 339.
7. E. Dinkler in *Neutestamentliche Studien für R. Bultmann*, Berlin (1957²), 125.
8. E. Hirsch, 'Zwei Fragen zu Gal. 6', *ZNW* 29 (1930), 192-97. He rightly denies that the vision may have caused some eyetroubles which could be στίγματα, because according to Acts 26.13, 14 (cf. 9.8) all his companions fell to the ground.
9. Luther (*Galatians*, 566), Adeney, Burton, Duncan, Lightfoot, Schlier, Sieffert; J.H. Moulton, 'The Marks of Jesus', *ExpT* 21 (1910), 283ff.; Betz, *TDNT*, VIII, 663; T. Schmidt, *Der Leib Christi*, Leipzig (1919), 212; O. Schmitz, *Die Christus-Gemeinschaft des Paulus im Lichte seines Genitivgebrauchs*, Gutersloh (1924), 185ff.
10. T.W. Crafer, 'The Stoning of St. Paul at Lystra and the Epistle to the Galatians', *Expositor* VI (8th series) (1913), 375-84. On the other hand, we are unable to accept Stauffer's identification of στίγματα as 'the marks of his suffering as a confessor at Ephesus' (*Theology of the NT*, 185), because it is doubtful if Galatians was written after he had been to Ephesus.
11. A. Schweitzer, *Mysticism of St. Paul the Apostle*, London (1937), 230. A. Wikenhauser, *Pauline Mysticism*, London (1960), 155.
12. H. Grundmann, ἀνάγκη, *TDNT*, I, 346.
13. Bertram, στενοχωρία, *TDNT*, VII, 607.
14. See Chapter 1.
15. J.T. Müller, *The Epistles to the Philippians and Philemon*, London (1956), 49; cf. also NEB.
16. K. Barth, *Philippians*, 26; Schweitzer, *Mysticism*, 125.
17. E. Lohse, *Qumrantexte*, 119; Vermes, *Dead Sea Scrolls*, 155.
18. J. Moffatt, *Expositor's Greek Testament* (1910), *in loc.*; Frame, *in loc..*
19. M. Dibelius, *An die Thessalonischer I und II*, *in loc.*; Simon, *Die Psychologie des Apostels Paulus* (1897), 63.

20. T. Ling, *The Significance of Satan*, London (1961), 39; O. Everling, *Die paulinische Angelologie und Dämonologie* (1888), 74.

21. W.M. Ramsay, *St. Paul the Traveller and the Roman Citizen*, London (1897), 230-31.

22. R.B. Rackham, *The Acts of the Apostles*, London (1901), 298. See also Grenfell and Hunt, *Oxyrhynchus Papyri* II, no. 294 (dating about AD 22).

23. See Chapter 2.

24. J. Weiss, *Der erste Korintherbrief, in loc.*; Weiss, *Earliest Christianity*, I, New York (1959), 321.

25. Lietzmann, *An die Korinther*, 83.

26. See also J. Weiss; Lightfoot, *Galatians*; Parry, *1 Corinthians*; G.S. Duncan, *Paul's Ephesian Ministry* (1929), 66ff.; Acts of Paul 7 (Hennecke, II, 369f.); L. Vouaux, *Les Actes de Paul et ses lettres apocryphes* (1913), 112ff.

27. Appian, *B.C.*, 763: οἵοις θηρίοις μαχόμεθα; Plato, *Phaedo*, 240B; Aristophanes, *Nub.* 184, which describes brutal men as beasts; Ignatius, *Ad Rom.* 5; *Ad Tars.* 1; *Ad Smyrn..* 4; Tit. 1.12; 2 Tim. 4.17. See above, Chapter 2; C.H. Dodd, *New Testament Studies*, Manchester (1953), 100f.

28. J.W. Hunkin, '1 Cor. 15.32', *ExpT* 39 (1927), 281-82.

29. T.L. Shear, 'Excavations in the Theatre District of Corinth in 1926', *AJA* (2nd series) 30 (1926), 453; R.E. Osborne, 'Excavations at Corinth in 1925', *AJA* 29 (1925), 381-97; O. Broneer, 'Corinth', *Biblical Archaeology* 14 (1951), 78-96.

30. R.E. Osborne, 'Paul and the Wild Beasts', *JBL* 80 (1966), 225-30. On the basis of 1QpHab 2.17 he identifies the opponents of Paul as the Judaizers. Hab. 2.17 reads: 'The violence done to Lebanon will overwhelm you; the destruction of the beasts will terrify you'. The Qumran commentary on that is: 'For Lebanon is the Council of the Community; the beasts are the Simple of Judah who keep the Law'. However, there is not much evidence of Jewish influence during Paul's sojourn at Corinth.

31. Some MSS, e.g. ℵ, 31, 81, add μου to παθήμασιν.

32. W. Michaelis, παθῆμα, *TDNT*, V, 930-35; E. Kamlah, 'Wie beurteilt Paulus sein Leiden? Ein Beitrag zur Untersuchung seiner Denkstruktur', *ZNW* 54 (1963), 217-32.

33. Seneca, *de Consolatione* 13.6; *Ad Polybium* 16.2; 1.4; *Epist.* 21.33.

34. Seneca, *Ad Marciam* 24; *Ad Polybium* 2.1.5; *Epist.* 96.6; Cicero, *Disp. Tusc.* 3.32.77. R. Liechtenhan, 'Die Uberwindung des Leides bei Paulus und in der zeitgenossischen Stoa', *ZTK* 3 (1922), 377ff.

35. Barrett, *Romans*, 240.

36. Conzelmann, χαρά, *TDNT*, IX, 369.

37. In view of the parallelism καί, which links the two parts of the verse, has the force of the Semitic *w*, i.e. it is a connective 'where more discriminating usage would call for other particles' (Arndt–Gingrich, 393). In other words καί gives another reason for the joy.

38. Lohse, *Märtyrer und Gottesknecht*, 200-203.

39. G. Kittel, *ZSysTh* 18 (1941), 186-91, translates ἀνταναπληρῶ, 'to fulfil', referring to the fulfilment of Jesus' prediction that his disciples and followers would come under attack. But this theory does not commend itself to us for the reason that it would be a most unusual way of referring to the fulfilment of scripture or even a dominical teaching. Further, the association of Col. 1.24 with specific words of Jesus about suffering is rather dubious.

40. J. Schneider, *Die Passionsmystik des Paulus*, Leipzig (1929), 24f.

41. K. Staab, *Die Gefangenschaftsbriefe, in loc.*

42. It is an issue whether ἐν τῇ σαρκί μου goes with ἀνταναπληρῶ or with the phrase that follows, i.e. τὰ ὑστερήματα . . . Χριστοῦ. Kremer argues for the former view because (a) if it were going with τῶν θλιψεῶν τοῦ Χριστοῦ, the article would have been expected after Χριστοῦ. (b) Though ἐν τῇ σαρκί μου is a good antithesis of ὑπὲρ ὑμῶν, it is better taken with ἀνταναπληρῶ. But we are not convinced by his argument: first, the omission of the definite article is easily done by a writer like Paul. Second, the obvious parallelism between ἐν τῇ σαρκί μου and ὑπὲρ τοῦ σώματος αὐτοῦ excludes Kremer's thesis. Indeed, as Moir points out, the very position of the phrase detaches it from ἀνταναπληρῶ (*ExpT* 42 [1931], 479f.). Besides, the very sense of the words compels us to take ἐν τῇ σαρκί μου with what follows. Cf. E. Schweizer, *TDNT*, VII, 136.

43. Wikenhauser, *op. cit.*, 161.

44. *Mek.* Ex. 16.25 (58b); 16.29 (59a); b.*Shub.* 118a; b.*Pes.* 118a; Strack–Billerbeck, I, 950. Lohse, *Colossians and Philemon*, 69f.

45. Bammel in a personal communication has suggested that despite the criticism mentioned above, there still is some truth in the theory that the thought here is of Messianic Woes. He argues that since apocalypticism is the general background of Paul's theology, the idea may come up without special reason. We ourselves are not so persuaded.

46. A. Deissmann, *Paul*, 162f., 181f., 202; O. Schmitz, *Die Christus-Gemeinschaft des Paulus im Lichte seines Genetivgebrauchs*, 190-96; J. Schneider, *op. cit.*

47. Lohse, *Colossians and Philemon*, 69.

48. E. Lohmeyer, *Die Briefe an die Philipper, an die Kolosser und an Philemon, in loc.*. See also E. Percy, *Die Probleme der Kolosser- und Epheser-Briefe*, 128-34.

NOTES TO CHAPTER 6

1. The use of the Greek Bible *hapax legomenon* σαίνεσθαι may be a hint at another theological tenet. Literally it means in the active 'wag the tail', 'fawn' or 'flatter'. So it came metaphorically to mean to 'deceive' or 'beguile'. With that meaning Paul sees the persecution as a means to beguile the Thessalonian Christians away from Christ. That act of beguiling is, of

course, the work of Satan, the great deceiver. There may thus be another martyrological motif, depicting the persecution as the work of Satan (cf. 1 Thess. 2.18; 3.5). That in itself is the other side of the coin, namely zeal for the Lord. See H. Chadwick, '1 Thess. 3.3, σαίνεσθαι', *JTS* (1950), 156-58; F. Lang, σαίνω, *TDNT*, VII, 54-56.

2. F. Büchsel, κεῖμαι, *TDNT*, III, 654.

3. J.L. Houlden, *Paul's Letters from Prison*, Harmondsworth (1970), 66.

4. M. Buber, 'Imitatio Dei' in *Israel and the World*, New York (1963), 66ff.; J. Schoeps, *Aus frühchristlicher Zeit: Religionsgeschichtliche Untersuchungen*, Tübingen (1950), ch. 13; W. Michaelis, μιμέομαι, *TDNT*, IV, 661ff.

5. W. Foerster, διάβολος, *TDNT*, II, 79.

6. E. Best, *The First and Second Epistles to the Thessalonians*, London (1972), 255.

7. Sanday and Headlam, *Romans, in loc.*; K.E. Kirk, *Romans*, 213.

8. W. Foerster, κλῆρος, *TDNT*, III, 712. J. Bonsirven, *Le Judaisme palestinien*, I, Paris (1934), 307-21; D.S. Russell, *Method and Message of Jewish Apocalyptic*, 286ff.; Stauffer, *Theology*, 76f. and n. 189.

13. Frame, *Thessalonians*, 169.

14. Bicknell, *Thessalonians*, 44-45.

15. Frame, *op. cit.*, 170.

16. Von Dobschütz, *Thessalonischerbrief*, 191; Moule, *Idiom Book*, 57.

17. K. Lake, *The Earlier Epistles of St. Paul* (1911), 88.

18. οἱ περιλειπόμενοι = *hns'rym*. That and its synonym οἱ κατάλοιποι appear to be terms for the purified, faithful remnant: cf. Is. 4.3; 2 Kgs 24.14; 4 Macc. 12.6; 13.7; Josephus, *Ap.* I.35; 2 Macc. 8.14; Apoc. Baruch 29.4; 40.2; 70.8f.; 71; 4 Esdr. 6.25; 7.25f.; 9.7; 12.34; 13.48.

19. Deissmann, *Light*, 368; Oepke, παρουσία, *TDNT*, V, 858-71.

20. Russell, *Method and Message*, 92ff., 380ff.

21. E. Preuschen, 'Und liesse meinen Leib brennen, 1 Cor. 13.3', *ZNW* 16 (1915), 127-31. He argues against the martyr interpretation on the ground that that type of punishment was unknown in the Graeco-Roman world. But that is unconvincing, for it did occur in the Seleucid and Roman societies; see C.J. Ball, *Apocrypha*, II, 362; *Records of the Past*, I, 77; IX, 56. Furthermore, his objection that 'if we think in terms of martyrdom, it is hard to maintain voluntariness' does not stand up to scrutiny in the light of our discussion of the zealot-theme in Chapter 2.

22. F.J. Dolger, *Antike und Christentum*, I (1929), 254.

23. 4 Macc. 5.32; 6.24f.; 7.4, 12; 8.13; 9.17, 19ff.; Heb. 11.24; cf. Deissmann, *Paul*, 95 n. 9.

24. K.L. Schmidt, *TDNT*, III, 466.

25. L. Baeck, *Judaism and Christianity*, 46.

26. Cf. 4 Macc. 4.23; 11.4; Philo, *Flacc.* 54.

27. Burton, *Galatians*, 44.

SELECT BIBLIOGRAPHY

Aalen, S. *Die Begriffe 'Licht' und 'Finsternis' im alten Testament, im Spätjudentum und Rabbinismus.* Oslo, 1951.

Abel, F.-M. *Histoire de la Palestine depuis la conquête d'Alexandre jusqu'à l'invasion arabe.* Paris, 1952.

Abrahams, I. *Studies in Pharisaism and the Gospel.* 2nd Series. Cambridge, 1927.

Adler, H. *Synagogue Service, Day of Atonement.* New York, 1928.

Arehoevel, D. 'Die Eschatologie der Makkabäerbucher', *TLZ* (1963), 259ff.

Bacher, W. *Die Aggada der Tannaiten.* 2 vols. Strasbourg, 1844-1890.

Bacon, B.W. 'The Festival of Lives Given for the Nation in Jewish and Christian Faith', *HJ* 15 (1916-17), 256-78.

Baeck, L. *Judaism and Christianity.* Philadelphia, 1964.

Bammel, E. 'Zum jüdischen Märtyrerkult', *TLZ* (1953), 119-26.

— 'Zum Kapitalrecht in Kyrene', *ZRGG* 71 (1954), 356.

— 'Jüdenverfolgung und Naherwartung zur Eschatologie des ersten Thessalonischerbriefs', *ZTK* 56 (1959), 294-315.

Bammel, E. (ed.) *The Trial of Jesus.* London, 1969.

Barrett, C.K. 'The Background of Mark 10.45', *New Testament Essays. Studies in Memory of T.W. Manson*, ed. A.J.B. Higgins. London (1959), 1-18.

Bauer, A. 'Heidnische Märtyrerakten', *Archiv für Papyrusforschung* 1 (1901), 29-47.

Baumeister, T. *Die Anfänge der Theologie des Martyriums.* Münster, 1980.

Baumgartner, W. 'Ein Vierteljahrhundert Danielforschung', *TR* (1939), 58-83, 125f., 201-28.

Baynes, N.H. 'The Death of Julian the Apostate in a Christian Legend', *JRS* 27 (1937), 22-29.

Bengtson, H. *Griechische Geschichte von die Anfängen bis in die römische Kaiserzeit.* Munich, 1965.

Betz, O. 'Die Donnersöhne', *RQ* 3 (1961-62), 41-70.

Bevan, E. *Jerusalem under the High Priests.* London, 1958.

Bevan, E. *The House of Seleucus.* London, 1902.

Bickermann, E. *Der Gott der Makkabäer.* Berlin, 1939.

Blank, S.H. 'The Death of Zechariah in Rabbinic Literature', *HUCA* 12-13 (1937-38), 327-346.

Blinzler, J. *Der Prozess Jesu.* Regensburg, 1960.

Bousset, W. *The Anti-Christ Legend.* London, 1896.

— *Hauptprobleme.* Göttingen, 1907.

— *Kyrios Christos.* Göttingen, 1921².

— *Die Religion des Judentums in späthellenistischen Zeitalter.* 3rd edition by H. Gressman, Tübingen, 1926.

Braude, W.C. *The Midrash on Psalms.* New York, 1959.

Braun, H. *Gerichtsgedanke und Rechtfertigungslehre bei Paulus.* Leipzig, 1930.

— *Spätjudisch-häretischer und frühchristlicher Radikalismus.* Tübingen, 1957.

Brox, N. *Zeuge und Märtyrer.* Munich, 1961.

Bruston, C. 'Les consequences du vrai sens de ἱλαστήριον', *ZNW* (1906), 77-81.

Büchler, A. *Studies in Sin and Atonement in the Rabbinic Literature of the First Century.* New York, 1927.

Buzy, D. 'L'adversaire et l'obstacle (II Thess. II 3-12)', *RSR* (1934), 402-31.

Canfield, L.H. *The Early Persecutions of the Christians.* New York, 1913.

Cerfaux, L. & Tondriau, J. *Le Culte des souverains dans la civilisation gréco-romaine.* Tournai, 1957.

Conrat, M. *Die Christenverfolgungen in römischen Reiche von Standpunkt des Juristen.* Leipzig, 1894.

Corssen, P. 'Begriff und Wesen des Märtyrers in der alten Kirche', *NJKAG* (1915), 481-500.

— 'Martus und *pseudomartur*', *NJKAG* 37 (1916), 424-27.

Crafer, T.W. 'The Stoning of St. Paul at Lystra and the Epistle to the Galatians', *Expositor* 6 (8th series) (1913), 375-84.

Cullmann, O. *Peter, Disciple, Apostle and Martyr.* London, 1962.

— *Christology of the New Testament.* London, 1963.

— *Jesus and the Revolutionaries.* New York, 1970.

— 'Le caractère eschatologique du devoir missionaire et de la conscience apostolique de St. Paul. Étude sur le κατέχον(-ων) de II Thess. 2.6-7', *RHPR* 16 (1936), 51-76.

de St Croix, G.E.M. 'Why were the Early Christians Persecuted?', *Past and Present* 26 (1963), 6-38.

Daly, R.J. 'The Soteriological Significance of the Sacrifice of Isaac', *CBQ* 39 (1977), 45-75.

Danby, H. *The Mishnah.* Oxford, 1933.

— 'The Bearing of the Rabbinical Criminal Code on the Jewish Trial Narratives in the Gospels', *JTS* 21 (1919), 51-76.

Daube, D. 'The Last Chapter of Esther', *JQR* 37 (1946), 139-47.

Davies, P.O. 'Did Jesus die a Martyr-Prophet?', *BR* 2 (1957), 19-34.

De Vaux, R. *Studies in Old Testament Sacrifice.* Cardiff, 1964.

140   *Persecution & Martyrdom in Paul*

Delling, G. *Der Kreuzestod Jesu in der urchristlichen Verkündigung.* Göttingen, 1972.

Dillman, A. *Ascensio Isaie, aethiopice et latine.* Leipzig, 1877.

Dorrie, H. *Leid und Erfahrung, Die Wort- und Sinn-Verbindung* patheinmathein *im griechischen Denken.* Mainz, 1959.

Downing, J. 'Jesus and Martyrdom', *JTS* 14 (1963), pp. 279-293. *Neotestamentica et Semitica. Studies in honour of M. Black ed. E.E. Ellis and M. Wilcox.* Edinburgh, 1969.

Esking, E. 'Das Martyrium als theologisch-exegetisches Problem', In Memoriam Ernst Lohmeyer, ed. W. Schmauch. Stuttgart, 1951.

Finkelstein, L. *Akiba, Scholar, Saint and Martyr.* New York, 1936.

Fischel, H.A. 'Martyr and Prophet', *JQR* 36 (1946-47), 265-80, 363-86.

Flusser, D. 'The Apocryphal Book of Ascensio Isaiae and the Dead Sea Sect', *IEJ* 3 (1953), 30-47.

Freese, N.F. 'τὸ κατέχον und ὁ κατέχων', *ThStKr* 93 (1920-21), 73-77.

Frend, W.H.C. *Martyrdom and Persecution in the Early Church.* Oxford, 1965.

— 'The Persecutions: Some Links Between Judaism and the Early Church', *JEH* 9 (1958), 141-61.

— 'The Failure of Persecutions in the Roman Empire', *Past and Present* 16 (1959), 10-30.

Gauger, J.D. *Beiträge zur jüdischen Apologetik. Untersuchungen zur Authentizität von Urkunden bei Flavius Josephus und im I Makkabäerbuch.* Bonn, 1977.

Ginzberg, L. *The Legends of the Jews. 8 vols.* Philadelphia, 1911-38.

Gnilka, J. 'Martyriumsparänese und Sühnetod in synoptisches und jüdischen Tradition', *Die Kirche des Anfangs. Festschrift für H. Schürmann.* Leipzig, 1977, 223-46.

Gubler, M.-L. *Die frühesten Deutungen des Todes Jesu.* (Orbis Biblicus et Orientalis, 15). Fribourg and Göttingen, 1977.

Gunther, E. 'Zeuge und Märtyrer', *ZNW* 47 (1956), 145-61.

Guterman, S.C. *Religious Toleration and Persecution in Ancient Rome.* London, 1957.

Güttgemanns, E. *Der leidende Apostel und sein Herr.* Göttingen, 1966.

Harnack, A. 'Das ursprüngliche Motiv der Abfassung von Märtyrer- und Heilungsakten in der Kirche', *SBA* (1910), 106-25.

Harnack, A. 'κόπος (κοπιᾶν, οἱ κοπιῶντες) im frühchristlichen Sprachgebrauch', *ZNW* 27 (1928), 1-10.

Hengel, M. *Judaism and Hellenism. Studies in their Encounter in Palestine in the Early Hellenistic Period.* London, 1974.

Hengel, M. *Was Jesus a Revolutionary?* Philadelphia, 1977.

— *Victory over Violence.* Philadelphia, 1973.

— *The Atonement.* London, 1981.

Bibliography   141

— *Crucifixion*. London, 1977.
— *Die Zeloten*. Leiden, 1976².
Higgins, A.J.B. (ed.) *New Testament Essays in Memory of T.W. Manson*. Manchester, 1959.
Hirsch, E. 'Zwei Fragen zu Gal. 6', *ZNW* 29 (1930), 192-97.
Holl, K. *Gesammelte Aufsätze zur Kirchengeschichte*. 2 vols. Tübingen, 1928.
Hooker, M.D. *Jesus and the Servant*. London, 1959.
Hunkin, J.W. 'I Cor. 15.32', *ExpT* (1927-28), 281.
Husband, R.W. *The Prosecution of Jesus*. Princeton, 1986.
Jeremias, J. *Heiligengräber in Jesu Umwelt*. Göttingen, 1958.
Jeremias, J. *The Eucharistic Words of Jesus*. London, 1966.
Jeremias, J. 'Das Lösegeld für Viele', *Judaica* 3-4 (1947-48), 249-64.
Jones, A.H.M. *Studies in Roman Government and Law*. Oxford, 1960.
Kamlah, E. 'Wie beurteilt Paulus sein Leiden? Ein Beitrag zur Untersuchung seiner Denkstruktur', *ZNW* 54 (1963), 217-32.
Kattenbusch, F. 'Der Märtyrertitel', *ZNW* 4 (1903), 111-27.
Kellermann, U. *Auferstanden in den Himmel. 2 Makkabäer 7 und die Auferstehung der Märtyrer*. Stuttgart, 1979.
Kilian, R. *Isaaks Opferung*. Stuttgart, 1970.
Kilpatrick, G.D. *The Trial of Jesus*. Oxford, 1953.
Kittel, G. 'Col. 1 v. 24', *ZSysTh* 18 (1941), 186-91.
Kraeling, C.H. 'The Jewish Community at Antioch', *JBL* 51 (1932), 130-60.
Kremer, J. *Was an den Leiden Christi noch mangelt?* Bonn, 1956.
Krüger, G. 'Zur Frage nach der Enstehung der Märtyrertitel', *ZNW* 17 (1916), 264-69.
Larsson, E. *Christus als Vorbild*. Uppsala, 1962.
Last, H. 'The Study of the Persecutions', *JRS* 27 (1937).
Leaney, A.R.C. 'The Eschatological Significance of Human Suffering in the Old Testament and Dead Sea Scrolls', *SJT* 16 (1963), 286-96.
Leipoldt, J. *Der Tod bei Griechen und Juden*. Leipzig, 1942.
Leitzmann, H. *Der Prozess Jesu*. Berlin, 1931.
Lévi, I. 'Le sacrifice d'Isaac et la mort de Jésus', *RÉJ* 64 (1912), 161-84.
Licht, J. 'Taxo or the Apocalyptic Doctrine of Vengeance', *JJS* 12 (1961), 95-103.
Liechtenhan, R. 'Die Überwindung des Leides bei Paulus und in der zeitgenossischen Stoa', *ZTK* 3 (1922), 308-99.
Lohmeyer, E. 'Die Idee des Martyriums in Judentum und Urchristentum', *ZSysTh* 5 (1927), 231-49.
Lohse, E. *Märtyrer und Gottesknecht*. Göttingen, 1955.
Maas, W. 'Die Maccabäer als christliche Heilige', *MGWJ* 44 (1900), 145-56.
Malone, E.S. 'The Monk and the Martyr', *Studia Anselmiana* 38 (1956), 201-28.

142   *Persecution & Martyrdom in Paul*

Manson, T.W. 'Martyrs and Martyrdom', *BJRL* 39 (1957), 463-84.
Marquardt, J. *Römische Staatsverwaltung*. 2 vols. Leipzig, (1878).
Michel, O. *Prophet und Märtyrer*. Gütersloh, 1932.
Mommsen, T. *Römisches Strafrecht*. Leipzig, 1899.
— 'Der Religionsfrevel nach römischen Recht', *HZ* 64 (1890), 390-429.
— 'Die Rechtsverhältnisse des Apostels Paulus', *ZNW 2* (1901), 81ff.
Morris, L. *The Apostolic Preaching of the Cross*. London, 1965².
— 'The Biblical Use of ἱλάσκεσθαι etc. in Biblical Greek', *ExpT* 63 (1951-52), 227.
Morris, L. 'The Biblical Use of the Term Blood', *JTS* 3 (1952-53), 216-27.
Moule, C.F.D. *The Birth of the New Testament*. London, 1962.
Moule, C.F.D. *The Origin of Christology*. London, 1977.
Moule, C.F.D. 'From Defendant to Judge and Deliverer: an Enquiry into the use and limitation of the theme of Vindication in the New Testament', *BSNTS* 1-3 (1950-52; reprint 1963), 40-53.
Moulton, J.H. 'The Marks of Jesus', *ExpT* 21 (1910), 283.
Nauck, W. 'Freude im Leiden', *ZNW* 46 (1955), 68-80.
Nelis, J. 'L'Antithèse littéraire Ζωή–Θάνατος dans les Épîtres pauliniennes', *ETL* 20 (1943), 22.
Obermann, J. 'The Sepulchre of the Maccabaean Martyrs', *JBL* 50 (19), 250-65.
Osborne, R.E. 'Paul and the Wild Beasts', *JBL* 85 (1966), 225-230.
A.F. von Pauly and G. Wissowa (eds.) *Realencyclopädie für der classischen Altertumswissenschaft*. Stuttgart, 1894.
Peake, A.S. *The Problem of Suffering in the Old Testament*. London, 1907.
Plitt, G.L. (ed.) *Realencyclopädie für protestantische Theologie und Kirche*. Vol. XII. Leipzig, 1883.
Preuschen, E. 'Und liesse meinen Leib brennen (I Cor. 13.3)', *ZNW* 16 (1915), 127.
Rahner, K. *On the Theology of Death*. New York, 1961.
Riddle, D.W. *The Martyrs—A Study in Social Control*. Chicago, 1931.
Robinson, H.W. *Suffering, Human and Divine*. New York, 1939.
Roloff, J. 'Anfänge der soteriologischen Deutung des Todes Jesu', *NTS* 19 (1972), 38-64.
Rostovtsev, M.I. *Die hellenistische Welt*. Stuttgart, 1955-56.
Rowley, H.H. *Submission in Suffering*. Cardiff, 1957.
Sanders, J.A. *Suffering as Divine Discipline in the Old Testament and Postbiblical Judaism*. Rochester, 1955.
Schechter, S. *Some Aspects of Rabbinic Theology*. London, 1909.
Schelkle, K.H. *Die Passion Jesu in der Verkündigung des Neuen Testaments*. Heidelberg, 1949.
Schlatter, A. *Der Märtyrer in der Anfängen der Kirche*. Gütersloh, 1915.
Schmauch, W. (ed.) *In Memoriam E. Lohmeyer*. Stuttgart, 1951.

Schmidt, H.W. 'Das Kreuz Christi bei Paulus', *ZSysTh* 21 (1950-52), 145-59.

Schmidt, K.L. 'Ἰησοῦς Χριστὸς κολαφιζόμενος und die Colaphisation der Juden', *Aux Sources de la tradition chrétienne. Mélanges offerts à M. Goguel.* Neuenberg, 1950.

Schmitz, O. *Die Christus-Gemeinschaft des Paulus im Lichte seines Genetivgebrauchs.* Gütersloh 1924.

Schneider, J. *Die Passionsmystik des Paulus.* Leipzig, 1926.

Schoeps, H.J. *Aus frühchristlicher Zeit. Religionsgeschichtliche Untersuchungen.* Tübingen, 1950.

— 'Die jüdischen Prophetenmorde', *Aus frühchristlicher Zeit*, 126-43.

Scott, C.A. 'The Sufferings of Christ. A Note on I Pet. 1.11', *Expositor* 12 (6th series) (1905), 234-40.

Shear, T.L. 'Excavations in the Theatre District of Corinth in 1926', *AJA* (2nd series) 30 (1926), 444-463.

Sherwin-White, A.N. *Roman Society and Roman Law in the New Testament.* Oxford, 1963.

— 'Early Persecutions and Roman Law', *JTS* 3 (1952-53), 199-213.

Stählin, G. *Skandalon.* Gütersloh, 1934.

Stamm, J.J. *Erlösen und Vergeben im Alten Testament.* Bern, 1940.

— *Das Leiden des Unschuldigen in Babylon und Israel.* Zürich, 1946.

Stauffer, E. 'Märtyrertheologie und Tauferbewegung', *ZK* 3 (1933), 545-609.

— 'Der gekreuzigte Thoralehrer', *ZRGG* 8 (1956), 250ff.

Steubing, A. *Der paulinische Begriff Christusleiden.* Darmstadt, 1905.

Strack, H.L. & Billerbeck, P. *Kommentar zum neuen Testament aus Talmud und Midrasch.* 4 vols. Munich, 1956².

Strathmann, H. μαρτύς, *Theological Dictionary of the New Testament*, IV, 474-514.

Surkau, H.W. *Martyrien in jüdäischer und frühchristlicher Zeit.* Göttingen, 1938.

Tarn, W.W. *Hellenistic Civilization.* London, 1936.

Tarn, W.W. *Alexander the Great.* New York, 1948-1950.

Tarn, W.W. & Griffith, G.T. *Hellenistic Civilization.* London, 1952. London, 1932.

Taylor, L.R. *The Divinity of the Roman Emperor.* Connecticut, 1931.

Taylor, V. *Jesus and His Sacrifice.* London, 1937.

Tcherikover, A. *Hellenistic Civilization and the Jews.* Philadelphia, 1959.

Thyen, H. *Studien zur Sündervergebung im Neuen Testament und seinen alttestamentlichen und jüdischen Voraussetzungen.* Göttingen, 1970.

Violet, B. *Die Apokalypsen des Esdras und des Baruch in deutscher Gestalt.* Leipzig, 1924.

Von Campenhausen, H.F. *Die Idee des Martyriums in der alten Kirche.* Göttingen, 1959.

Whiteley, D.E.H. 'St. Paul's Thoughts on the Atonement', *JTS* 8 (1957), 240-55.

Wichmann, W. *Die Leidenstheologie*. Stuttgart, 1930.

Wiencke, G. *Paulus über Jesus Tod*. Gütersloh, 1939.

Williams, S.K. *Jesus' Death as Saving Event: The Background and Origins of a Concept*. Missoula, 1975.

INDEXES

INDEX OF BIBLICAL PASSAGES

INDEX OF MODERN AUTHORS

JOURNAL FOR THE STUDY OF THE NEW TESTAMENT
Supplement Series